Alfred Lord Tennyson's *In Memoriam*

Reading Guides to Long Poems

Published:

John Milton's Paradise Lost: *A Reading Guide*
Noam Reisner
Hbk: 978 0 7486 3999 1
Pbk: 978 0 7486 4000 3

Edmund Spenser's The Faerie Queene: *A Reading Guide*
Andrew Zurcher
Hbk: 978 0 7486 3956 4
Pbk: 978 0 7486 3957 1

Homer's Odyssey: *A Reading Guide*
Henry Power
Hbk: 978 0 7486 4110 9
Pbk: 978 0 7486 4109 3

Alfred Lord Tennyson's In Memoriam: *A Reading Guide*
Anna Barton
Hbk: 978 0 7486 4135 2
Pbk: 978 0 7486 4134 5

Elizabeth Barrett Browning's Aurora Leigh: *A Reading Guide*
Michele Martinez
Hbk: 978 0 7486 3971 7
Pbk: 978 0 7486 3972 4

Alfred Lord Tennyson's
In Memoriam
A Reading Guide

Anna Barton

EDINBURGH
University Press

For Dad, who read to me.

© Anna Barton, 2012

Edinburgh University Press Ltd
22 George Square, Edinburgh

www.euppublishing.com

Typeset in 10.5/13 Sabon
by Servis Filmsetting Ltd, Stockport, Cheshire, and
printed and bound in Great Britain by
CPI Group (UK) Ltd, Croydon, CR0 4YY

A CIP record for this book is available from the British Library

ISBN 978 0 7486 4135 2 (hardback)
ISBN 978 0 7486 4134 5 (paperback)
ISBN 978 0 7486 4912 9 (webready PDF)
ISBN 978 0 7486 4914 3 (epub)
ISBN 978 0 7486 4913 6 (Amazon)

The right of Anna Barton
to be identified as author of this work
has been asserted in accordance with
the Copyright, Designs and Patents Act 1988.

Contents

Acknowledgements

First thanks go to David Amigoni, who suggested I write this book, to Jackie Jones for her help towards its publication and to Sally Bushell for her patient and encouraging editorial work. I am grateful for the keen eyes and thoughtful suggestions of Iain Kee Vaughan and of my father, who both read drafts of the manuscript. I acknowledge Faber and Faber for granting permission for the inclusion of extracts from 'In Memoriam' by T.S. Eliot and Berlin Associates for granting permission to reproduce Max Beerbohm's cartoon, 'Mr Tennyson, reading "In Memoriam" to his Sovereign.' I would also like to acknowledge the support of my colleagues at the Universities of Keele and Sheffield, whose research and teaching have provided and continue to provide stimulation and inspiration for my own work. Finally, I would like to thank my students, whose ideas about and responses to *In Memoriam* inform this book throughout.

Editions

The text of *In Memoriam* included in this Guide is based on the nine-volume *Eversley Tennyson*, ed. Hallam Lord Tennyson, London: Macmillan, 1907–8. This edition has been cross-referenced with Christopher Ricks, ed. (1987), *The Poems of Tennyson in Three Volumes*, Harlow: Longman, and Susan Shatto and Marion Shaw, eds (1982), *In Memoriam*, Oxford: Clarendon. All other quotations from Tennyson are taken from the Ricks edition.

Abbreviations

Two sources quoted a number of times throughout the Guide are abbreviated as follows:

EN   Tennyson's notes to the Eversley edition of *In Memoriam*.
Memoir Hallam Lord Tennyson (1897), *Alfred Lord Tennyson: A Memoir By His Son*, 2 vols, London: Macmillan.

Series Editors' Preface

The form of the long poem has been of fundamental importance to Literary Studies from the time of Homer onwards. The *Reading Guides to Long Poems Series* seek to celebrate and explore this form in all its diversity across a range of authors and periods. Major poetic works – *The Odyssey, The Faerie Queene, Paradise Lost, The Prelude, In Memoriam, The Waste Land* – emerge as defining expressions of the culture which produced them. One of the main aims of the series is to make contemporary readers aware of the importance of the long poem for our literary and national heritage.

How 'long' is a long poem? In 'The Philosophy of Composition' Edgar Allan Poe asserted that there is 'a distinct limit, as regards length, to all works of literary art – the limit of a single sitting'. Defined against this, a long poem must be one which *exceeds* the limit of a single sitting, requiring sustained attention over a considerable period of time for its full appreciation. However, the concept of poetic length is not simply concerned with the number of lines in a poem, or the time it takes to read it. In 'From Poe to Valéry' T. S. Eliot defends poetic length on the grounds that 'it is only in a poem of some length that a variety of moods can be expressed . . . These parts can form a whole more than the sum of the parts; a whole such that the pleasure we derive from the reading of any part is enhanced by our grasp of the whole.' Along with Eliot, the Series Editors believe that poetic length creates a unique space for a varied play of meaning and tone, action and reflection, that results in particular kinds of reading and interpretation not possible for shorter works. The *Reading Guides* are therefore concerned with communicating the pleasure and enjoyment of engaging with the form in a range of ways – focusing on particular episodes, tracing out patterns of poetic imagery, exploring form, reading and rereading the text – in order to allow the reader to experience the multiple interpretative layers that the long poem holds within it. We also believe that a self-awareness about *how* we read the long poem may help to provide the modern reader with a necessary fresh perspective upon the genre.

The *Reading Guides to Long Poems Series* will engage with major works in new and innovative ways in order to revitalise the form of the long poem for a new generation. The series will present shorter 'long poems' in their entirety, while the longest are represented by a careful selection of essential parts. Long poems have often been read aloud, imitated or even translated in excerpts, so there is good precedent for appreciating them through selective reading. Nevertheless, it is to be hoped that readers will use the *Guides* alongside an appreciation of the work in its entirety or, if they have not previously done so, go on to read the whole poem.

Ultimately, the *Edinburgh Reading Guides to Long Poems Series* seeks to be of lasting value to the discipline of Literary Studies by revitalising a form which is in danger of being marginalised by the current curriculum but is central to our understanding of our own literature, history and culture.

Sally Bushell with Isobel Armstrong and Colin Burrow

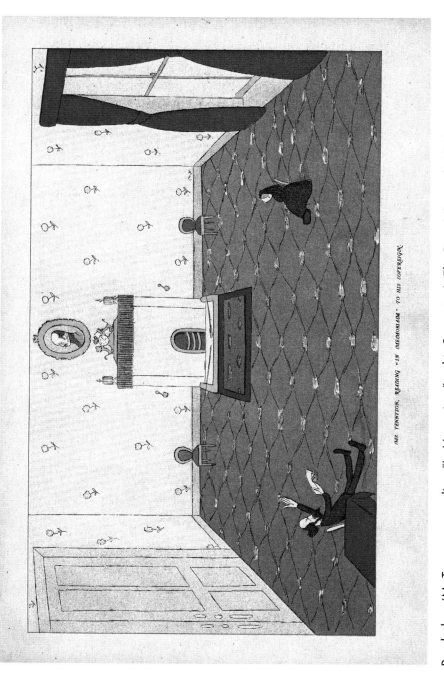

MR. TENNYSON, READING "IN MEMORIAM" TO HIS SOVEREIGN.

Max Beerbohm, 'Mr Tennyson, reading "In Memoriam" to his Sovereign', *The Poets' Corner* (1904)

Introduction

In 1904, caricaturist Max Beerbohm produced a cartoon entitled 'Mr Tennyson, reading "In Memoriam" to his Sovereign'. The cartoon pictures a large, almost empty room decorated with heavy curtains, four small chairs and a fireplace with an empty grate, above which sits an ornamental clock. The walls are decorated with floral wallpaper and hung with a single portrait of Prince Albert. In the room sit Alfred Tennyson and Queen Victoria. Tennyson, hair and beard flapping, arms gesturing widely and legs lifted straight out in front of him, reads from sheets of paper that he holds in his hand. Victoria, dressed in black, seated with her hands demurely in her lap and her feet resting on a foot stool, looks straight ahead, past Tennyson, towards the door.

Tennyson, who became Poet Laureate (the poet of the nation, an honour bestowed by the monarch) in 1850, met Queen Victoria on a number of occasions. He also enjoyed reading his poetry aloud. However, Tennyson never read *In Memoriam* to Queen Victoria. By imagining this encounter, Beerbohm, who was famous for satirising the culture and celebrities of his day, pokes fun at poet, queen and poem. He also tells us something about the cultural identity of *In Memoriam* at the end of the nineteenth century. Beerbohm identifies *In Memoriam* with the Victorian establishment and with the Victorian culture of mourning that found its best example in Victoria's own extended period of mourning for Prince Albert, who died in 1862. His cartoon is probably based on reports that *In Memoriam* and the Bible were the two texts in which the Queen found comfort after her husband's death, a widely reported fact which bestows the poem with a near-religious authority.[1] Beerbohm recognises that authority, but he also calls it into question by inviting us to laugh at it.

The reason the cartoon is funny has to do with its scale. The room is far too big for the two figures that sit in it. Victoria's body more or less fits in a single square of the carpet's enormous pattern and her head is the size of one of the wallpaper flowers. She and Tennyson, almost swallowed up by the room, are also sitting a long way apart. In this way, Beerbohm effectively communicates the awkwardness of this encounter to the viewer, who can imagine the strained atmosphere as Tennyson recites his poem enthusiastically, while his sovereign sits, motionless. A reading of *In Memoriam*'s more than 20,000 words is itself an event made absurd by its scale, so that we might begin to feel sorry for Queen Victoria and to wonder whether she is tempted to tug at one of the bell-pulls that are positioned on either side of the fireplace so that someone will come and take the poet and his long poem away.

In an earlier version of the cartoon, the flowers that pattern the wallpaper are replaced by a skull and crossbones motif, a repetitive pattern on the theme of mortality much like the pattern of stanzas that form *In Memoriam* (Bevis 2003: 432). The over-large room, an uncomfortable mixture of room of state and private, domestic interior, might therefore suggest that the poem itself is likewise a grossly exaggerated space: an intimate expression of grief, transformed into an empty, monumental public performance that alienates readers rather than touching them.

For readers encountering *In Memoriam* for the first time, this satirical representation of Tennyson's long elegy might ring true. *In Memoriam* is excessive, repetitive, monumental, and decked out with the furnishings of Victorian domestic sentiment. As its opening words, in which the speaker addresses himself to the 'Strong Son of God', make clear, it is both a prayer and a public / published declaration of Christian faith. However, Tennyson's long elegy is made up of lyric fragments that are often doubtful, questioning, private and subversive. It is a poem published by a middle-aged man, engaged to be married and well on his way to being recognised as one of the greatest poets of the century; but it is also a collection of brief sketches of mourning, some of which were written by a young man of twenty-four, struggling to come to terms with the death of a close friend whom he describes, in one of the first cantos he composed, as 'the brother of my love' (IX, 16): a bereavement that left the poet, as he writes in the same canto, 'widowed' (IX, 18).[2]

In its published form, *In Memoriam* is a long poem that charts the three years of the mourner's life following his bereavement. However, during its composition there is evidence that Tennyson thought of the poem, not as a single text, but as a number of separate poems, written on loosely the same theme. In his letters and in the letters and diaries of friends who read early drafts of *In Memoriam*, it is referred to as 'some beautiful Elegies', 'the memorial poems', 'a volume of poems' and simply 'those poems'.[3] None of these descriptions suggests that the elegiac stanzas written by Tennyson constitute one complete piece of work. The title of the published text, *In Memoriam*, was not decided until just before its publication. As Christopher Ricks points out, Tennyson also considered *The Way of the Soul*, a title that would have more clearly identified the poem as a narrative of spiritual progress, and *Fragments of an Elegy*, which, by contrast, allows the text to be permeable, broken and unfinished (Ricks 1989: 202).

The answer to the question, 'what kind of poem is *In Memoriam*?', is therefore not straightforward, but by beginning to negotiate these questions of fragmentation and wholeness, lyricism and length, it becomes possible for us to find ways to engage with *In Memoriam* as readers. A poem's form or forms constitute(s) the terms of our engagement with it. The shape of a text on the page invites us to inhabit a particular kind of space: public or private, open or enclosed, comfortable or uncomfortable, familiar or strange. By reading *In Memoriam* we enter two kinds of space at once and so, to understand it, we are required to employ a kind of double vision. In her influential study of Victorian Poetry, Isobel Armstrong coins the term 'double poem' to describe the distinctive qualities of poetry written after 1830 (Armstrong 1993: 13). This term is helpful when thinking about the best way to approach *In Memoriam*. Armstrong argues that a double poem is both a representation of the culture in which it is composed and published, and also a way in which that same culture can be brought into question, challenged and even transformed. By suggesting that Victorian poetry at once constructs and deconstructs its own historical moment, Armstrong finds a new role for the reader, whom she describes as 'active': 'The active reader is compelled to be internal to the poem's contradictions and recomposes the poem's processes in the act of comprehending them as ideological struggle' (Armstrong 1993: 17). Part of what Armstrong means by this is that reading is an act of composition: that as readers we should not just enter a poem and sit demurely with our hands in our laps, but that we should rearrange the furniture, or even pull down the walls and rebuild them.

This Guide explores the way in which *In Memoriam* invites this kind of reading. It provides information about *In Memoriam*, its composition and its context, but it also suggests strategies for reading the poem that enable the reader to engage actively with its multiple, monumental form. Like other Guides in this series, it acknowledges the fact that the long poem is an unfamiliar and potentially daunting form for a modern readership. As readers, we are happy to immerse ourselves in a long novel. Habituated to the devices of narrative, plot and character, we are experts at navigating the forms that structure our novel-reading experience. The novel is a descendent of epic poetry (Marxist critic Georg Lukács famously defined the novel as 'the epic of a world that has been abandoned by God' (Lukács [1916] 1971: 88)), but, in learning to read the novel, we have forgotten how to read the long poem; its forms have become alien and so they prohibit, rather than enable our understanding. *In Memoriam*, one of the youngest poems to be covered by this series, was published in the Age of the Novel, of the Brontës, Dickens and Eliot, and in one sense the anxiety that it expresses when it asks 'What hope is there for modern rhyme [. . .] ?' (LXXVII, 1) is justified. It is a poem that is all too aware of its own belatedness, of the way the cultural tide was turning. As readers, we are inheritors of that Victorian turn to the novel and it is for that reason that the literary world of *Jane Eyre*, *Middlemarch* or *Bleak House* feels much more familiar than that of *In Memoriam*.

This Guide, along with others in this series, aims to reacquaint readers with the long poem by addressing the challenges that it poses, by introducing some of the formal practices that it employs and by exploring some of the literary traditions with which it engages. It is by no means the last word on *In Memoriam*, but a series of starting points, from which readers might feel encouraged to find their own ways through the poem. The opening chapter offers information about the poem's biographical and literary genesis. Addressing *In Memoriam* as a whole, it introduces some of its key formal elements and considers its relationship with the elegiac tradition. The main body of the Guide, which includes the full text of *In Memoriam*, reads Tennyson's elegy from four different perspectives, each of which traces a particular thematic motif through the poem. Following on from this, I provide a selection of primary material that documents some significant elements of *In Memoriam*'s contexts and reception. The Guide concludes with a chapter that addresses the challenges and opportunities of teaching the poem, which is accompanied by an annotated bibliography.

Notes

1. For a detailed discussion of Queen Victoria as a reader of *In Memoriam*, see Kirstie Blair (2001), 'Touching Hearts: Queen Victoria and the Curative Properties of *In Memoriam*', *Tennyson Research Bulletin 5*, pp. 246–54.
2. Many critics have commented on this double identity. To take just two, J. H. Buckley writes that the poem 'was to serve the whole generation as a sort of Victorian *Essay on Man*', but also comments on the poem's 'virtually formless structure' and 'large, loose argument' (Buckley 1960: 108 and 112); and Alan Sinfield identifies the poem as containing the opposing aesthetics of the Romantics and the neo-Classicists (Sinfield 1971: 16–40).
3. These descriptions are included in Christopher Ricks's account of the poem's composition and publication, in *The Poems of Tennyson in Three Volumes*, pp. 345–7.

Chapter 1

Mapping and Making

This first chapter provides an overview of *In Memoriam*'s subject matter, summarises relevant biographical information about Tennyson and 'A. H. H.', and introduces some of the key questions and contexts that inform the way Tennyson's poem is read: Who is the speaker? Who is he speaking to / about? Where does the poem begin? What is the relationship between its different sections? What is the relationship between its content and its form? Beginning with a consideration of the different ways that *In Memoriam* can be defined and described – from fragmentary lyric to long poem, from elegy to epic, moving on to talk about the composition of the poem and the development of the *In Memoriam* stanza form, and ending by positioning the poem within the elegiac tradition, the chapter aims to encourage readers to think, when they read *In Memoriam*, not just about *what* they read, but also about *how* they read and how *In Memoriam* forms the reader in relation to its own complex and multiple forms.

Monuments and Fragments

A. H. H.

In Memoriam was published anonymously.[1] The identity of its author was no great secret; many people knew that Tennyson had been working on a long elegiac composition for a number of years and Tennyson's name was accidentally printed in some of the advertisements for the work. However, according to Tennyson's demand, the first and all subsequent editions of the poem were printed with a title page that read simply: *In Memoriam A. H. H.* The open secret of *In Memoriam*'s authorship is an interesting place to start when thinking about the poem in relation to its biographical context. It gives the poem an identity that is both private and universal. The author keeps himself and his grief out of the public eye; but he also gives his grief over to the public. The speaker of the poem could be anybody and so the speaker becomes, potentially, everybody.

Tennyson addresses this question in some remarks on the poem that are published in his biography: '[*In Memoriam*] is a poem, *not* an actual biography [. . .] "I" is not always the author speaking of himself, but the voice of the human race speaking thro' him' (*Memoir* I, 305). What Tennyson describes here is typical of the function of the 'lyric I', or the first-person speaker of lyric poetry. Lyric ('song-like') poetry, as opposed to narrative or dramatic poetry, is poetry that voices the thoughts and feelings of a single speaker. It is often associated with the sincere expression of extreme or intense emotion, usually love (as in a sonnet) or grief (as in an elegy). As Tennyson's comment suggests, the 'I' who speaks a lyric poem is never straightforwardly the poet. Even if the poem is inspired by the poet's own experiences and feelings, the act of *formulating* those feelings into words on a page initiates a disconnect between poet and text, poet and 'I'. By using a shared or common language, a poet allows the feelings the words describe to be recognised as common and so enables the reader to become the speaker, 'speaking through' the poet. Therefore reading a lyric poem, we feel both that we are listening in on a private confession of love or grief and also that we inhabit that love or grief ourselves.

The title of *In Memoriam* also expresses this kind of lyric tension. The reader is not told the identity of A. H. H., so reading the poem becomes rather like coming across a private document, meant only for the eyes of those for whom the initials have meaning. At the same time, 'In Memoriam', Latin for 'to the memory of', adopts the formal language of public memorials and so confers that same kind of public identity on the poem. The publicly private nature of *In Memoriam* suggests that the relationship between the anonymous poet and A. H. H. is at once central and peripheral to the concerns of the reader.

The initials A. H. H., which appear on the title page of *In Memoriam*, stand for Arthur Henry Hallam, who was the eldest son of a wealthy and influential political historian, Henry Hallam. Hallam met Alfred Tennyson, the third son of a Lincolnshire clergyman, at Trinity College, Cambridge, in 1829. Tennyson, who was a year older than Hallam, had been a student at Cambridge since 1827; Hallam had enrolled in 1828. Hallam had been a pupil at Eton, along with those who were to become important figures in nineteenth-century political and cultural life; his closest school-friend was William Ewart Gladstone, who later became Prime Minister. Tennyson's older brother Frederick had also been to Eton, but Tennyson's father was not wealthy enough to give all his sons such an expensive education and so Alfred had been educated at a local day school and then by his father at home. Both Tennyson and Hallam were considered to be young men of great promise, but neither had any substantial achievements to their name. Hallam's death, four years later, which prevented him from living up to the expectations of his youth, was also the event that led Tennyson to compose those poems that were the making of his career.

Tennyson's friendship with Hallam was a product of the intense, cloistered, masculine environment of early nineteenth-century Cambridge. They first became friends when both men submitted a poem to a university competition (Tennyson's poem won). Both men were also members of the Apostles, or the Society, an exclusive club that met in the private rooms of its members to discuss political, philosophical and literary questions. In 1830, Hallam found Tennyson a publisher for his first signed volume of poems (and, it is likely, provided financial backing for the project), *Poems, Chiefly Lyrical*, and wrote an essay that compared Tennyson with Keats and Shelley, two of the most popular poets of the day. In the same year, Hallam became engaged to Tennyson's sister Emily, an event that promised the brotherhood that Tennyson talks about in section IX of *In Memoriam*. Between 1829 and 1833 the two young men also travelled together, making an ill-advised trip to Spain in 1830 in an attempt to support a short-lived revolution against the Spanish monarchy, and visiting the Rhine country in 1832. At the end of 1832, Tennyson, who had by now left Cambridge following the death of his father in 1831, published his second signed volume, *Poems*, to mixed reviews. In August 1833 Hallam set off on a tour of Europe with his father. He died suddenly in Venice, of a brain haemorrhage, a month later. After the autopsy, his body was brought back to England by boat and he was buried in Clevedon, Somerset, in January, 1834.

Mapping Grief

Tennyson learned of Hallam's death through a letter, sent by Henry Hallam, which reached Tennyson in early October. It is at this point, one could argue, that we meet our mourner. The first canto of the poem voices the overwhelming grief of a man who cannot conceive of anything that will make up for the loss that he has suffered: 'But who shall so forecast the years / And find in loss a gain to match?' (I, 5) and declares his resolve to revel in his grief in order to keep alive his love for his lost friend:

Let Love clasp Grief lest both be drowned,
　　Let darkness keep her raven gloss:
　　Ah sweeter to be drunk with loss,
To dance with death, to beat the ground,
　　　　　(I, 9–12)

This description of the initial throes of grief is also a statement of purpose for the poem that is to follow. The speaker suggests that the best way to express his grief is through a Bacchanalian frenzy of wild dancing. He resolves to overindulge in his grief, as one might overindulge in alcohol, so that he is taken beyond the bounds of reason or social propriety. *In Memoriam* becomes part of this excess: a spontaneous, heartfelt cry. However, a dance, even a Bacchanalian 'dance with death', involves form, or some sort of public ritual. These opening lines therefore also suggest an element of performance, an 'acting out' of grief that immediately complicates any reading of the poem's spontaneity. By resolving to become 'drunk with loss', the mourner reveals, not that he *is* drunk with loss, but that he considers this to be the best response to his situation. This is the first of many examples of *In Memoriam*'s meta-poetic or meta-elegiac identity. It is a poem about grief, but it is also a poem that repeatedly asks how best to write about grief in poetry.

This meta-poetic discourse is present from the outset of the section, which begins, 'I held it truth, with him who sings / To one clear harp in diverse tones' (I, 1–2). This reference to another singer and another song (which I return to a number of times in this Guide) suggests that, by writing his poem, the mourner engages in a literary dialogue with other writers. According to Tennyson, the singer he refers to here is Goethe (1749–1832), an early nineteenth-century German author, one of the most influential and controversial of his day.[2] By making an oblique reference to Goethe, Tennyson indicates something of his literary identity and professional ambition.

There is also something else going on here. By opening his poem with a singer and a harp, Tennyson suggests that his poem is not an elegy, or not just an elegy, but an epic.[3] Epics, long narrative poems that tell the story of the birth of a culture or a nation, form a tradition that originates with Homer's *Iliad*, a long poem that narrates the fall of Troy, and Homer's *Odyssey*, which follows a hero in the Greek army, Odysseus, as he makes his eventful journey home from Troy to Ithaca. Traditionally, therefore, epics are stories of war, adventure, heroic action and physical struggle. They are rooted in an oral tradition whereby a culture gained a sense of communal identity by passing their mythologised histories from one generation to the next. Different from the private song of lyric, epic is public and communal. The opening lines of *The Iliad* call out: 'Sing, goddess, the anger of Peleus' son Achilleus' (Homer 1987: 3). Likewise, *The Odyssey* begins by commanding the Muse to 'Sing to me of the man, Muse, the man of twists and turns / driven time and again off course, once he had plundered / the hallowed heights of Troy' (Homer 2006: 77). *Paradise Lost*, John Milton's fifteenth-century English epic, conforms to this convention as well: 'Of Man's First disobedience, and the Fruit / Of that Forbidden Tree [. . .] Sing Heav'nly Muse' (Milton 1968: 5). Tennyson's opening reference to a singer and a harp (although he is not the singer, nor is his the harp) might be read as an epic allusion. Again, this complicates the lyric identity of Tennyson's text. *In Memoriam* is an elegy, and therefore a lyric, but it also suggests itself as epic, not simply by its size, but also through its self-conscious construction as a poem that will, in some way, tell the story of nineteenth-century Britain. As lyric epic (a contradiction in terms) it turns its gaze inward, lending the scope and scale of heroic battles between men and nations to the emotional, psychological and spiritual experience of a recently bereaved young man.

Setting Out

But what sort of journey is this? And does it really begin here? The answer to the second of these questions – both yes and no – points us back towards *In Memoriam*'s multiple structures and forms in a way that begins to equip us as active readers of the text. As we have seen, section I is, in many significant, not to say obvious, ways, the opening of *In Memoriam*; it echoes the opening lines of classical epics and it describes the initial, overwhelming shock of personal loss, from which a reader might expect a journey of recovery to begin. It also comes at the start of the poem. However, there are two other sections that might also be identified as the beginning of *In Memoriam*. The first is the Prologue. The second is section IX, the first section that Tennyson composed.

The Prologue consists of a declaration of faith that acts as both an apology and a disclaimer for what follows:

> Forgive my grief for one removed,
>   Thy creature, whom I found so fair.
>   I trust he lives, in thee, and there
> I find him worthier to be loved
>
> Forgive these wild and wandering cries,
>   Confusions of a wasted youth;
>   Forgive them when they fail in truth,
> And in thy wisdom make me wise.
>   (Prologue, 37–44)

In published versions of the poem, these lines are dated 1849, the year before the poem was published. One of the last sections composed by Tennyson and a section that apologises for the 'wild and wandering cries' of a youth from which the speaker has moved on, the Prologue is surely as much an end as it is a beginning. Its position nevertheless demands that it be read first. By beginning at the end in this way, Tennyson offers some sense of the nature of the journey on which his mourner embarks; it is a journey from despair to hope, from doubt to faith. But he also implies that the journey is somehow circular: that it begins and ends in the same place. The reader is given confidence in the mourner's progress, but this confidence is tempered by an understanding that the progress the mourner makes is not linear but cyclical, repeatedly returning on itself.

The other claim that the Prologue makes is that this cyclical journey is not finished. The mourner's prayer describes his faith as faith in an event that has not happened yet. He writes, 'Thou wilt not leave us in the dust' (9), a statement that admits that he, along with the rest of humankind, is still in the dust at the time of writing. He describes God-given knowledge as 'a beam in darkness' which must 'grow', continuing:

> Let knowledge grow from more to more,
>   But more of reverence in us dwell;
>   That mind and soul, according well,
> May make one music as before'
>   (Prologue, 25–8)

The end that the Prologue looks towards is the end of the world, when humanity will be reunited with God. In this context everything, including the poem that we are about to read, is unfinished, or 'broken' (19).

This ultimate end is also described in terms of music and song. The mourner imagines the mind and soul in harmony with one another and with God, making 'one music'. In this way, he invites a direct comparison with his poem. He suggests that *In Memoriam* does not achieve the perfect music that it strives towards and that it therefore remains in some way unfinished. However, even the ultimate end alluded to in the Prologue is a return to the beginning. The 'as before' that concludes the phrase describes a progress back as well as forward. Tennyson's notes to the poem say that 'as before' refers to 'the ages of faith', which is conveniently vague, but 'before' might also be read as a reference to a pre-lapsarian world – a world before the Fall of humanity as described in Genesis (I return to this reading in the 'Lost for Words' section of the Reading Guide).

Although the manuscript evidence for the precise order in which Tennyson composed the various cantos of *In Memoriam* is inconclusive, it is likely that section IX was among the first that Tennyson wrote. It is contained in a notebook that also includes sections XVII and XVIII. In the notebook, Tennyson labels XVII and XVIII, 'II' and 'III'. Along with section IX, these two sections form a series of reflections on the return of Hallam's body by boat to England. The mourner prays for the ship to be brought safely and quickly home, and gains small comfort from the thought of Hallam's burial in familiar earth. Again, this little sequence makes sense as a beginning. Nowhere in the poem are we told about the death of Hallam, or the moment when Tennyson hears of his friend's death, and so the 'fair ship' lyrics begin the narrative of the events of the mourner's grief.

However, the beginning described in these sections is very different from both the Prologue and section I. Although these two sections might initially be read as opposites – an expression of sincere faith followed by an expression of sincere doubt, they both employ a similar epic register. The mourner – and it is much more clearly 'the mourner' here – speaks in universal terms, adopting a collective voice that refers to 'we', 'us' and 'our', inviting the reader to acknowledge a shared experience. By contrast, sections IX, XVII and XVIII maintain a much narrower focus. Like the Prologue, section IX is a prayer of sorts, but it is also one of the few sections to refer to Arthur by name and so, rather than being interpellated ('hailed' or recognised and included) as mourners within a shared experience of mourning, the reader is positioned outside, looking in on a private moment of grief, felt by one individual for another. Another journey within *In Memoriam*, then, is Tennyson's transformation from young anonymous poet into the bard of an age and a nation. This journey is neither cyclical nor linear. It is broken up and absorbed into the poem's final published form, so that the personal and the public rub alongside one another, creating varying degrees of tension.

Looking at the order in which the sections of *In Memoriam* were composed is one way of mapping the poem. By considering the difference between the poem's published form and the fragments of manuscript that Tennyson amassed over the seventeen years of the poem's composition, it is possible to appreciate *In Memoriam*, not as a 'wild and wandering cry', but as a carefully constructed, formed and performed literary work.[4] And yet Tennyson's elegy continues to draw attention to the fragmentary nature of its progress, leaving traces of other routes to be mapped by the reader. For example, section XVII concludes, 'The dust of him I shall not see / 'Till all my widowed race be run,' lines that are an imperfect repetition of section IX: 'My Arthur, whom I shall not see / 'Till all my widowed race be run,' so that the poem appears at this point to collapse back on itself, its progress stalled. At the same time, the line works as a moment of self-citation and the phrase ''Till all my widowed race be run' is transformed from spontaneous lyric expression to elegiac convention, marking a step away from the immediacy of grief (it is interesting that, on the second occasion this line is used, 'my Arthur' has become an anonymous 'him'). It is this kind of mapping of *In Memoriam*'s patterns of images and themes that I employ as a method for reading the poem in the Reading Guide section of this book. Before I come to that, the final two parts of this introductory chapter will consider ways to approach the stanza form of the poem and discuss some of the works that make up *In Memoriam*'s literary context.

The *In Memoriam* Stanza

Mapping Time

So far, I have discussed the way *In Memoriam* charts the progress of the speaker's grief, considering the form of the poem as an – albeit fragmented – whole: its multiple beginnings, its open endings, its cycles and repetitions. It is equally important to think about the formal elements that make up this whole: its stanza form, metre and rhyme scheme. In his introduction to poetic rhythm, Derek Attridge writes about the relationship between rhythm and movement:

> although strictly speaking the idea of movement implies travel through *space*, rhythm is what makes a physical medium (the body, the sound of speech or music) seem to move with deliberatedness through *time*, recalling what has happened (by repetition) and projecting into the future (by setting up expectations), rather than just letting time pass by. (Attridge 1995: 4)

What Attridge suggests here is that rhythm maps time. It transforms time from something that is shapeless and difficult to grasp (time can seem to drag, fly past or stop) into something that can be seen, heard and, as we shall see in a moment, felt. This kind of mapping can be understood as the central work of *In Memoriam*, which is concerned both with remembrance ('recalling what has happened') and with recovery ('projecting into the future'). The regular metre and verse form of the poem constantly recalls itself, while at the same time creating a pattern that compels onward movement.

This pattern or map of grief is visual; the passing of time is represented by the shape of the stanzas on the page, which draw the eye from left to right, top to bottom. It is also physical. Attridge again: 'rhythm is *felt* as much as it is heard or seen [. . .] it enables muscular movements to happen with a certain evenness and predictability' (Attridge 1995: 4). Attridge is keen to emphasise the way that poetic rhythm is experienced by the body of the reader. The passage of time is marked by a regular pulse that is created by the muscles of the body when a poem is read aloud. *In Memoriam* reflects on these kinds of bodily rhythms on a couple of occasions:

> in the dusk of thee, the clock
> Beats out the little lives of men.
> (II, 7–8)

But, for the unquiet heart and brain,
  A use in measured language lies;
  The sad, mechanic exercise,
Like dull narcotics, numbing pain.
           (V, 5–8)

In the first of these, Tennyson describes a ticking clock that lends rhythm to the passing time. Its beats are mirrored by the iambic beat of the line and so the reader is invited to think about the poem as a kind of clock, a way for the poet to measure out his hours, or to pass time, now that his friend is dead. The other thing that 'beats out the little lives of men' is the heart: so we might also understand the beat of the poem as a kind of pulse, bound up in the workings of our living, breathing bodies. Seamus Perry points out that 'to beat out' also means 'to put an end to', 'like beating out a fire' (Perry 2004: 130), so these lines not only describe the way the poem marks time, but also the way it works steadily towards its own end, which, in this stanza, is associated with the end of life.

In the second example the mourner talks more directly about poetic rhythm, but the connection with the rhythm of the living body remains strong. Here, the mourner, who holds little hope that his words will adequately express his grief (for more on this see the 'Lost for Words' section of the Reading Guide), nevertheless declares that 'measured' (metrical) language is useful because its regular, mechanic motion is soothing. The measure of language is set against 'the unquiet heart and brain' and so poetic rhythm is again understood as something that acts on or through the body, regulating heartbeat. Yet, here again, the poem seems barely to suppress a desire to beat itself out. An unquiet heart is a troubled heart, but its opposite – a quiet heart – sounds more like one that has stopped beating altogether. The desire to quiet an unquiet heart might be interpreted as a suicidal impulse. Therefore the regular rhythm of *In Memoriam* is both the thing that connects past and future by balancing memory with anticipation, and also a bodily pulse that marks the difference or distance of the speaker from the friend he mourns; a distance that the poem repeatedly attempts and fails to bridge.

Ballad Metre

Tennyson's description of metre as something that controls or dulls distressed emotion echoes an essay by William Wordsworth, major Romantic poet and Tennyson's predecessor as Poet Laureate. Wordsworth writes:

The end of poetry is to produce excitement in co-existence with an over-balance of pleasure [. . .] But, if the words by which this excitement is produced are in themselves powerful, or the images and feelings have an undue proportion of pain connected with them, there is some danger that the excitement may be carried beyond its proper bounds. Now the presence of something regular, something to which the mind has been accustomed in various moods and in a less excited state, cannot but have great efficacy in tempering and restraining the passion by an intertexture of ordinary feeling. (Wordsworth [1800] 1991: 264)

Wordsworth's remarks offer a different perspective on the 'use' of 'measured language'. Rather than 'dulling' or 'numbing', Wordsworth talks about rhythm in terms of regulating, tempering and restraining. This sense of the regularity of metre might lead us to think about metre and regulation, or metre and rules or laws. One of the functions of law is to organise individuals into functioning social units. The regulation of metre might be understood to serve a similar purpose, regulating private, individual emotions to public, social rhythms. Perhaps what Wordsworth means, then, when he talks about the way metre tempers and restrains emotion is that it transforms something personal and inward into something communal and public, which is part of a recognised, sanctioned, cultural discourse. The example that Wordsworth offers to illustrate his point is 'the metre of the old Ballads'. Ballads are English folk songs that originated as part of an oral tradition of poetry, whereby poems would be spoken aloud or sung, passed down and preserved through community memory, rather than being written down, printed or published. Wordsworth has his own reasons for naming ballads in particular. His essay was published as the preface to *Lyrical Ballads*, an experimental volume of poetry, which aimed at a recovery and adaptation of the ballad tradition. However, his choice of example is also helpful for thinking about the metre and stanza form of *In Memoriam*. The ballad metre to which Wordsworth refers consists of four-line stanzas of alternating iambic tetrameter (four units of rhythm, each consisting of an unstressed syllable followed by a stressed syllable) and iambic trimeter, following an ABAB rhyme scheme. Wordsworth employed this form in a number of poems published in lyrical ballads. A good example of this is a poem called simply 'Song' (another word for ballad):

> She dwelt among th'untrodden ways
> Beside the springs of Dove
> A maid whom there was none to praise
> And very few to love.
>   (Wordsworth [1800] 1991: 153)

When he uses this form, Wordsworth consciously references a literary tradition from a time much earlier than his own, identifying his work with a particular idea of national identity and history.[5] The rhythm and rhyme scheme lend themselves to being memorised; the end words of lines 1 and

2 set up cues for the end words of lines 3 and 4, and the iambic metre sets up a momentum that carries each line through to its conclusion. If we think back to what Attridge says about rhythm being experienced by the body, then a rhythm like this that feels familiar or natural causes the reader, singer or listener to recognise that their body has something in common with the bodies of the people who composed and sang ballads in the past, creating a sense of community across time and bearing witness to a shared cultural identity.

The oral, communal, narrative poetry of the ballad is therefore very different from the individual, emotional poetry we are likely to associate with *In Memoriam*. However, the *In Memoriam* stanza, like the stanza of Wordsworth's 'Song' and the ballads that it imitates, is made up of four lines of iambic tetrameter. By choosing this verse form, Tennyson references, or places his poem in relation to, the ballad tradition. Like the epic, the ballad connotes a desire to speak on behalf of a community and to use poetry to establish and sustain a shared identity. In this case, because ballad metre is a British form, Tennyson characterises that shared identity in national terms, speaking with the cultural voice of the British people. Remember also that *In Memoriam* was published anonymously. Although this decision to keep authorial identity hidden could be interpreted as part of the poem's aesthetic of privacy, it might also be compared with the ballad, which has no single author because it belongs to no single voice.

In section VI, the mourner addresses this theme of universal mourning, describing the 'commonplaces' that are offered as inadequate comfort to his grief:

> One writes that 'Other friends remain',
>   That 'Loss is common to the race' –
>   And common is the commonplace
> And vacant chaff well meant for grain.
>
> That loss is common would not make
>   My own less bitter, rather more:
>   Too common! Never morning wore
> To evening but some heart did break.
>   (VI, 1–8)

Taking up the word 'common' that is used in the letter from his well-wisher, he broods upon it, considering the fact that the loss he feels is experienced by countless people every day. He concludes that this common experience is no comfort because bereavement is experienced as isolated instances of heartbreak, so that the tragedy of grief is that it is common but can never be shared. Ballad metre is sometimes referred to as 'common metre' and so this tension that Tennyson identifies between the commonplace and the particular, the individual and the race, is one way to think about the *In Memoriam* stanza, which both alludes to and separates itself from the communal poetry of the ballad.

The two main differences between the ballad stanza and the *In Memoriam* stanza can be seen clearly if we compare the stanzas we have just been looking at with the opening stanzas of 'Sir Patrick Spens', a ballad that was published in an influential anthology of traditional ballads that would have been familiar to both Wordsworth and Tennyson:

> The king sits in Dumferling toune,
>   Drinking the blude-reid wine:
> O whar will I get a guid sailor
>   To sail this ship of mine?
>   (Percy 1765: 72–4)

The stanzas of 'Sir Patrick Spens' are divided clearly into two linked pairs of lines. The end of the first two lines is marked by a silent beat, where the reader is forced to pause; and, as we have seen, the first pair create, or anticipate, the second pair by setting up an end rhyme that lines three and four complete. In *In Memoriam* these divisions are not so pronounced, nor are the linked continuations so clear.[6] All four lines of each stanza make full use of their tetrameter (four-beat) length so that the movement from line to line is continuous; and the rhyme scheme creates two pairs of lines that do not so much follow one another as mirror one another, so that AB is reflected back as BA. Ballad metre lends itself to the work of narrative, whereby one event leads to another. The king sits and then he speaks, asking a question, which ensures the presence of another character, who offers an answer, naming a third character, whom the King summons, and so the story unfolds. The rhythm and rhyme scheme of *In Memoriam* obstructs narrative. There are no pauses to mark the end of one event and the beginning of another, so that time, although measured, is featureless, like a flat plane of land; and each stanza begins back where it started so that if the poem moves forward at all, it does so always looking back over one shoulder. This sets up something more like inertia than momentum, a reluctant progress that, in this particular example, is at one with the mourner's response to his letter of condolence. The mourner is not moved by the letter (to reply, to act, even to view his situation differently); instead he dwells upon it, going over and over the same ground, deepening his friend's shallow commonplace, but not really getting anywhere. His lack of progress is emphasised by the description of the progress of the day, from morning to evening. Time passes but each day is the same, because each day brings death and grief. The effect of time passing in this passage is the cumulative effect of repetition (more 'bitter' for being 'common'), rather than the onward march of progress.

I began this section by suggesting that metre was a way of measuring out, or giving form to, the time of grief. However, the *In Memoriam* stanza provides a form that constantly threatens to disintegrate or unravel itself. Again, the poem holds itself in tension: between fragmentation and wholeness, between the universal and the individual, between progress and stasis, between structure and chaos.

Remembering the Elegy

So far, thinking about the various ways that *In Memoriam* is pieced together, I have talked about the allusions that it makes to epic, ballad and lyric; but, as we saw in the letters written by Tennyson and his friends, *In Memoriam* is most often identified as an elegy. I have already discussed how the proposed title, 'Fragments of an Elegy', draws attention to the poem's fragility and incompleteness, but it is important also to consider what it is that *In Memoriam* fragments and / or collects back together. 'Fragments of an Elegy' implies that the elegy itself is broken in a way that must bear some relation to the broken body of Arthur Hallam. We are led to think about the elegy as a kind of poetry that is likewise lost and that is likewise mourned, or imperfectly remembered, by *In Memoriam*.

Elegy, loosely defined, is any kind of writing about any kind of loss. The word elegy comes from the Greek word *elegos*, which means 'mournful song' and originally referred to the form and performance of a poem rather than its content. Elegies were poems written in elegiac couplets that were often performed to the accompaniment of a particular kind of flute. The elongated length of the poetic lines and the melancholy tone of the flute meant that elegy came to be associated with reflective or solemn themes. Eventually, these themes – in other words, the content rather than the form of the elegy – became its defining feature. Developing out of this tradition, and influenced by the work of particular Ancient Greek writers (Theocritus, Bion and Moschus), the English Elegiac tradition more firmly established elegy as the poetry of grief, mourning and remembrance. Jahan Ramazani argues that *In Memoriam* represents a turning point for elegy, a break with or breakdown of the conventions of what he refers to as 'classical elegy' and the creation of 'modern elegy' (Ramazani 1994; 4). This is helpful when thinking about *In Memoriam* as fragments of an elegy. The elegy that *In Memoriam* fragments, in a way that allows it to be made new by modern authors, is the classical funeral elegy.

If the sonnet is a form of lyrical poetry in which a man expresses desire for a woman who is out of reach, then the classical elegy is a type of lyrical poetry in which a man expresses his grief for another man who is out of reach through death (of course, elegies, like sonnets, have been written by women, but this kind of elegy, like the sonnet, nevertheless remains a masculine tradition). This kind of elegy originates in the sixteenth century with 'Astrophel', Edmund Spenser's elegy for Sir Philip Sidney, a fellow poet who died in battle, aged thirty-two. Two other important elegies written within this tradition are *Lycidas* (1637/45), Milton's elegy for his classmate, Edward King, who drowned at the age of twenty-six, and *Adonais* (1821), Shelley's elegy for John Keats, who died in Rome of tuberculosis, aged twenty-five.[7] Each of these elegies, like *In Memoriam*, mourns the early death of a contemporary who, although not in every case a close friend, was of great significance to the author. Because of this shared circumstance, each elegist makes reference to, and employs the conventions of, earlier elegies in order both to elevate their subject and to elevate themselves: 'the elegist borrows [the] uniform of his predecessors to convince us of his seriousness and depth of feeling, so that elegy, more than any other genre of poetry, is a poem made out of other poems' (Kennedy 2007: 5). In other words, *all* elegies remember the elegies that have gone before them and so, even in its breaking down and piecing back together of elegiac tradition, *In Memoriam* takes part in the traditions of elegy. As Seamus Perry writes, Tennyson's poem 'elude[s] the expectation of classical elegy, while constantly evoking their possibility' (Perry 2004: 129).

To get a clearer sense of exactly how *In Memoriam* conforms to and subverts the patterns established by earlier elegies, it is helpful to compare Tennyson's poem directly with that group of elegies that make up its genealogy. In his important history of the elegy, Peter Sacks identifies a set of conventions that characterise the classical funeral elegy. For the purposes of this study, I have chosen to focus on just three: contest and inheritance, performance and the pastoral, and the movement from despair to consolation and resurrection.

Contest and Inheritance

In the masculine elegiac tradition, where a young male poet writes about the death of another young male poet, elegy's compensatory relationship with the loss that it mourns is intensified. The elegist voices his awareness that by writing a poem for a poet who can no longer write, he is walking in the shoes of a dead man. Therefore, comparison becomes one of the central conventions of elegy. These comparisons consistently favour the mourned object over the mourner, elevating his status by insisting that he is without equal and therefore cannot be replaced. Milton writes, 'For Lycidas is dead, dead ere his prime, / Young Lycidas, and hath not left his peer' (8–9),[8] and Shelley describes Keats as poetry's 'extreme hope, the loveliest and the last' (51).[9] 'Last' could simply mean most recent, but the reader is invited to understand that Keats's death represents for Shelley the untimely death of poetry itself.

Having insisted on the peerlessness of his subject, the elegist then reflects modestly on the inadequacy of his own skill, drawing himself into unfavourable comparisons with the great talent that has been lost. It is worth noting that, even by the seventeenth century, this is recognised as part of the conventional performance of elegy. Milton calls on the 'gentle Muse' of tragedy, who will begin the poem 'with denial vain and coy excuse' (18). It is a convention to which Milton nevertheless conforms, figuring himself as an 'uncouth swain' (186) and implying that his song is likewise crude and basic. However, these gestures of modesty in fact draw attention to, rather than masking, the sophistication of Milton's work, which manipulates elegiac conventions in order to construct a complex, extended political metaphor. Milton therefore employs his performance of grief at the death of a promising young poet to stage his own arrival on the literary and political scene. Likewise, Shelley stages his entrance on to the scene of mourning: 'one frail Form / A phantom among men; companionless' (271–2), describing himself as Keats's natural successor, and concluding his elegy with an image of himself sailing in a boat towards 'the inmost veil of Heaven' where 'the soul of Adonais, like a star, / Beacons from the abode where the Eternal are' (493–5). The 'Eternal' are those poets who have gained immortality through fame, and it is no accident that two of those poets that Shelley refers to directly in the poem are Milton and Sidney, the author and subject of two canonical elegies. In so doing, he offers a clear indication of his intentions for his elegy and identifies himself as the heir of Keats and of Spenser and Milton. In this respect, an elegy is as much a monument to the living promise of the elegist as it is a monument to the lost promise of the person mourned. An elegy is, paradoxically, a coming-of-age poem.

This is equally true of *In Memoriam*, which alludes to other poets and other elegies in order to indicate the high rank of both the poet's grief and his poetic skill. Section LXIX, for example, describes a dream in which the mourner imagines making and wearing a crown of thorns:

> I wandered from the noisy town,
>   I found a wood with thorny boughs:
>   I took the thorn to bind my brows,
> I wore it like a civic crown.
>   (LXIX, 5–8)

The mourner's dream alludes to Shelley's description of himself in *Adonais*: 'He answered no, but with a sudden hand / Made bare his branded and

ensaguined brow, / Which was like Cain's or Christ's' (304–6). By employing this image of poet as Christ-figure, Tennyson also draws a comparison
between himself and Shelley (*Adonais* was a poem that held particular significance for Tennyson because its publication, which occurred after Shelley
himself had died, was organised by the Apostles, the university society to
which Tennyson and Hallam had both belonged). However, the dream framework that Tennyson places around this self-image perhaps implies a certain
scepticism of the Shelleyan Poet-Christ, a suspicion that the religious power of
poetry that Shelley describes is an illusion. Both the fact of Tennyson's poetic
inheritance and its value are described as fantasy. Tennyson commented on
these lines: 'I tried to make my grief into a crown of these poems – but it is
not to be taken too closely – To write verses about grief and death is to wear
a crown of thorns which ought to be put by, as people say' (*EN*). A crown
of thorns also suggests a laurel wreath – a classical symbol of public honour
(root of the term 'Poet Laureate') and so this section also self-consciously
betrays the ambition invested in this kind of intertextual allusion.

In Memoriam's main contest, however, is with Hallam. The identity of the
mourner and mourned object are constituted via comparisons, the one with
the other:

> I vex my heart with fancies dim
>   He still outstript me in the race;
>   It was but unity of place
> That made me dream I ranked with him.
>   (XLII, 1–4)

In this case the mourner describes his friend's death as the experience of
being woken from a dream in which the two of them were equal. Here, and
throughout, *In Memoriam* conforms to the elegiac convention that insists on
the superiority of the mourned object. However, whereas in other elegies the
mourner implicitly gains the advantage in what David Kennedy describes as
the elegy's 'heroic performance of survival' (Kennedy 2007: 29), Tennyson
complicates the outcome of this elegiac contest through repeated references to
his friend's onward journey in death. In *Lycidas*, straightforward replacement
of dead voice by living voice takes place. The mourner, having established
that 'Lycidas' was a poet who 'knew / Himself to sing, and build the lofty
rhyme' (10–11), immediately refers to his own song: 'He must not float upon
the watery bier / Unwept, and welter to the paraching wind, / Without the
need of some melodious tear' (12–14). Milton's confidence that he can supply
a song that will both pay tribute to and sing in place of 'Lycidas' (King) is
complicated by Shelley, who insists that Adonais (Keats) has 'awakened from
the dream of life' (344) and that the living 'decay / Like corpses in a charnel'

(348–9) . He is nevertheless able to make this charnel into a lush poetic space where he can display his talents at length. Adonais has travelled ahead of the mourner, but at the end of the poem we see the mourner confidently following him.

As I will discuss in the 'Lost for Words' section of the Reading Guide, Tennyson's elegy, although much longer than either Milton's or Shelley's, constantly doubts its own adequacy to voice the absence of the poet's friend, stating: 'I leave thy praises unexpressed' and 'So here shall silence guard thy fame' (LXXV, 1 and 16). The speaker also dwells on the difference or distance between himself and his friend, which he often views as an insurmountable problem. Hallam is not imagined as a beacon that will guide Tennyson to an eventual reunion; instead Tennyson imagines how he must look to his friend as he gazes down on him: 'How dimly charactered and slight, / How dwarfed a growth of cold and night, / How blanched with darkness must I grow' (LXI, 6–8), so that the poet's inferiority is reasserted from this heavenly perspective. Survival is never heroic in *In Memoriam*: the poem stages a contest that Tennyson has always already lost.

Pastoral

Section XXXVII of *In Memoriam* abruptly introduces a set of classical references that seem to belong to another poem. The mourner is addressed by Urania and Melpemone, two Ancient Greek Muses (female personifications of different kinds of inspiration) associated with elegy. Here Tennyson gestures back through the English Elegiac tradition to its classical ancestry: the pastoral elegies of Theocritus, in which a shepherd calls on the Muses to help him express his grief at the death of a fellow shepherd. Pastoral literature is literature that figures the countryside as a location of leisure, retreat, simplicity and renewal. Within the pastoral elegy, the mourner-poet finds the time and space to mourn and the opportunity to re-establish the natural order that has been upset by the untimely death they mourn. As David Kennedy puts it, pastoral elegy 'examines change and loss against continuity' (Kennedy 2007: 17).

English elegies establish themselves within the privileged natural environment of the pastoral by gesturing towards the figures and tropes that populate classical pastoral elegies. The retreat of the English elegist to simple, natural surroundings can therefore also be understood as a retreat from the present into the past. *Lycidas* and *Adonais* achieve a more wholesale engagement with the pastoral mode. In *Lycidas*, Milton represents himself and King as fellow shepherds, tending their flocks and playing rustic music together in a fantastic rural idyll: 'Meanwhile the rural ditties were not mute / Tempered to the oaten flute, / Rough satyrs danced, and fawns with cloven heel / From the glad sound would not be absent long' (32–5). Shelley also retreats to the landscape of classical pastoral to mourn Keats, whom he transforms into Adonais, a derivation of a character from Greek myth. Both Milton and Shelley are self-consciously artful in their employment of the pastoral mode, constructing complex extended metaphors from the pastoral's props and furnishings. In *Lycidas*, the sheep and shepherds become a metaphor for failings in the English church, and in *Adonais*, Keats's poems are figured as his 'flocks, whom near the living streams / Of his young spirit he fed' (75–6). Both also test and play with the conventions of pastoral, challenging the natural order that pastoral asserts. Nevertheless, in both poems the performance of pastoral is sustained throughout.

In Memoriam is scarcely a pastoral elegy at all.[10] The poem's setting is as often urban as it is rural. It might be possible to draw a comparison between the dramatised voice of Tennyson's mourner and the masks adopted by authors of other pastoral elegies, but the mask of the mourner is closely modelled on the features of its wearer rather than borrowed from the classics. Any references to the classical tradition of pastoral elegy are made piecemeal, appearing as single, detached fragments that refuse to be integrated into any kind of complete reading. In section C the mourner looks out from the top of a hill and finds 'no place that does not breathe / Some gracious memory of my friend'. The scene stretched out before him is pastoral:

> Nor rivulet tinkling from the rock,
>   Nor pastoral rivulet that swerves
>   To left and right through meadow curves,
> That feed the mothers of the flock.
>   (C, 13–16)

But this pastoral moment extends only brief comfort:

> But each has pleased a kindred eye,
>   And each reflects a kindlier day;
>   And leaving these, to pass away
> I think once more he seems to die
>   (C, 17–20)

Whereas, for earlier elegists, the pastoral represents a place of imaginative return to the past, Tennyson's mourner can only observe it from a distance, regarding it as something irretrievably lost, from which he must 'pass away'. In these moments, where the pastoral comes briefly into view, *In Memoriam* performs the rejection of the pastoral mode and its failure to provide relief. This rejection might be understood as an assertion of modernity, which can be read in the context of *In Memoriam*'s engagement with

Victorian science and the profound challenges that it presented to the consolations of the natural world (a theme I return to in more detail later in the Guide).

Consolation and Resurrection

The consolation offered by nature and religion form a third important convention of traditional masculine elegy, which moves towards a restoration of the natural order and the promise of resurrection. In *Lycidas* these two related ends are enabled by the pastoral framework of the poem. The poem, which begins by demanding that melodious tears be shed, concludes with an injunction to 'Weep no more, woeful shepherds, weep no more, / For Lycidas your sorrow is not dead' (165–6). It compares Lycidas to the sun which sets at night only to rise again in the morning: 'So Lycidas sunk low, but mounted high, / Through the dear might of him that walked the waves' (172–3). God in Christ works in harmony with the cycle of nature to confirm Lycidas's immortality. Death ends with rebirth, and the shepherd is able to move on to the 'fresh woods and pastures new' (193) because he has been restored by the work of elegy. In the same way, Shelley, who begins, 'I weep for Adonais – he is dead!', concludes, 'Peace, peace! he is not dead, he does not sleep, / He hath awakened from the dream of life' (343–4). For Shelley, natural consolation and religious resurrection are one and the same. His elegy ascribes to a neo-Platonic belief system that recognises the creative and immortal power of nature, to which Keats has returned, and through which he now lives. Shelley is also more concerned with the power of his own poetry to immortalise (both himself and Keats), so that the final image of Shelley travelling towards Keats's star in a boat mingles nature, life and poetry as a single 'breath' that carries the poet onward.

The breakdown of pastoral in *In Memoriam* means that it can neither perform, nor confidently look forward to, the resurrection of Hallam. Throughout, the elegy returns to images of natural consolation and Christian resurrection, but rather than finding comfort in them, it interrogates them, subjecting them to the mourner's sceptical gaze. Section XXXI considers the gospel story of the resurrection of Lazarus, and focuses on Mary's question to her brother: 'Where were't thou brother, those four days?' The mourner is troubled by the fact that, in the gospel account, Mary receives no answer:

Behold a man raised up by Christ!
  The rest remaineth unrevealed;
  He told it not; or something sealed
The lips of the Evangelist.
                (XXXI, 13–16)

Like Mary, the mourner wants to know the answer to that child-like question, 'where do we go when we die?' His suspicion is that the answer is unspeakable, and his fear is that the place or the experience of death is something so foreign that his friend (referred to later as 'strange friend') will be transformed beyond recognition, so that resurrection is not, in fact, the same as day returning after night, but is a more radical and disruptive change that should be feared as much as looked forward to.

Other sections of *In Memoriam* are happier to accept the consolation offered by the elegiac conventions of natural renewal and Christian resurrection. Section XLIII considers death and resurrection in terms of night and day, sleep and waking, arguing that, 'If Sleep and Death be truly one' then 'love will last as pure and whole / As when he loved me here in Time, / And at the spiritual prime / Rewaken with the dawning soul' (XLIII, 1 and 13–16). But unlike Shelley's or Milton's confident formulations of these elegiac tropes, Tennyson's description of death as a peaceful and changeless sleep is conditional. By saying '*If* Sleep and Death be truly one', the speaker opens up the possibility of an 'If *not*' that exists as an unwritten contradiction to faith and hope. The section that follows reopens the question, immediately disrupting the fragile optimism of the previous lines, 'How fares it with the happy dead?' (XLIV, 1), and the mourner again expresses doubt that his friend will ever know him again. Any consolation that *In Memoriam* achieves is temporary and doubtful. In fact, the only thing that *In Memoriam* is ever confident about is its doubt: 'There lives more faith in honest doubt. / Believe me, than in half the creeds' (XCI, 11–12). *In Memoriam*'s paradoxical declaration of doubtful faith or faithful doubt suggests that faith is not proved by the repetition of creeds (which are formal confessions of faith, often said as part of a religious service), but by testing and questioning the conventions of those creeds, conventions that inform the conventions of elegy. I return to these questions in more detail in the 'Cycle and Ritual' section of this Guide, but it is important to recognise poetry and religion as mutually informing traditions, so that form falters with faith.

As *In Memoriam* draws to a close, it returns to those elegiac conventions that it has thrown into doubt. Tennyson's mourner comes round to the idea that his friend survives in God, in nature and in himself:

> Known and unknown; human, divine;
> > Sweet human hand and lips and eye;
> > Dear heavenly friend that canst not die,
> Mine, mine forever, ever mine;
> > > > (CXXIX, 5–8)

On first reading this section, we might argue that elegy achieves its moment of resurrection at the moment when it takes possession of its subject: 'Mine,

mine forever, ever mine' (8). However, on a second reading, this triumphant cry begins to sound strained or desperate (in *Maud*, a poem published five years after the publication of *In Memoriam*, Tennyson puts similar words into the mouth of a mad man, who deludes himself into thinking that the women he loves belongs to him: 'Mine, mine by a right, from birth till death. / Mine, mine – our fathers have sworn' (725–6)). Whereas we believe Shelley, when he expresses his faith that 'He lives, he wakes – 'tis Death is dead, not he' (361), there is something about this moment of reconciliation that does not ring true. Although Milton and Shelley profess different religious faiths, both their elegies express complete faith in the power of poetry to resurrect and immortalise. Tennyson's belief in the ability of elegy to defy death is never so secure. In this section, the mourner's hold on his friend is called into question by the paradoxes that he uses, which describe the conclusions that his elegy has reached. Hallam is a 'strange friend', 'known and unknown', 'so far, so near', 'past, present and to be'. Christopher Ricks makes sense of some of these paradoxes for us:

> The suggestion of paradox in 'Strange friend' (the dead friend cannot but be almost a stranger) is [. . .] taken up in 'Loved deeplier, darklier understood' – when you love someone deeply you do indeed understand them more and yet the understanding is not simply illumination – love makes you more aware of the mysteriousness of another, makes you understand 'darklier' the person that you understandingly love. (Ricks 1989: 223)

Ricks is right, but it is worth noting that *In Memoriam* leaves the sense of these lines unmade, holding these opposites in tension and allowing the reader to appreciate their difference from one another. These paradoxes are a much more accurate representation of the kind of double-edged consolation that *In Memoriam* finds in itself. Unlike *Adonais* and *Lycidas*, it does not achieve an untroubled harmony or wholeness at its conclusion; instead it finds a way to accommodate, without solving, the questions, doubts and deep loss caused by death.

Notes

1. For the best, recent biographical account of Tennyson and Hallam's friendship and *In Memoriam*'s publication, see Robert Martin's biography of Tennyson (1980). For more detailed biographical information about Arthur Hallam, see *A Life Lived Quickly* by Martin Blocksidge (2010).
2. Shatto and Shaw quote Tennyson, 'I alluded to Goethe's creed. Among his last words were [. . .] "from changes to higher changes".' They also note that there is no record of these words belonging to Goethe (Shatto and Shaw 1982: 162).
3. For readings of other nineteenth-century epics, see Herbert Tucker (2008), *Epic: Britain's Heroic Muse 1790–1910*.
4. For more detailed and extensive analysis of the *In Memoriam* manuscripts, see

Christopher Ricks's annotated edition of the poem (1987) and Susan Shatto and Marion Shaw's excellent single-volume edition (1982).

5. Anne Janowitz explores the changing political significance of the ballad form at the turn of the nineteenth century in *Lyric and Labour in the Romantic Tradition* (1998).

6. A. C. Bradley's early and influential commentary on *In Memoriam* (1901) offers a helpful discussion of Tennyson's development of the *In Memoriam* stanza. See also Perry 2004: 135–6.

7. A. C. Bradley also carries out a comparison between *Lycidas*, *Adonais* and *In Memoriam* (Bradley 1901: 23).

8. All quotations from *Lycidas* are taken from John Milton (1971), *The Complete Shorter Poems*, ed. John Carey, London: Longman, pp. 232–54.

9. All quotations from *Adonais* are taken from P. B. Shelley (1970), *Complete Poems*, ed. Thomas Hutchinson, 2nd edn, London: Oxford University Press, pp. 430–44.

10. Other critics argue that *In Memoriam* identifies itself more closely with the pastoral mode. See, for example, Buckley (1960), pp. 115–17; Sinfield (1971), pp. 64–5.

Chapter 2

The Poem

The Reading Guide aims to lead the reader through *In Memoriam* and should be read alongside the text of the poem, which is printed, in full, below. Initially, it is important to read *In Memoriam* from beginning to end in order to gain an appreciation of the poem's shape and the narrative that it outlines. To help with this, I provide a summary of the poem and a brief accompanying glossary indicating sections addressed in the commentary. However, because *In Memoriam* is a poem of fragments that both construct and threaten to disassemble the whole, the Guide, which follows the full text of the poem, does not perform a straightforwardly chronological reading of the poem. Instead, it selects four different pathways through the text, each focusing on a particular theme: language, touch, economies of loss, and cycles and rituals.[1] Taking the poem apart and piecing it back together in different ways will give a sense of the wide variety of images, metaphors, ideas and arguments that *In Memoriam* strains to hold together within its length and of the different ways that they work with and against one another. The themes I have chosen provide just a sample of the different ways through *In Memoriam*, and in the 'Teaching the Text' section that concludes this book I suggest others that readers might want to trace for themselves. At the beginning of each reading, I list those sections of the poem on which the reading focuses and it is a good idea to reread those sections before coming to the commentary text. In each case, the commentary will explain some of the key ideas that underpin the reading and then explore how these ideas find expression in *In Memoriam*, and how they inform and structure the elegy.

Outline

As we have seen, *In Memoriam* does not describe a sequence of events that can be neatly summarised. However, in an article by Tennyson's friend, James Knowles, published in 1893, in which Knowles records Tennyson's own comments about his elegy, Tennyson argues that the poem can be divided up into a number of groups (Knowles 1893: 182). I use these groups as the basis for a 'map' of *In Memoriam*, offering brief summaries of the content of each group.

Prologue (not mentioned in Knowles's article): A prayer in which the mourner expresses faith in God and asks forgiveness for moments of doubt caused by grief.

Sections I to VIII: The mourner describes the initial shock and despair of loss.

Sections IX to XXI: The 'fair ship' lyrics, which focus on the return of Hallam's body from Austria to England.

Sections XXII to XXVII: The mourner reflects on his friendship with A. H. H. and considers the end of their shared life.

Sections XXVIII to XLIX: The first of three Christmases. The speaker and his family celebrate and mourn together. In the sections that follow, the mourner's grief is tempered by a tentative renewal of faith.

Sections L to LVIII: These sections consider different kinds of progress: the progress of A. H. H. as he moves on ahead of the mourner in death, and the progress of the species, which is called into question by the proofs of evolutionary science.

Sections LIX to LXXI: Returning again to think about the change that his friend has undergone in death, the mourner wonders whether the distance that separates them from one another will ever be bridged. He describes the temporary, illusory reunion offered by sleep and dreams and expresses a desire to be haunted.

Sections LXXII to XCVIII: This group, which begins on the anniversary of Hallam's death and which includes the elegy's second Christmas, begins to trace a more certain recovery, a return to the concerns of everyday life and a resignation or reconciliation to the death of A. H. H.

Sections XCIX to CIII: This small group begins on the same day one year later and refers to the move from the family home at Somersby to a new home at Dalby, made by the Tennyson family in 1837.

Sections CIV to CXXXI: The last group begins with the third Christmas, spent in an unfamiliar location that offers the possibility of a new beginning. As the poem draws to a close, winter moves into spring and the mourner begins to look towards the future with renewed faith, both in God and in his own work.

Epilogue (not mentioned in Knowles's article): Describes the marriage of Tennyson's sister, Cecilia, and his friend, Edmund Lushington.

The Poem

The text of *In Memoriam* is taken from the Eversley Edition (1907–8), edited by Tennyson's son, Hallam Tennyson. The only editorial change to the text is the removal of apostrophised abbreviations (so that 'thro'' becomes 'through', 'possess'd' becomes 'possessed', and so on). Explanatory notes that were provided by Tennyson and included in an appendix to the Eversley are also given as footnotes. Notes in languages other than English are given in translation.

IN MEMORIAM A. H. H.
OBIT MDCCCXXXIII

```
1    Strong Son of God, immortal Love,*
2        Whom we, that have not seen thy face,
3        By faith, and faith alone, embrace,
4    Believing where we cannot prove;

5    Thine are these orbs of light and shade;*
6        Thou madest Life in man and brute;
7        Thou madest Death; and lo, thy foot
8    Is on the skull which thou hast made.

9    Thou wilt not leave us in the dust:
10       Thou madest man, he knows not why,
11       He thinks he was not made to die;
12   And thou hast made him: thou art just.

13   Thou seemest human and divine,
14       The highest, holiest manhood, thou:
15       Our wills are ours, we know not how;
16   Our wills are ours, to make them thine.

17   Our little systems have their day;
18       They have their day and cease to be:
19       They are but broken lights of thee,
20   And thou, O Lord, art more than they.

21   We have but faith: we cannot know;
22       For knowledge is of things we see;
```

The Prologue is an affirmation of Christian faith that praises God as the author of creation, expresses belief in a divine wisdom that exceeds human knowledge and hope that humanity will eventually return to perfect knowledge of and union with God. See: 'Lost for Words'.

---

1 The footnotes that follow reproduce Tennyson's notes to the poem. This might be taken in a St John sense.
5 Sun and Moon.

23   And yet we trust it comes from thee,
24   A beam in darkness: let it grow.

25   Let knowledge grow from more to more,
26   But more of reverence in us dwell;
27   That mind and soul, according well,
28   May make one music as before,*

29   But vaster. We are fools and slight;
30   We mock thee when we do not fear:
31   But help thy foolish ones to bear;
32   Help thy vain worlds to bear thy light.

33   Forgive what seemed my sin in me;
34   What seemed my worth since I began;
35   For merit lives from man to man,
36   And not from man, O Lord, to thee.

37   Forgive my grief for one removed,
38   Thy creature, whom I found so fair.
39   I trust he lives in thee, and there
40   I find him worthier to be loved.

41   Forgive these wild and wandering cries,
42   Confusions of a wasted youth;
43   Forgive them where they fail in truth,
44   And in thy wisdom make me wise.

1849

I.

1   I held it truth, with him who sings
2   To one clear harp in divers tones,
3   That men may rise on stepping-stones
4   Of their dead selves to higher things.*

5   But who shall so forecast the years
6   And find in loss a gain to match?
7   Or reach a hand through time to catch
8   The far-off interest of tears?*

The mourner begins in a state of intense doubt, unable to escape the immediate circumstances of his grief. See: 'Losing Touch' and 'Profit and Loss'.

28 As in the ages of faith.
4 I alluded to Goethe's creed. Among his last words were these [. . .] 'from changes to higher changes'.
8 The good that grows for us out of grief.

9   Let Love clasp Grief lest both be drowned,
10   Let darkness keep her raven gloss:
11   Ah, sweeter to be drunk with loss,
12   To dance with death, to beat the ground,

13   Than that the victor Hours should scorn
14   The long result of love, and boast,
15   'Behold the man that loved and lost,
16   But all he was is overworn.'*

II.

The mourner compares himself with a tree that stands in a graveyard. See: 'Lost for Words' and 'Losing Touch'.

1   Old Yew, which graspest at the stones
2   That name the under-lying dead,
3   Thy fibres net the dreamless head,*
4   Thy roots are wrapt about the bones.

5   The seasons bring the flower again,
6   And bring the firstling to the flock;
7   And in the dusk of thee, the clock
8   Beats out the little lives of men.

9   O not for thee the glow, the bloom,
10   Who changest not in any gale,
11   Nor branding summer suns avail
12   To touch thy thousand years of gloom:

13   And gazing on thee, sullen tree,
14   Sick for thy stubborn hardihood,
15   I seem to fail from out my blood
16   And grow incorporate into thee.

III.*

The mourner listens to the voice of Sorrow, who insinuates doubts about the meaning and purpose of life and death. See: 'Losing Touch'.

1   O Sorrow , cruel fellowship,
2   O Priestess in the vaults of Death,
3   O sweet and bitter in a breath,
4   What whispers from thy lying lip?

5   'The stars,' she whispers, 'blindly run;
6   A web is woven across the sky;

16 Yet it is better to bear the wild misery of extreme grief than that Time should obliterate the sense of loss and deaden the power of love.
3 'The powerless heads of the dead' (*Odyssey* X, 521 etc.).
III First realization of blind sorrow.

7   From out waste places comes a cry,
8   And murmurs from the dying sun:*

9   'And all the phantom, Nature, stands –
10   With all the music in her tone,
11   A hollow echo of my own, –
12   A hollow form with empty hands.'

13   And shall I take a thing so blind,
14   Embrace her as my natural good;
15   Or crush her, like a vice of blood,
16   Upon the threshold of the mind?

      IV.

1   To Sleep I give my powers away;
2   My will is bondsman to the dark;
3   I sit within a helmless bark,
4   And with my heart I muse and say:

5   O heart, how fares it with thee now,
6   That thou should'st fail from thy desire,
7   Who scarcely darest to inquire,
8   'What is it makes me beat so low?'

9   Something it is which thou hast lost,
10   Some pleasure from thine early years.
11   Break, thou deep vase of chilling tears,
12   That grief hath shaken into frost!*

13   Such clouds of nameless trouble cross
14   All night below the darkened eyes;
15   With morning wakes the will, and cries,
16   'Thou shalt not be the fool of loss.'

      V.

1   I sometimes hold it half a sin
2   To put in words the grief I feel;
3   For words, like Nature, half reveal
4   And half conceal the Soul within.

The mourner surrenders himself to sleep and to unconscious thought. See: 'Profit and Loss'.

This section expresses the mourner's doubts about his own ability to express his grief accurately in poetry. See: 'Lost for Words' and 'Losing Touch'.

---

8 Expresses the feeling that sad things in nature affect him who mourns.

12 Water can be brought below freezing point and not turn into ice – if it be kept still; but if it be moved, suddenly it turns into ice and may break the vase.

5   But, for the unquiet heart and brain,
6   A use in measured language lies;
7   The sad mechanic exercise,
8   Like dull narcotics, numbing pain.

9   In words, like weeds, I'll wrap me o'er,
10   Like coarsest clothes against the cold:
11   But that large grief which these enfold
12 Is given in outline and no more.

            VI.
1   One writes, that 'Other friends remain,'
2   That 'Loss is common to the race'–
3   And common is the commonplace,
4   And vacant chaff well meant for grain.

The mourner describes the inadequate
consolation offered by letters of
condolence.
See: 'Lost for Words'.

5   That loss is common would not make
6   My own less bitter, rather more:
7   Too common! Never morning wore
8   To evening, but some heart did break.

9   O father, wheresoe'er thou be,
10   Who pledgest now thy gallant son;
11   A shot, ere half thy draught be done,
12 Hath stilled the life that beat from thee.

13 O mother, praying God will save
14   Thy sailor, – while thy head is bowed,
15   His heavy-shotted hammock-shroud
16 Drops in his vast and wandering grave.

17 Ye know no more than I who wrought
18   At that last hour to please him well;
19   Who mused on all I had to tell,
20 And something written, something thought;

21 Expecting still his advent home;
22   And ever met him on his way
23   With wishes, thinking, 'here to-day,'
24 Or 'here to-morrow will he come.'

25 O somewhere, meek, unconscious dove,
26   That sittest ranging golden hair;

27   And glad to find thyself so fair,
28   Poor child, that waitest for thy love!

29   For now her father's chimney glows
30   In expectation of a guest;
31   And thinking 'this will please him best,'
32   She takes a riband or a rose;

33   For he will see them on to-night;
34   And with the thought her colour burns;
35   And, having left the glass, she turns
36   Once more to set a ringlet right;

37   And, even when she turned, the curse
38   Had fallen, and her future Lord
39   Was drowned in passing through the ford,
40   Or killed in falling from his horse.

41   O what to her shall be the end?
42   And what to me remains of good?
43   To her, perpetual maidenhood,
44   And unto me no second friend.

VII.

1   Dark house, by which once more I stand
2   Here in the long unlovely street,
3   Doors, where my heart was used to beat
4   So quickly, waiting for a hand,

5   A hand that can be clasped no more –
6   Behold me, for I cannot sleep,
7   And like a guilty thing I creep
8   At earliest morning to the door.

9   He is not here; but far away
10   The noise of life begins again,
11   And ghastly through the drizzling rain
12   On the bald street breaks the blank day.

The mourner visits his friend's home and stands at the door.
See: 'Losing Touch'.

VIII.

1   A happy lover who has come
2   To look on her that loves him well,
3   Who 'lights and rings the gateway bell,
4   And learns her gone and far from home;

The mourner compares himself to a lover who visits the house of his beloved, only to find that she has gone away. He compares his poem to a flower that he plants on the tomb of his friend.
See: 'Lost for Words'.

5   He saddens, all the magic light
6   Dies off at once from bower and hall,
7   And all the place is dark, and all
8   The chambers emptied of delight:

9   So find I every pleasant spot
10   In which we two were wont to meet,
11   The field, the chamber and the street,
12 For all is dark where thou art not.

13 Yet as that other, wandering there
14   In those deserted walks, may find
15   A flower beat with rain and wind,
16 Which once she fostered up with care;

17 So seems it in my deep regret,
18   O my forsaken heart, with thee
19   And this poor flower of poesy
20 Which little cared for fades not yet.

21 But since it pleased a vanished eye,
22   I go to plant it on his tomb,
23   That if it can it there may bloom,
24 Or dying, there at least may die.

IX.

1   Fair ship, that from the Italian shore
2   Sailest the placid ocean-plains
3   With my lost Arthur's loved remains,
4   Spread thy full wings, and waft him o'er.

5   So draw him home to those that mourn
6   In vain; a favourable speed
7   Ruffle thy mirrored mast, and lead
8   Through prosperous floods his holy urn.

9   All night no ruder air perplex
10   Thy sliding keel, till Phosphor,* bright
11   As our pure love, through early light
12 Shall glimmer on the dewy decks.

The mourner addresses the ship that
brings Arthur's body back from
Austria for burial in England.
See: 'Cycle and Ritual'.

10 Star of dawn.

13   Sphere all your lights around, above;
14   Sleep, gentle heavens, before the prow;
15   Sleep, gentle winds, as he sleeps now,
16   My friend, the brother of my love;

17   My Arthur, whom I shall not see
18   Till all my widowed race be run;
19   Dear as the mother to the son,
20   More than my brothers are to me.

X.

1   I hear the noise about thy keel;
2   I hear the bell struck in the night:
3   I see the cabin-window bright;
4   I see the sailor at the wheel.

The mourner continues his address, imagining all the things that a ship might bring and reflecting on the importance of the ritual of burial. See: 'Losing Touch' and 'Cycle and Ritual'.

5   Thou bringest the sailor to his wife,
6   And travelled men from foreign lands;
7   And letters unto trembling hands;
8   And, thy dark freight, a vanished life.

9   So bring him: we have idle dreams:
10   This look of quiet flatters thus
11   Our home-bred fancies: O to us,
12   The fools of habit, sweeter seems

13   To rest beneath the clover sod,
14   That takes the sunshine and the rains,
15   Or where the kneeling hamlet drains
16   The chalice of the grapes of God;

17   Than if with thee the roaring wells
18   Should gulf him fathom-deep in brine;
19   And hands so often clasped in mine,
20   Should toss with tangle* and with shells.

XI.

1   Calm is the morn without a sound,
2   Calm as to suit a calmer grief,
3   And only through the faded leaf
4   The chestnut pattering to the ground:

---

20 *Tangle*, or 'oar-weed'.

5   Calm and deep peace on this high wold,*
6   And on these dews that drench the furze,
7   And all the silvery gossamers
8   That twinkle into green and gold:

9   Calm and still light on yon great plain
10   That sweeps with all its autumn bowers,
11   And crowded farms and lessening towers,
12 To mingle with the bounding main:

13 Calm and deep peace in this wide air,
14   These leaves that redden to the fall;
15   And in my heart, if calm at all,
16 If any calm, a calm despair:

17 Calm on the seas, and silver sleep,
18   And waves that sway themselves in rest,
19   And dead calm in that noble breast
20 Which heaves but with the heaving deep.

        XII.
1   Lo, as a dove when up she springs
2   To bear through Heaven a tale of woe,
3   Some dolorous message knit below
4   The wild pulsation of her wings;

5   Like her I go; I cannot stay;
6   I leave this mortal ark behind,*
7   A weight of nerves without a mind,
8   And leave the cliffs, and haste away

9   O'er ocean-mirrors rounded large,
10   And reach the glow of southern skies,
11   And see the sails at distance rise,
12 And linger weeping on the marge,

13 And saying; 'Comes he thus, my friend?
14   Is this the end of all my care?'
15   And circle moaning in the air:
16 'Is this the end? Is this the end?'

5 A Lincolnshire wold or upland from which the whole range of marsh to the sea is visible.
6 My spirit flies from out my material self.

17   And forward dart again, and play
18   About the prow, and back return
19   To where the body sits, and learn
20   That I have been an hour away.

XIII.

1   Tears of the widower, when he sees
2   A late-lost form that sleep reveals,
3   And moves his doubtful arms, and feels
4   Her place is empty, fall like these;

5   Which weep a loss for ever new,
6   A void where heart on heart reposed;
7   And, where warm hands have prest and closed,
8   Silence, till I be silent too.

9   Which weep the comrade of my choice,
10   An awful thought, a life removed,
11   The human-hearted man I loved,
12   A Spirit, not a breathing voice.

13   Come Time, and teach me, many years,
14   I do not suffer in a dream;
15   For now so strange do these things seem,
16   Mine eyes have leisure for their tears;

17   My fancies time to rise on wing,
18   And glance about the approaching sails,
19   As though they brought but merchants' bales,
20   And not the burthen that they bring.

The mourner compares his tears to the tears of a widower.
See: 'Lost for Words'.

XIV.

1   If one should bring me this report,
2   That thou hadst touched the land to-day,
3   And I went down unto the quay,
4   And found thee lying in the port;

5   And standing, muffled round with woe,
6   Should see thy passengers in rank
7   Come stepping lightly down the plank,
8   And beckoning unto those they know;

9   And if along with these should come
10   The man I held as half-divine;

The mourner imagines what might happen if Arthur were to return, alive.
See: 'Losing Touch'.

11   Should strike a sudden hand in mine,
12   And ask a thousand things of home;

13   And I should tell him all my pain,
14   And how my life had drooped of late,
15   And he should sorrow o'er my state
16   And marvel what possessed my brain;

17   And I perceived no touch of change,
18   No hint of death in all his frame,
19   But found him all in all the same,
20   I should not feel it to be strange.

XV.

1   To-night the winds begin to rise
2   And roar from yonder dropping day:
3   The last red leaf is whirled away,
4   The rooks are blown about the skies;

5   The forest cracked, the waters curled,
6   The cattle huddled on the lea;
7   And wildly dashed on tower and tree
8   The sunbeam strikes along the world:

9   And but for fancies, which aver
10   That all thy motions gently pass
11   Athwart a plane of molten glass,*
12   I scarce could brook the strain and stir

13   That makes the barren branches loud;
14   And but for fear it is not so,
15   The wild unrest that lives in woe
16   Would dote and pore on yonder cloud

17   That rises upward always higher,
18   And onward drags a labouring breast,
19   And topples round the dreary west,
20   A looming bastion fringed with fire.

XVI.

1   What words are these have fallen from me?
2   Can calm despair and wild unrest

The mourner turns once more to the subject of his own writing. See: 'Lost for Words'.

11 A calm sea.

```
3      Be tenants of a single breast,
4      Or sorrow such a changeling be?

5      Or doth she only seem to take
6          The touch of change in calm or storm;
7          But knows no more of transient form
8      In her deep self, than some dead lake

9      That holds the shadow of a lark
10         Hung in the shadow of a heaven?
11         Or has the shock, so harshly given,
12     Confused me like the unhappy bark

13     That strikes by night a craggy shelf,
14         And staggers blindly ere she sink?
15         And stunned me from my power to think
16     And all my knowledge of myself;

17     And made me that delirious man
18         Whose fancy fuses old and new,
19         And flashes into false and true,
20     And mingles all without a plan?
```

XVII.

```
1      Thou comest, much wept for: such a breeze
2          Compelled thy canvas, and my prayer
3          Was as the whisper of an air
4      To breathe thee over lonely seas.

5      For I in spirit saw thee move
6          Through circles of the bounding sky,
7          Week after week: the days go by:
8      Come quick, thou bringest all I love.

9      Henceforth, wherever thou may'st roam,
10         My blessing, like a line of light,
11         Is on the waters day and night,
12     And like a beacon guards thee home.

13     So may whatever tempest mars
14         Mid-ocean, spare thee, sacred bark;
15         And balmy drops in summer dark
16     Slide from the bosom of the stars.
```

The mourner blesses the ship as he imagines its approach.
See: 'Cycles and Rituals'.

17   So kind an office hath been done,
18   Such precious relics brought by thee;
19   The dust of him I shall not see
20   Till all my widowed race be run.

      XVIII.

1   'Tis well; 'tis something; we may stand
2   Where he in English earth is laid,
3   And from his ashes may be made
4   The violet of his native land.*

5   'Tis little; but it looks in truth
6   As if the quiet bones were blest
7   Among familiar names to rest
8   And in the places of his youth.

9   Come then, pure hands, and bear the head
10   That sleeps or wears the mask of sleep,
11   And come, whatever loves to weep,
12   And hear the ritual of the dead.

13   Ah yet, even yet, if this might be,
14   I, falling on his faithful heart,
15   Would breathing through his lips impart
16   The life that almost dies in me;

17   That dies not, but endures with pain,
18   And slowly forms the firmer mind,
19   Treasuring the look it cannot find,
20   The words that are not heard again.

      XIX.

1   The Danube to the Severn gave*
2   The darkened heart that beat no more;
3   They laid him by the pleasant shore,
4   And in the hearing of the wave.

5   There twice a day the Severn fills;
6   The salt sea-water passes by,

Returns to the theme of the burial.
See: 'Cycle and Ritual'.

---

   4 Cf. 'Lay her in the earth, / And from her fair and unpolluted flesh / May violets spring' (*Hamlet*, V, i, 232–4).
   1 He died at Vienna and was brought to Clevedon to be buried.

7   And hushes half the babbling Wye,
8   And makes a silence in the hills.*

9   The Wye is hushed nor moved along,
10   And hushed my deepest grief of all,
11   When filled with tears that cannot fall,
12   I brim with sorrow drowning song.

13   The tide flows down, the wave again
14   Is vocal in its wooded walls;
15   My deeper anguish also falls,
16   And I can speak a little then.

XX.

1   The lesser griefs that may be said,
2   That breathe a thousand tender vows,
3   Are but as servants in a house
4   Where lies the master newly dead;

5   Who speak their feeling as it is,
6   And weep the fulness from the mind:
7   'It will be hard,' they say, 'to find
8   Another service such as this.'

9   My lighter moods are like to these,
10   That out of words a comfort win;
11   But there are other griefs within,
12   And tears that at their fountain freeze;

13   For by the hearth the children sit
14   Cold in that atmosphere of Death,
15   And scarce endure to draw the breath,
16   Or like to noiseless phantoms flit:

17   But open converse is there none,
18   So much the vital spirits sink
19   To see the vacant chair, and think,
20   'How good! how kind! and he is gone.'

Draws a comparison between 'lesser griefs', which can be expressed, and 'other griefs' that cannot.
See: 'Lost for Words' and 'Profit and Loss'.

XXI.

1   I sing to him that rests below,
2   And, since the grasses round me wave,

Written in the pastoral mode, this section addresses questions about the place of elegiac, lyric verse in the modern world.
See: 'Lost for Words'.

8 Taken from my own observation – the rapids of the Wye are stilled by the incoming sea.

3   I take the grasses of the grave,
4   And make them pipes whereon to blow.

5   The traveller hears me now and then,
6   And sometimes harshly will he speak:
7   'This fellow would make weakness weak,
8   And melt the waxen hearts of men.'

9   Another answers, 'Let him be,
10   He loves to make parade of pain
11   That with his piping he may gain
12   The praise that comes to constancy.'

13   A third is wroth: 'Is this an hour
14   For private sorrow's barren song,
15   When more and more the people throng
16   The chairs and thrones of civil power?

17   'A time to sicken and to swoon,
18   When Science reaches forth her arms
19   To feel from world to world, and charms
20   Her secret from the latest moon?'

21   Behold, ye speak an idle thing:
22   Ye never knew the sacred dust:
23   I do but sing because I must,
24   And pipe but as the linnets sing:

25   And one is glad; her note is gay,
26   For now her little ones have ranged;
27   And one is sad; her note is changed,
28   Because her brood is stolen away.

XXII.
1   The path by which we twain did go,
2   Which led by tracts that pleased us well,
3   Through four sweet years arose and fell,
4   From flower to flower, from snow to snow:

5   And we with singing cheered the way,
6   And, crowned with all the season lent,
7   From April on to April went,
8   And glad at heart from May to May:

9   But where the path we walked began
10   To slant the fifth autumnal slope,
11   As we descended following Hope,
12   There sat the Shadow feared of man;

13   Who broke our fair companionship,
14   And spread his mantle dark and cold,
15   And wrapt thee formless in the fold,
16   And dulled the murmur on thy lip,

17   And bore thee where I could not see
18   Nor follow, though I walk in haste,
19   And think, that somewhere in the waste
20   The Shadow sits and waits for me.

             XXIII.
1   Now , sometimes in my sorrow shut,
2   Or breaking into song by fits,
3   Alone, alone, to where he sits,
4   The Shadow cloaked from head to foot,

5   Who keeps the keys of all the creeds,*
6   I wander, often falling lame,
7   And looking back to whence I came,
8   Or on to where the pathway leads;

9   And crying, How changed from where it ran
10   Through lands where not a leaf was dumb;
11   But all the lavish hills would hum
12   The murmur of a happy Pan:

13   When each by turns was guide to each,
14   And Fancy light from Fancy caught,
15   And Thought leapt out to wed with Thought
16   Ere Thought could wed itself with Speech;

17   And all we met was fair and good,
18   And all was good that Time could bring,
19   And all the secret of the Spring*
20   Moved in the chambers of the blood;

---

5 After death we shall learn the truth of all beliefs.
19 Reawakening of life.

21 And many an old philosophy
22   On Argive heights divinely sang,
23   And round us all the thicket rang
24 To many a flute of Arcady.

      XXIV.
1 And was the day of my delight
2   As pure and perfect as I say?
3   The very source and fount of Day
4 Is dashed with wandering isles of night.*

5 If all was good and fair we met,
6   This earth had been the Paradise
7   It never looked to human eyes
8 Since our first Sun arose and set.

9 And is it that the haze of grief
10   Makes former gladness loom so great?
11   The lowness of the present state,
12 That sets the past in this relief?

13 Or that the past will always win
14   A glory from its being far;
15   And orb into the perfect star
16 We saw not, when we moved therein?

      XXV
1 I know that this was Life,* – the track
2   Whereon with equal feet we fared;
3   And then, as now, the day prepared
4 The daily burden for the back.

5 But this it was that made me move
6   As light as carrier-birds in air;
7   I loved the weight I had to bear,
8 Because it needed help of Love:

9 Nor could I weary, heart or limb,
10   When mighty Love would cleave in twain
11   The lading of a single pain,
12 And part it, giving half to him.

4 Sun-spots.
1 Chequered, but the burden was shared.

XXVI.

1   Still onward winds the dreary way;
2   I with it; for I long to prove
3   No lapse of moons can canker Love,
4   Whatever fickle tongues may say.

5   And if that eye which watches guilt*
6   And goodness, and hath power to see
7   Within the green the mouldered tree,
8   And towers fallen as soon as built –

9   Oh, if indeed that eye foresee
10   Or see (in Him is no before)
11   In more of life true life no more
12 And Love the indifference to be,

13 Then might I find, ere yet the morn
14   Breaks hither over Indian seas,
15   That Shadow waiting with the keys,
16 To shroud me from my proper scorn.*

XXVII.

1   I envy not in any moods
2   The captive void of noble rage,
3   The linnet born within the cage,
4   That never knew the summer woods:

5   I envy not the beast that takes
6   His license in the field of time,
7   Unfettered by the sense of crime,
8   To whom a conscience never wakes;

9   Nor, what may count itself as blest,
10   The heart that never plighted troth
11   But stagnates in the weeds of sloth;
12 Nor any want-begotten rest.

13 I hold it true, whate'er befall;
14   I feel it, when I sorrow most;
15   'Tis better to have loved and lost
16 Than never to have loved at all.

5 The Eternal Now. I AM.
16 Scorn of myself.

XXVIII.

1 The time draws near the birth of Christ:
2   The moon is hid; the night is still;
3   The Christmas bells from hill to hill
4 Answer each other in the mist.

5 Four voices of four hamlets round,
6   From far and near, on mead and moor,
7   Swell out and fail, as if a door
8 Were shut between me and the sound:

9 Each voice four changes on the wind,
10   That now dilate, and now decrease,
11   Peace and goodwill, goodwill and peace,
12 Peace and goodwill, to all mankind.

13 This year I slept and woke with pain,
14   I almost wished no more to wake,
15   And that my hold on life would break
16 Before I heard those bells again:

17 But they my troubled spirit rule,
18   For they controlled me when a boy;
19   They bring me sorrow touched with joy,
20 The merry merry bells of Yule.

XXIX.

1 With such compelling cause to grieve
2   As daily vexes household peace,
3   And chains regret to his decease,
4 How dare we keep our Christmas-eve;

5 Which brings no more a welcome guest
6   To enrich the threshold of the night
7   With showered largess of delight
8 In dance and song and game and jest?

9 Yet go, and while the holly boughs
10   Entwine the cold baptismal font,
11   Make one wreath more for Use and Wont,
12 That guard the portals of the house;

13 Old sisters of a day gone by,
14   Gray nurses, loving nothing new;

The following three sections describe the first Christmas. See: 'Cycle and Ritual'.

15   Why should they miss their yearly due
16   Before their time? They too will die.

XXX.

1   With trembling fingers did we weave
2   The holly round the Christmas hearth;
3   A rainy cloud possessed the earth,
4   And sadly fell our Christmas-eve.

5   At our old pastimes in the hall
6   We gambolled, making vain pretence
7   Of gladness, with an awful sense
8   Of one mute Shadow watching all.

9   We paused: the winds were in the beech:
10   We heard them sweep the winter land;
11   And in a circle hand-in-hand
12   Sat silent, looking each at each.

13   Then echo-like our voices rang;
14   We sung, though every eye was dim,
15   A merry song we sang with him
16   Last year: impetuously we sang:

17   We ceased: a gentler feeling crept
18   Upon us: surely rest is meet:
19   'They rest,' we said, 'their sleep is sweet,'
20   And silence followed, and we wept.

21   Our voices took a higher range;
22   Once more we sang: 'They do not die
23   Nor lose their mortal sympathy,
24   Nor change to us, although they change;

25   'Rapt from the fickle and the frail
26   With gathered power, yet the same,
27   Pierces the keen seraphic flame
28   From orb to orb, from veil to veil.'

29   Rise, happy morn, rise, holy morn,
30   Draw forth the cheerful day from night:
31   O Father, touch the east, and light
32   The light that shone when Hope was born.

XXXI.*

1 When Lazarus left his charnel-cave,
2   And home to Mary's house returned,
3   Was this demanded—if he yearned
4 To hear her weeping by his grave?

5 'Where wert thou, brother, those four days?'
6   There lives no record of reply,
7   Which telling what it is to die
8 Had surely added praise to praise.

9 From every house the neighbours met,
10   The streets were filled with joyful sound,
11   A solemn gladness even crowned
12 The purple brows of Olivet.

13 Behold a man raised up by Christ!
14   The rest remaineth unrevealed;
15   He told it not; or something sealed
16 The lips of that Evangelist.

The mourner imagines the reaction of Lazarus's sister, after her brother has been raised from the dead.
See: 'Lost for Words'.

XXXII.

1 Her eyes are homes of silent prayer,
2   Nor other thought her mind admits
3   But, he was dead, and there he sits,
4 And he that brought him back is there.

5 Then one deep love doth supersede
6   All other, when her ardent gaze
7   Roves from the living brother's face,
8 And rests upon the Life indeed.

9 All subtle thought, all curious fears,
10   Borne down by gladness so complete,
11   She bows, she bathes the Saviour's feet
12 With costly spikenard and with tears.

13 Thrice blest whose lives are faithful prayers,
14   Whose loves in higher love endure;
15   What souls possess themselves so pure,
16 Or is there blessedness like theirs?

XXXI 'She goeth unto the grave to weep there' (St John XI: 31).

XXXIII.

1   O thou that after toil and storm
2   Mayst seem to have reached a purer air,
3   Whose faith has centre everywhere,
4   Nor cares to fix itself to form,

5   Leave thou thy sister when she prays,
6   Her early Heaven, her happy views;
7   Nor thou with shadowed hint confuse
8   A life that leads melodious days*

9   Her faith through form is pure as thine,
10   Her hands are quicker unto good:
11   Oh, sacred be the flesh and blood
12   To which she links a truth divine!

13   See thou, that countest reason ripe
14   In holding by the law within,
15   Thou fail not in a world of sin,
16   And even for want of such a type.

XXXIV.

1   My own dim life should teach me this,
2   That life shall live for evermore,
3   Else earth is darkness at the core,
4   And dust and ashes all that is;

5   This round of green, this orb of flame,
6   Fantastic beauty; such as lurks
7   In some wild Poet, when he works
8   Without a conscience or an aim.

9   What then were God to such as I?
10   'Twere hardly worth my while to choose
11   Of things all mortal, or to use
12   A little patience ere I die;

13   'Twere best at once to sink to peace,
14   Like birds the charming serpent draws,
15   To drop head-foremost in the jaws
16   Of vacant darkness and to cease.

---

8 'As if afraid to disturb the Pierian days and music-haunted slumbers of tranquil Vopiscus' (Statius, *Silvae* I, iii, 22–3).

XXXV.

1 Yet if some voice that man could trust
2   Should murmur from the narrow house,
3   'The cheeks drop in; the body bows;
4 Man dies: nor is there hope in dust:'

5 Might I not say? 'Yet even here,
6   But for one hour, O Love, I strive
7   To keep so sweet a thing alive:'
8 But I should turn mine ears and hear

9 The moanings of the homeless sea,
10   The sound of streams that swift or slow
11   Draw down Æonian hills, and sow
12 The dust of continents to be;

13 And Love would answer with a sigh,
14   'The sound of that forgetful shore*
15   Will change my sweetness more and more,
16 Half-dead to know that I shall die.'

17 O me, what profits it to put
18   An idle case? If Death were seen
19   At first as Death, Love had not been,
20 Or been in narrowest working shut,

21 Mere fellowship of sluggish moods,
22   Or in his coarsest Satyr-shape
23   Had bruised the herb and crushed the grape,
24 And basked and battened in the woods.

Considers the permanence of the mourner's love in the face of mortality and temporal change. See: 'Profit and Loss'.

XXXVI.

1 Though truths in manhood darkly join,
2   Deep-seated in our mystic frame,
3   We yield all blessing to the name
4 Of Him that made them current coin;

5 For Wisdom dealt with mortal powers,
6   Where truth in closest words shall fail,
7   When truth embodied in a tale
8 Shall enter in at lowly doors.*

Describes the transmission of divine truth via the gospel narrative. See: 'Losing Touch'.

14 The land where all things are forgotten.
8 For divine Wisdom had to deal with the limited powers of humanity, to which truth logically argued out would be ineffectual, whereas truth coming in the story of the gospel can influence the poorest.

9   And so the Word had breath, and wrought
10   With human hands the creed of creeds
11   In loveliness of perfect deeds,
12   More strong than all poetic thought;

13   Which he may read that binds the sheaf,
14   Or builds the house, or digs the grave,
15   And those wild eyes* that watch the wave
16   In roarings round the coral reef.

XXXVII.
1   Urania speaks with darkened brow:
2   'Thou pratest here where thou art least;
3   This faith has many a purer priest,
4   And many an abler voice than thou.

5   'Go down beside thy native rill,
6   On thy Parnassus set thy feet,
7   And hear thy laurel whisper sweet
8   About the ledges of the hill.'

9   And my Melpomene replies,
10   A touch of shame upon her cheek:
11   'I am not worthy even to speak
12   Of thy prevailing mysteries;

13   'For I am but an earthly Muse,
14   And owning but a little art
15   To lull with song an aching heart,
16   And render human love his dues;

17   'But brooding on the dear one dead,
18   And all he said of things divine,
19   (And dear to me as sacred wine
20   To dying lips is all he said),

21   'I murmured, as I came along,
22   Of comfort clasped in truth revealed;
23   And loitered in the master's field,*
24   And darkened sanctities with song.'

15 By this is intended the Pacific Islanders, 'wild' having a sense of the 'barbarian' in it.
23 The province of Christianity.

XXXVIII.

1 With weary steps I loiter on,
2   Though always under altered skies
3   The purple from the distance dies,
4 My prospect and horizon gone.

5 No joy the blowing season* gives,
6   The herald melodies of spring,
7   But in the songs I love to sing
8 A doubtful gleam of solace lives.

9 If any care for what is here
10   Survive in spirits rendered free,
11   Then are these songs I sing of thee
12 Not all ungrateful to thine ear.

XXXIX.

1 Old warder of these buried bones,
2   And answering now my random stroke
3   With fruitful cloud and living smoke,*
4 Dark yew, that graspest at the stones

5 And dippest toward the dreamless head,
6   To thee too comes the golden hour
7   When flower is feeling after flower;
8 But Sorrow – fixt upon the dead,

9 And darkening the dark graves of men, –
10   What whispered from her lying lips?
11   Thy gloom is kindled at the tips,
12 And passes into gloom again.*

XL.

1 Could we forget the widowed hour
2   And look on Spirits breathed away,
3   As on a maiden in the day
4 When first she wears her orange-flower!

5 When crowned with blessing she doth rise
6   To take her latest leave of home,

Compares the parting of death with
the parting of a woman from her
family on her wedding day.
See: 'Lost for Words'.

5 The blossoming season.
3 The yew, when flowering, in a wind or if struck sends up its pollen like smoke.
13 In section II, as in the last two lines of this section, Sorrow saw only the winter gloom of the foliage.

7   And hopes and light regrets that come
8   Make April of her tender eyes;

9   And doubtful joys the father move,
10   And tears are on the mother's face,
11   As parting with a long embrace
12   She enters other realms of love;

13   Her office there to rear, to teach,
14   Becoming as is meet and fit
15   A link among the days, to knit
16   The generations each with each;

17   And, doubtless, unto thee is given
18   A life that bears immortal fruit
19   In those great offices that suit
20   The full-grown energies of heaven.

21   Ay me, the difference I discern!
22   How often shall her old fireside
23   Be cheered with tidings of the bride,
24   How often she herself return,

25   And tell them all they would have told,
26   And bring her babe, and make her boast,
27   Till even those that missed her most
28   Shall count new things as dear as old:

29   But thou and I have shaken hands,
30   Till growing winters lay me low;
31   My paths are in the fields I know,
32   And thine in undiscovered lands.

            XLI.
1   Thy spirit ere our fatal loss
2   Did ever rise from high to higher;
3   As mounts the heavenward altar-fire,
4   As flies the lighter through the gross.

5   But thou art turned to something strange,
6   And I have lost the links that bound
7   Thy changes; here upon the ground,
8   No more partaker of thy change.

9 Deep folly! yet that this could be –
10   That I could wing my will with might
11   To leap the grades of life and light,
12 And flash at once, my friend, to thee.

13 For though my nature rarely yields
14   To that vague fear implied in death;
15   Nor shudders at the gulfs beneath,
16 The howlings from forgotten fields;

17 Yet oft when sundown skirts the moor
18   An inner trouble I behold,
19   A spectral doubt which makes me cold,
20 That I shall be thy mate no more,

21 Though following with an upward mind
22   The wonders that have come to thee,
23   Through all the secular to-be,
24 But evermore a life behind.

XLII.

1 I vex my heart with fancies dim:
2   He still outstript me in the race;
3   It was but unity of place
4 That made me dream I ranked with him.

5 And so may Place retain us still,
6   And he the much-beloved again,
7   A lord of large experience, train
8 To riper growth the mind and will:

9 And what delights can equal those
10   That stir the spirit's inner deeps,
11   When one that loves but knows not, reaps
12 A truth from one that loves and knows?

XLIII.*

1 If Sleep and Death be truly one,
2   And every spirit's folded bloom

Considers the distance that separated the mourner and his friend in life and continues to separate them in death. See: 'Profit and Loss'.

The mourner wonders whether the dead remember their past lives. See: 'Losing Touch' and 'Cycle and Ritual'.

XLIII If the immediate life after death be only sleep, and the spirit between this life and the next should be folded like a flower in a night slumber, then the remembrance of the past might remain, as the smell and colour do in the sleeping flower; and in that case the memory of our love would last as true, and would live pure and whole within the spirit of my friend until it was unfolded at the breaking of morn, when the sleep was over.

3   Through all its intervital gloom*
4   In some long trance should slumber on;

5   Unconscious of the sliding hour,
6   Bare of the body, might it last,
7   And silent traces of the past
8   Be all the colour of the flower:

9   So then were nothing lost to man;
10   So that still garden of the souls
11   In many a figured leaf enrolls
12   The total world since life began;

13   And love will last as pure and whole
14   As when he loved me here in Time,
15   And at the spiritual prime*
16   Rewaken with the dawning soul.

                XLIV.
1   How fares it with the happy dead?
2   For here the man is more and more;
3   But he forgets the days before
4   God shut the doorways of his head.*

5   The days have vanished, tone and tint,
6   And yet perhaps the hoarding sense
7   Gives out at times (he knows not whence)
8   A little flash, a mystic hint;

9   And in the long harmonious years
10   (If Death so taste Lethean springs),
11   May some dim touch of earthly things
12   Surprise thee ranging with thy peers.

13   If such a dreamy touch should fall,
14   O turn thee round, resolve the doubt;
15   My guardian angel will speak out
16   In that high place, and tell thee all.

---

3 In the passage between this life and the next.
15 Dawn of the spiritual life hereafter.
4 Closing of the skull after babyhood.

XLV.

1   The baby new to earth and sky,
2   What time his tender palm is prest
3   Against the circle of the breast,
4   Has never thought that 'this is I:'

5   But as he grows he gathers much,
6   And learns the use of 'I', and 'me,'
7   And finds 'I am not what I see,
8   And other than the things I touch.'

9   So rounds he to a separate mind
10   From whence clear memory may begin,
11   As through the frame that binds him in
12 His isolation grows defined.

13 This use may lie in blood and breath,
14   Which else were fruitless of their due,
15   Had man to learn himself anew
16 Beyond the second birth of Death.

Describes the development of individual consciousness. See: 'Losing Touch' and 'Cycle and Ritual'.

XLVI.

1   We ranging down this lower track,
2   The path we came by, thorn and flower,
3   Is shadowed by the growing hour,
4   Lest life should fail in looking back.

5   So be it: there no shade can last
6   In that deep dawn behind the tomb,
7   But clear from marge to marge shall bloom
8   The eternal landscape of the past;

9   A lifelong tract of time revealed;
10   The fruitful hours of still increase;
11   Days ordered in a wealthy peace,
12 And those five years its richest field.

13 O Love, thy province were not large,
14   A bounded field, nor stretching far;
15   Look also, Love, a brooding star,
16 A rosy warmth from marge to marge.

Describes life as a landscape, surveyed retrospectively, from a distance. See: 'Profit and Loss'.

XLVII.*

1   That each, who seems a separate whole,
2   Should move his rounds, and fusing all
3   The skirts of self again, should fall
4   Remerging in the general Soul,

5   Is faith as vague as all unsweet:
6   Eternal form shall still divide
7   The eternal soul from all beside;
8   And I shall know him when we meet:

9   And we shall sit at endless feast,
10   Enjoying each the other's good:
11   What vaster dream can hit the mood
12   Of Love on earth? He seeks at least

13   Upon the last and sharpest height,
14   Before the spirits fade away,
15   Some landing-place, to clasp and say,
16   'Farewell! We lose ourselves in light.'

Considers death as the surrender of individual identity.
See: 'Cycle and Ritual'.

XLVIII.

1   If these brief lays, of Sorrow born,
2   Were taken to be such as closed
3   Grave doubts and answers here proposed,
4   Then these were such as men might scorn:

5   Her care is not to part and prove;
6   She takes, when harsher moods remit,
7   What slender shade of doubt may flit,
8   And makes it vassal unto love:

9   And hence, indeed, she sports with words,
10   But better serves a wholesome law,
11   And holds it sin and shame to draw
12   The deepest measure from the chords:

13   Nor dare she trust a larger lay,
14   But rather loosens from the lip
15   Short swallow-flights of song, that dip
16   Their wings in tears, and skim away.

XLVII The individuality lasts after death and we are not utterly absorbed into the Godhead. If we are to be finally merged in the Universal Soul, Love asks to have at least one more parting before we lose ourselves.

XLIX.

1 From art, from nature, from the schools,
2   Let random influences glance,
3   Like light in many a shivered lance
4 That breaks about the dappled pools:

5 The lightest wave of thought shall lisp,
6   The fancy's tenderest eddy wreathe,
7   The slightest air of song shall breathe
8 To make the sullen surface crisp.

9 And look thy look, and go thy way,
10   But blame not thou the winds that make
11   The seeming-wanton ripple break,
12 The tender-pencilled shadow play.

13 Beneath all fancied hopes and fears
14   Ay me, the sorrow deepens down,
15   Whose muffled motions blindly drown
16 The bases of my life in tears.

L.

1 Be near me when my light is low,
2   When the blood creeps, and the nerves prick
3   And tingle; and the heart is sick,
4 And all the wheels of Being slow.

5 Be near me when the sensuous frame
6   Is racked with pangs that conquer trust;
7   And Time, a maniac scattering dust,
8 And Life, a Fury slinging flame.

9 Be near me when my faith is dry,
10   And men the flies of latter spring,
11   That lay their eggs, and sting and sing
12 And weave their petty cells and die.

13 Be near me when I fade away,
14   To point the term of human strife,
15   And on the low dark verge of life
16 The twilight of eternal day.

LI.

Considers the implications of the presence of the dead among the living. See: 'Cycle and Ritual'.

1   Do we indeed desire the dead
2   Should still be near us at our side?
3   Is there no baseness we would hide?
4   No inner vileness that we dread?

5   Shall he for whose applause I strove,
6   I had such reverence for his blame,
7   See with clear eye some hidden shame
8   And I be lessened in his love?

9   I wrong the grave with fears untrue:
10   Shall love be blamed for want of faith?
11   There must be wisdom with great Death:
12 The dead shall look me through and through.

13 Be near us when we climb or fall:
14   Ye watch, like God, the rolling hours
15   With larger other eyes than ours,
16 To make allowance for us all.

LII.

The 'Spirit of true love' responds to the mourner's frustration concerning the limitations of his poetry. See: 'Lost for Words' and 'Profit and Loss'.

1   I cannot love thee as I ought,
2   For love reflects the thing beloved;
3   My words are only words, and moved
4   Upon the topmost froth of thought.

5   'Yet blame not thou thy plaintive song,'
6   The Spirit of true love replied;
7   'Thou canst not move me from thy side,
8   Nor human frailty do me wrong.

9   'What keeps a spirit wholly true
10   To that ideal which he bears?
11   What record? not the sinless years
12 That breathed beneath the Syrian blue:

13 'So fret not, like an idle girl,
14   That life is dashed with flecks of sin.
15   Abide:* thy wealth is gathered in,
16 When Time hath sundered shell from pearl.'

15 Wait without wearying.

LIII.*
1   How many a father have I seen,
2   A sober man, among his boys,
3   Whose youth was full of foolish noise,
4   Who wears his manhood hale and green:

5   And dare we to this fancy give,
6   That had the wild oat not been sown,
7   The soil, left barren, scarce had grown
8   The grain by which a man may live?

9   Or, if we held the doctrine sound
10   For life outliving heats of youth,
11   Yet who would preach it as a truth
12   To those that eddy round and round?

13   Hold thou the good: define it well:
14   For fear divine Philosophy
15   Should push beyond her mark, and be
16   Procuress to the Lords of Hell.

LIV.
1   Oh yet we trust that somehow good
2   Will be the final goal of ill,
3   To pangs of nature, sins of will,
4   Defects of doubt, and taints of blood;

5   That nothing walks with aimless feet;
6   That not one life shall be destroyed,
7   Or cast as rubbish to the void,
8   When God hath made the pile complete;

9   That not a worm is cloven in vain;
10   That not a moth with vain desire
11   Is shrivelled in a fruitless fire,
12   Or but subserves another's gain.

13   Behold, we know not anything;
14   I can but trust that good shall fall
15   At last – far off – at last, to all,
16   And every winter change to spring.

The mourner describes his faith in a divine plan for creation, but then dismisses that faith as 'a dream'. See: 'Lost for Words' and 'Profit and Loss'.

LIII There is a passionate heat of nature in a rake sometimes. The nature that yields emotionally may turn out straighter than a prig's. Yet we must not be making excuses, but we must set before ourselves a rule of good for young and old.

17   So runs my dream: but what am I?
18   An infant crying in the night:
19   An infant crying for the light:
20   And with no language but a cry.

            LV.

1   The wish, that of the living whole
2   No life may fail beyond the grave,
3   Derives it not from what we have
4   The likest God within the soul?*

5   Are God and Nature then at strife,
6   That Nature lends such evil dreams?
7   So careful of the type she seems,
8   So careless of the single life;

9   That I, considering everywhere
10   Her secret meaning in her deeds,
11   And finding that of fifty seeds
12   She often brings but one to bear,

13   I falter where I firmly trod,
14   And falling with my weight of cares
15   Upon the great world's altar-stairs
16   That slope through darkness up to God,

17   I stretch lame hands of faith, and grope,
18   And gather dust and chaff, and call
19   To what I feel is Lord of all,
20   And faintly trust the larger hope.

            LVI.

1   'So careful of the type?' but no.
2   From scarpèd cliff and quarried stone
3   She cries, 'A thousand types are gone:
4   I care for nothing, all shall go.

5   'Thou makest thine appeal to me:
6   I bring to life, I bring to death:
7   The spirit does but mean the breath:
8   I know no more.' And he, shall he,

Encounters a crisis of faith, faced with evidence of the vulnerability of individual life.
See: 'Profit and Loss'.

The crisis deepens as the mourner considers the evidence of evolution.
See: 'Profit and Loss'.

4 The inner consciousness – the divine in man.

9   Man, her last work, who seemed so fair,
10   Such splendid purpose in his eyes,
11   Who rolled the psalm to wintry skies,
12   Who built him fanes of fruitless prayer,

13   Who trusted God was love indeed
14   And love Creation's final law –
15   Though Nature, red in tooth and claw
16   With ravine, shrieked against his creed –

17   Who loved, who suffered countless ills,
18   Who battled for the True, the Just,
19   Be blown about the desert dust,
20   Or sealed within the iron hills?

21   No more? A monster then, a dream,
22   A discord. Dragons of the prime,*
23   That tare each other in their slime,
24   Were mellow music matched with him.

25   O life as futile, then, as frail!
26   O for thy voice to soothe and bless!
27   What hope of answer, or redress?
28   Behind the veil, behind the veil.

LVII.
1   Peace; come away: the song of woe
2   Is after all an earthly song:
3   Peace; come away: we do him wrong
4   To sing so wildly: let us go.

5   Come; let us go: your cheeks are pale;
6   But half my life I leave behind:
7   Methinks my friend is richly shrined;
8   But I shall pass; my work will fail.*

9   Yet in these ears, till hearing dies,
10   One set slow bell will seem to toll
11   The passing of the sweetest soul
12   That ever looked with human eyes.

22 The geological monsters of the early ages.
8 The poet speaks of these poems. Methinks I have built a rich shrine to my friend, but it will not last.

13   I hear it now, and o'er and o'er
14   Eternal greetings to the dead;
15   And 'Ave, Ave, Ave,' said,
16   'Adieu, adieu' for evermore.

LVIII.*

1   In those sad words I took farewell:
2   Like echoes in sepulchral halls,
3   As drop by drop the water falls
4   In vaults and catacombs, they fell;

5   And, falling, idly broke the peace
6   Of hearts that beat from day to day,
7   Half-conscious of their dying clay,
8   And those cold crypts where they shall cease.

9   The high Muse answered: 'Wherefore grieve
10   Thy brethren with a fruitless tear?
11   Abide a little longer here,
12   And thou shalt take a nobler leave.'

The mourner is advised to endure his life with patience. See: 'Profit and Loss'.

LIX.

1   O Sorrow, wilt thou live with me
2   No casual mistress, but a wife,
3   My bosom-friend and half of life;
4   As I confess it needs must be;

5   O Sorrow, wilt thou rule my blood,
6   Be sometimes lovely like a bride,
7   And put thy harsher moods aside,
8   If thou wilt have me wise and good.

9   My centred passion cannot move,
10   Nor will it lessen from to-day;
11   But I'll have leave at times to play
12   As with the creature of my love;

13   And set thee forth, for thou art mine,
14   With so much hope for years to come,
15   That, howsoe'er I know thee, some
16   Could hardly tell what name were thine.

LVIII 'Ulysses' was written soon after Hallam's death, and gave my feelings about the need of going forward and braving the struggle of life perhaps more simply than anything in *In Memoriam*.

LX.

1 He past; a soul of nobler tone:
2   My spirit loved and loves him yet,
3   Like some poor girl whose heart is set
4 On one whose rank exceeds her own.

5 He mixing with his proper sphere,
6   She finds the baseness of her lot,
7   Half jealous of she knows not what,
8 And envying all that meet him there.

9 The little village looks forlorn;
10   She sighs amid her narrow days,
11   Moving about the household ways,
12 In that dark house where she was born.

13 The foolish neighbours come and go,
14   And tease her till the day draws by:
15   At night she weeps, 'How vain am I!
16 How should he love a thing so low?'

> The mourner compares his love for his friend and the distance that separates them with the love of a woman for a man from a higher social class.
> See: 'Lost for Words'.

LXI.

1 If , in thy second state sublime,
2   Thy ransomed reason change replies
3   With all the circle of the wise,
4 The perfect flower of human time;

5 And if thou cast thine eyes below,
6   How dimly charactered and slight,
7   How dwarfed a growth of cold and night,
8 How blanched with darkness must I grow!

9 Yet turn thee to the doubtful shore,
10   Where thy first form was made a man;
11   I loved thee, Spirit, and love, nor can
12 The soul of Shakespeare love thee more.

> The mourner imagines how he must appear to his friend, who looks back at him from beyond the grave.
> See: 'Profit and Loss' and Cycle and Ritual'.

LXII.

1 Though if an eye that's downward cast
2   Could make thee somewhat blench or fail,
3   Then be my love an idle tale,
4 And fading legend of the past;

> The mourner requests that his friend not trouble himself with memories of the past.
> See: 'Profit and Loss'.

5   And thou, as one that once declined,
6   When he was little more than boy,
7   On some unworthy heart with joy,
8   But lives to wed an equal mind;

9   And breathes a novel world, the while
10   His other passion wholly dies,
11   Or in the light of deeper eyes
12 Is matter for a flying smile.

LXIII.

1   Yet pity for a horse o'er-driven,
2   And love in which my hound has part,
3   Can hang no weight upon my heart
4   In its assumptions up to heaven;

5   And I am so much more than these,
6   As thou, perchance, art more than I,
7   And yet I spare them sympathy,
8   And I would set their pains at ease.

9   So mayst thou watch me where I weep,
10   As, unto vaster motions bound,
11   The circuits of thine orbit round
12 A higher height, a deeper deep.

LXIV.

1   Dost thou look back on what hath been,
2   As some divinely gifted man,
3   Whose life in low estate began
4   And on a simple village green;

5   Who breaks his birth's invidious bar,
6   And grasps the skirts of happy chance,
7   And breasts the blows of circumstance,
8   And grapples with his evil star;

9   Who makes by force his merit known
10   And lives to clutch the golden keys,
11   To mould a mighty state's decrees,
12 And shape the whisper of the throne;

13 And moving up from high to higher,
14   Becomes on Fortune's crowning slope

The mourner speculates that his friend remembers his past life in the same way that a successful man remembers his humble origins.
See: 'Losing Touch'.

15 The pillar of a people's hope,
16 The centre of a world's desire;

17 Yet feels, as in a pensive dream,
18   When all his active powers are still,
19   A distant dearness in the hill,
20 A secret sweetness in the stream,

21 The limit of his narrower fate,
22   While yet beside its vocal springs
23   He played at counsellors and kings.
24 With one that was his earliest mate;

25 Who ploughs with pain his native lea
26   And reaps the labour of his hands,
27   Or in the furrow musing stands;
28 'Does my old friend remember me?'

LXV.

1 Sweet soul, do with me as thou wilt;
2   I lull a fancy trouble-tost
3   With 'Love's too precious to be lost,
4 A little grain shall not be spilt.'

5 And in that solace can I sing,
6   Till out of painful phases wrought
7   There flutters up a happy thought,
8 Self-balanced on a lightsome wing:

9 Since we deserved the name of friends,
10   And thine effect so lives in me,
11   A part of mine may live in thee
12 And move thee on to noble ends.

LXVI.

1 You thought my heart too far diseased;
2   You wonder when my fancies play
3   To find me gay among the gay,
4 Like one with any trifle pleased.

5 The shade by which my life was crost,
6   Which makes a desert in the mind,
7   Has made me kindly with my kind,
8 And like to him whose sight is lost;

9   Whose feet are guided through the land,
10   Whose jest among his friends is free,
11   Who takes the children on his knee,
12   And winds their curls about his hand:

13   He plays with threads, he beats his chair
14   For pastime, dreaming of the sky;
15   His inner day can never die,
16   His night of loss is always there.

      LXVII.
1   When on my bed the moonlight falls,
2   I know that in thy place of rest
3   By that broad water of the west,*
4   There comes a glory on the walls;

5   Thy marble bright in dark appears,
6   As slowly steals a silver flame
7   Along the letters of thy name,
8   And o'er the number of thy years.

9   The mystic glory swims away;
10   From off my bed the moonlight dies;
11   And closing eaves of wearied eyes
12   I sleep till dusk is dipt in gray:

13   And then I know the mist is drawn
14   A lucid veil from coast to coast,
15   And in the dark church like a ghost
16   Thy tablet glimmers to the dawn.*

      LXVIII.
1   When in the down I sink my head,
2   Sleep, Death's twin-brother, times my breath;
3   Sleep, Death's twin-brother, knows not Death,
4   Nor can I dream of thee as dead:

5   I walk as ere I walked forlorn,
6   When all our path was fresh with dew,

---

3 The Severn.
16 I myself did not see Clevedon till years after the burial of A. H. H. (Jan 3, 1834), and then in later editions of *In Memoriam* I altered the word 'chancel' (which was the word used by Mr Hallam in his *Memoir*) to 'dark church'.

7   And all the bugle breezes blew
8   Reveillée to the breaking morn.

9   But what is this? I turn about,
10   I find a trouble in thine eye,
11   Which makes me sad I know not why,
12   Nor can my dream resolve the doubt:

13   But ere the lark hath left the lea
14   I wake, and I discern the truth;
15   It is the trouble of my youth
16   That foolish sleep transfers to thee.

LXIX.*

1   I dreamed there would be Spring no more,
2   That Nature's ancient power was lost:
3   The streets were black with smoke and frost,
4   They chattered trifles at the door:

Describes a dream in which the mourner imagines that he is cast out from society. See: 'Losing Touch'.

5   I wandered from the noisy town,
6   I found a wood with thorny boughs:
7   I took the thorns to bind my brows,
8   I wore them like a civic crown:

9   I met with scoffs, I met with scorns
10   From youth and babe and hoary hairs:
11   They called me in the public squares
12   The fool that wears a crown of thorns:

13   They called me fool, they called me child:
14   I found an angel of the night;*
15   The voice was low, the look was bright;
16   He looked upon my crown and smiled:

17   He reached the glory of a hand,
18   That seemed to touch it into leaf:
19   The voice was not the voice of grief,
20   The words were hard to understand.

LXIX To write poems about death and grief is 'to wear a crown of thorns', which the people say ought to be laid aside.

14 But the Divine Thing in the gloom brought comfort.

LXX.

1   I cannot see the features right,
2   When on the gloom I strive to paint
3   The face I know; the hues are faint
4   And mix with hollow masks of night;

5   Cloud-towers by ghostly masons wrought,
6   A gulf that ever shuts and gapes,
7   A hand that points, and pallèd shapes
8   In shadowy thoroughfares of thought;

9   And crowds that stream from yawning doors,
10   And shoals of puckered faces drive;
11   Dark bulks that tumble half alive,
12 And lazy lengths on boundless shores;

13 Till all at once beyond the will
14   I hear a wizard music roll,
15   And through a lattice on the soul
16 Looks thy fair face and makes it still.

LXXI.

1   Sleep , kinsman thou to death and trance
2   And madness, thou hast forged at last
3   A night-long Present of the Past
4   In which we went through summer France.

5   Hadst thou such credit with the soul?
6   Then bring an opiate trebly strong,
7   Drug down the blindfold sense of wrong
8   That so my pleasure may be whole;

9   While now we talk as once we talked
10   Of men and minds, the dust of change,
11   The days that grow to something strange,
12 In walking as of old we walked

13 Beside the river's wooded reach,
14   The fortress, and the mountain ridge,
15   The cataract flashing from the bridge,
16 The breaker breaking on the beach.

LXXII.

1. Risest thou thus, dim dawn, again,
2.   And howlest, issuing out of night,
3.   With blasts that blow the poplar white,
4. And lash with storm the streaming pane?

5. Day, when my crowned estate begun
6.   To pine in that reverse of doom,
7.   Which sickened every living bloom,
8. And blurred the splendour of the sun;

9. Who usherest in the dolorous hour
10.   With thy quick tears that make the rose
11.   Pull sideways, and the daisy close
12. Her crimson fringes to the shower;

13. Who might'st have heaved a windless flame
14.   Up the deep East, or, whispering, played
15.   A chequer-work of beam and shade
16. Along the hills, yet looked the same,

17. As wan, as chill, as wild as now;
18.   Day, marked as with some hideous crime,
19.   When the dark hand struck down through time,
20. And cancelled nature's best: but thou,

21. Lift as thou mayst thy burthened brows
22.   Through clouds that drench the morning star,
23.   And whirl the ungarnered sheaf afar,
24. And sow the sky with flying boughs,

25. And up thy vault with roaring sound
26.   Climb thy thick noon, disastrous day;
27.   Touch thy dull goal of joyless gray,
28. And hide thy shame beneath the ground.

LXXIII.

1. So many worlds, so much to do,
2.   So little done, such things to be,
3.   How know I what had need of thee,
4. For thou wert strong as thou wert true?

5   The fame is quenched that I foresaw,
6   The head hath missed an earthly wreath:
7   I curse not nature, no, nor death;
8   For nothing is that errs from law.*

9   We pass; the path that each man trod
10   Is dim, or will be dim, with weeds:
11   What fame is left for human deeds
12   In endless age? It rests with God.

13   O hollow wraith of dying fame,
14   Fade wholly, while the soul exults,
15   And self-infolds the large results
16   Of force that would have forged a name.

LXXIV.

1   As sometimes in a dead man's face,
2   To those that watch it more and more,
3   A likeness, hardly seen before,
4   Comes out – to some one of his race:

5   So, dearest, now thy brows are cold,
6   I see thee what thou art, and know
7   Thy likeness to the wise below,
8   Thy kindred with the great of old.

9   But there is more than I can see,
10   And what I see I leave unsaid,
11   Nor speak it, knowing Death has made
12   His darkness beautiful with thee.

LXXV.

1   I leave thy praises unexpressed
2   In verse that brings myself relief,
3   And by the measure of my grief
4   I leave thy greatness to be guessed;

5   What practice howsoe'er expert
6   In fitting aptest words to things,
7   Or voice the richest-toned that sings,
8   Hath power to give thee as thou wert?

---

8 Cf. Zoroaster's saying, 'Nought errs from law.'

9   I care not in these fading days
10   To raise a cry that lasts not long,
11   And round thee with the breeze of song
12   To stir a little dust of praise.

13   Thy leaf has perished in the green*
14   And, while we breathe beneath the sun,
15   The world which credits what is done
16   Is cold to all that might have been.

17   So here shall silence guard thy fame;
18   But somewhere, out of human view,
19   Whate'er thy hands are set to do
20   Is wrought with tumult of acclaim.

LXXVI.

1   Take wings of fancy, and ascend,
2   And in a moment set thy face
3   Where all the starry heavens of space
4   Are sharpened to a needle's end;*

5   Take wings of foresight; lighten through
6   The secular abyss* to come,
7   And lo, thy deepest lays are dumb
8   Before the mouldering of a yew;

9   And if the matin songs,* that woke
10   The darkness of our planet, last,
11   Thine own shall wither in the vast,
12   Ere half the lifetime of an oak.

13   Ere these have clothed their branchy bowers
14   With fifty Mays, thy songs are vain;
15   And what are they when these remain
16   The ruined shells of hollow towers?

LXXVII.

1   What hope is here for modern rhyme
2   To him, who turns a musing eye
3   On songs, and deeds, and lives, that lie

13 At twenty-three.
4 So distant in void space that all our firmament would appear to be a needlepoint thence.
6 The ages upon ages to be.
9 The great early poets.

4   Foreshortened in the tract of time?

5   These mortal lullabies of pain
6   May bind a book, may line a box,
7   May serve to curl a maiden's locks;
8   Or when a thousand moons shall wane

9   A man upon a stall may find,
10   And, passing, turn the page that tells
11   A grief, then changed to something else.
12   Sung by a long-forgotten mind.

13   But what of that? My darkened ways
14   Shall ring with music all the same;
15   To breathe my loss is more than fame,
16   To utter love more sweet than praise.

LXXVIII.
1   Again at Christmas did we weave
2   The holly round the Christmas hearth;
3   The silent snow possessed the earth,
4   And calmly fell our Christmas-eve:

5   The yule-clog sparkled keen with frost,
6   No wing of wind the region swept,
7   But over all things brooding slept
8   The quiet sense of something lost.

9   As in the winters left behind,
10   Again our ancient games had place,
11   The mimic picture's breathing grace,*
12   And dance and song and hoodman-blind.

13   Who showed a token of distress?
14   No single tear, no mark of pain:
15   O sorrow, then can sorrow wane?
16   O grief, can grief be changed to less?

17   O last regret, regret can die!
18   No – mixt with all this mystic frame,
19   Her deep relations are the same,
20   But with long use her tears are dry.

The second Christmas.
See: 'Cycle and Ritual'.

11 *Tableaux vivants.*

LXXIX*

1 ' More than my brothers are to me,' –
2   Let this not vex thee, noble heart!
3   I know thee of what force thou art
4 To hold the costliest love in fee.

5 But thou and I are one in kind,
6   As moulded like in Nature's mint;
7   And hill and wood and field did print
8 The same sweet forms in either mind.

9 For us the same cold streamlet curled
10   Through all his eddying coves; the same
11   All winds that roam the twilight came
12 In whispers of the beauteous world.

13 At one dear knee we proffered vows,
14   One lesson from one book we learned,
15   Ere childhood's flaxen ringlet turned
16 To black and brown on kindred brows.

17 And so my wealth resembles thine,
18   But he was rich where I was poor,
19   And he supplied my want the more
20 As his unlikeness fitted mine.

LXXX.

1 If any vague desire should rise,
2   That holy Death ere Arthur died
3   Had moved me kindly from his side,
4 And dropt the dust on tearless eyes;

5 Then fancy shapes, as fancy can,
6   The grief my loss in him had wrought,
7   A grief as deep as life or thought,
8 But stayed in peace with God and man.

9 I make a picture in the brain;
10   I hear the sentence that he speaks;
11   He bears the burthen of the weeks
12 But turns his burthen into gain.

Imagines the situation reversed, so that the mourner had died in Arthur's place.
See: 'Profit and Loss'.

LXXIX This section is addressed to my brother Charles (Tennyson Turner).

13   His credit thus shall set me free;
14   And, influence-rich to soothe and save,
15   Unused example from the grave
16   Reach out dead hands to comfort me.

LXXXI.

1   Could I have said while he was here,
2   'My love shall now no further range;
3   There cannot come a mellower change,
4   For now is love mature in ear.'

5   Love, then, had hope of richer store:
6   What end is here to my complaint?
7   This haunting whisper makes me faint,
8   'More years had made me love thee more.'

9   But Death returns an answer sweet:
10   'My sudden frost was sudden gain,
11   And gave all ripeness to the grain,
12   It might have drawn from after-heat.'

Argues that the growth of his love for his friend was cut short by his untimely death.
See: 'Profit and Loss'.

LXXXII.

1   I wage not any feud with Death
2   For changes wrought on form and face;
3   No lower life that earth's embrace
4   May breed with him, can fright my faith.

5   Eternal process moving on,
6   From state to state the spirit walks;
7   And these are but the shattered stalks,
8   Or ruined chrysalis of one.

9   Nor blame I Death, because he bare
10   The use of virtue out of earth:
11   I know transplanted human worth
12   Will bloom to profit, otherwhere.

13   For this alone on Death I wreak
14   The wrath that garners in my heart;
15   He put our lives so far apart
16   We cannot hear each other speak.

Argues that the only thing he cannot come to terms with is the fact that he and his friend can no longer hear one another.
See: 'Profit and Loss'.

LXXXIII.

1 Dip down upon the northern shore,
2   O sweet new-year delaying long;
3   Thou doest expectant nature wrong;
4 Delaying long, delay no more.

5 What stays thee from the clouded noons,
6   Thy sweetness from its proper place?
7   Can trouble live with April days,
8 Or sadness in the summer moons?

9 Bring orchis, bring the foxglove spire,
10   The little speedwell's darling blue,
11   Deep tulips dashed with fiery dew,
12 Laburnums, dropping-wells of fire.

13 O thou, new-year, delaying long,
14   Delayest the sorrow in my blood,
15   That longs to burst a frozen bud
16 And flood a fresher throat with song.

LXXXIV.

1 When I contemplate all alone
2   The life that had been thine below,
3   And fix my thoughts on all the glow
4 To which thy crescent would have grown;

5 I see thee sitting crowned with good,
6   A central warmth diffusing bliss
7   In glance and smile, and clasp and kiss,
8 On all the branches of thy blood;

9 Thy blood, my friend, and partly mine;
10   For now the day was drawing on,
11   When thou should'st link thy life with one
12 Of mine own house,* and boys of thine

13 Had babbled 'Uncle' on my knee;
14   But that remorseless iron hour
15   Made cypress of her orange flower,
16 Despair of Hope, and earth of thee.

Considers the engagement between Arthur and Tennyson's sister, Emily. See: 'Losing Touch'.

12 The projected marriage of A. H. H. with Emily Tennyson.

17   I seem to meet their least desire,
18   To clap their cheeks, to call them mine.
19   I see their unborn faces shine
20   Beside the never-lighted fire.

21   I see myself an honoured guest,
22   Thy partner in the flowery walk
23   Of letters, genial table-talk,
24   Or deep dispute, and graceful jest;

25   While now thy prosperous labour fills
26   The lips of men with honest praise,
27   And sun by sun the happy days
28   Descend below the golden hills

29   With promise of a morn as fair;
30   And all the train of bounteous hours
31   Conduct by paths of growing powers,
32   To reverence and the silver hair;

33   Till slowly worn her earthly robe,
34   Her lavish mission richly wrought,
35   Leaving great legacies of thought,
36   Thy spirit should fail from off the globe;

37   What time mine own might also flee,
38   As linked with thine in love and fate,
39   And, hovering o'er the dolorous strait
40   To the other shore, involved in thee,

41   Arrive at last the blessèd goal,*
42   And He that died in Holy Land
43   Would reach us out the shining hand,
44   And take us as a single soul.

45   What reed was that on which I leant?
46   Ah, backward fancy, wherefore wake
47   The old bitterness again, and break
48   The low beginnings of content.

41 Cf. *Paradise Lost*, II: ''ere he arrive / The happy isle'.

LXXXV.

1	This truth came borne with bier and pall,
2	I felt it, when I sorrow'd most,
3	'Tis better to have loved and lost,
4	Than never to have loved at all –

A reflective passage that looks back over the first years of grief. See: 'Cycle and Ritual'.

5 O true in word, and tried in deed,
6   Demanding, so to bring relief
7   To this which is our common grief,
8 What kind of life is that I lead;

9 And whether trust in things above
10   Be dimmed of sorrow, or sustained;
11   And whether love for him have drained
12 My capabilities of love;

13 Your words have virtue such as draws
14   A faithful answer from the breast,
15   Through light reproaches, half exprest,
16 And loyal unto kindly laws.

17 My blood an even tenor kept,
18   Till on mine ear this message falls,
19   That in Vienna's fatal wall
20 God's finger touched him, and he slept.

21 The great Intelligences fair
22   That range above our mortal state,
23   In circle round the blessèd gate,
24 Received and gave him welcome there;

25 And led him through the blissful climes,
26   And showed him in the fountain fresh
27   All knowledge that the sons of flesh
28 Shall gather in the cycled times.

29 But I remained, whose hopes were dim,
30   Whose life, whose thoughts were little worth,
31   To wander on a darkened earth,
32 Where all things round me breathed of him.

33 O friendship, equal-poised control,
34   O heart, with kindliest motion warm,

35   O sacred essence, other form,
36   O solemn ghost, O crownèd soul!

37   Yet none could better know than I,
38   How much of act at human hands
39   The sense of human will demands
40   By which we dare to live or die.*

41   Whatever way my days decline,
42   I felt and feel, though left alone,
43   His being working in mine own,
44   The footsteps of his life in mine;

45   A life that all the Muses decked
46   With gifts of grace, that might express
47   All-comprehensive tenderness,
48   All-subtilising intellect:

49   And so my passion hath not swerved
50   To works of weakness, but I find
51   An image comforting the mind,
52   And in my grief a strength reserved.

53   Likewise the imaginative woe,
54   That loved to handle spiritual strife,
55   Diffused the shock through all my life,
56   But in the present broke the blow.

57   My pulses therefore beat again
58   For other friends that once I met;
59   Nor can it suit me to forget
60   The mighty hopes that make us men.

61   I woo your love: I count it crime
62   To mourn for any overmuch;
63   I, the divided half of such
64   A friendship as had mastered Time;

65   Which masters Time indeed, and is
66   Eternal, separate from fears:
67   The all-assuming months and years
68   Can take no part away from this:

40 Yet I know that the knowledge that we have free will demands from us action.

69   But Summer on the steaming floods,
70   And Spring that swells the narrow brooks,
71   And Autumn, with a noise of rooks,
72   That gather in the waning woods,

73   And every pulse of wind and wave
74   Recalls, in change of light or gloom,
75   My old affection of the tomb,
76   And my prime passion in the grave:

77   My old affection of the tomb,
78   A part of stillness, yearns to speak:
79   'Arise, and get thee forth and seek
80   A friendship for the years to come.

81   'I watch thee from the quiet shore;
82   Thy spirit up to mine can reach;
83   But in dear words of human speech
84   We two communicate no more.'

85   And I, 'Can clouds of nature stain
86   The starry clearness of the free?
87   How is it? Canst thou feel for me
88   Some painless sympathy with pain?'

89   And lightly does the whisper fall;
90   ''Tis hard for thee to fathom this;
91   I triumph in conclusive bliss,
92   And that serene result of all.'

93   So hold I commerce with the dead;
94   Or so methinks the dead would say;
95   Or so shall grief with symbols play
96   And pining life be fancy-fed.

97   Now looking to some settled end,
98   That these things pass, and I shall prove
99   A meeting somewhere, love with love,
100 I crave your pardon, O my friend;

101 If not so fresh, with love as true,
102   I, clasping brother-hands, aver
103   I could not, if I would, transfer
104 The whole I felt for him to you.

105 For which be they that hold apart
106   The promise of the golden hours?
107   First love, first friendship, equal powers,
108 That marry with the virgin heart.

109 Still mine, that cannot but deplore,
110   That beats within a lonely place,
111   That yet remembers his embrace,
112 But at his footstep leaps no more,

113 My heart, though widowed, may not rest
114   Quite in the love of what is gone,
115   But seeks to beat in time with one
116 That warms another living breast.

117 Ah, take the imperfect gift I bring,
118   Knowing the primrose yet is dear,
119   The primrose of the later year,
120 As not unlike to that of Spring.

              LXXXVI.*

1   Sweet after showers, ambrosial air,*
2   That rollest from the gorgeous gloom
3   Of evening over brake and bloom
4   And meadow, slowly breathing bare

5   The round of space, and rapt below
6   Through all the dewy-tasselled wood,
7   And shadowing down the hornèd flood
8   In ripples, fan my brows and blow

9   The fever from my cheek, and sigh
10   The full new life that feeds thy breath
11   Throughout my frame, till Doubt and Death,
12 Ill brethren, let the fancy fly

13 From belt to belt of crimson seas
14   On leagues of odour streaming far,
15   To where in yonder orient star*
16 A hundred spirits whisper 'Peace.'

The mourner experiences relief in nature.
See: 'Cycle and Ritual'.

LXXXVI Written at Barmouth.
1 It was a west wind.
15 Any rising star is here intended.

LXXXVII.*

1   I past beside the reverend walls
2   In which of old I wore the gown;
3   I roved at random through the town,
4   And saw the tumult of the halls;

5   And heard once more in college fanes
6   The storm their high-built organs make,
7   And thunder-music, rolling, shake
8   The prophet blazoned on the panes;

9   And caught once more the distant shout,
10   The measured pulse of racing oars
11   Among the willows; paced the shores
12 And many a bridge, and all about

13 The same gray flats again, and felt
14   The same, but not the same; and last
15   Up that long walk of limes I past
16 To see the rooms in which he dwelt.

17 Another name was on the door;
18   I lingered; all within was noise
19   Of songs, and clapping hands, and boys
20 That crashed the glass and beat the floor;

21 Where once we held debate, a band
22   Of youthful friends, on mind and art,
23   And labour, and the changing mart,
24 And all the framework of the land;

25 When one would aim an arrow fair,
26   But send it slackly from the string;
27   And one would pierce an outer ring,
28 And one an inner, here and there;

29 And last the master-bowman, he,
30   Would cleave the mark. A willing ear
31   We lent him. Who, but hung to hear
32 The rapt oration flowing free

LXXXVII Trinity College, Cambridge.

33   From point to point, with power and grace
34   And music in the bounds of law,
35   To those conclusions when we saw
36   The God within him light his face,

37   And seem to lift the form, and glow
38   In azure orbits heavenly-wise;
39   And over those ethereal eyes
40   The bar of Michael Angelo.*

LXXXVIII.*

1   Wild bird, whose warble, liquid sweet,
2   Rings Eden through the budded quicks,
3   O tell me where the senses mix,
4   O tell me where the passions meet,

5   Whence radiate: fierce extremes employ
6   Thy spirits in the darkening leaf,
7   And in the midmost heart of grief
8   Thy passion clasps a secret joy:

9   And I – my harp would prelude woe –
10   I cannot all command the strings;
11   The glory of the sum of things
12   Will flash along the chords and go.

LXXXIX.

1   Witch-elms that counterchange the floor
2   Of this flat lawn with dusk and bright;
3   And thou, with all thy breadth and height
4   Of foliage, towering sycamore;

The mourner remembers time spent at his family home with his friend. See: 'Cycle and Ritual'.

5   How often, hither wandering down,
6   My Arthur found your shadows fair,
7   And shook to all the liberal air
8   The dust and din and steam of town:

9   He brought an eye for all he saw;
10   He mixt in all our simple sports;
11   They pleased him, fresh from brawling courts
12   And dusty purlieus of the law.

40 The broad bar of frontal bone over the eyes of Michael Angelo.
LXXXVIII To the Nightingale.

13 O joy to him in this retreat,
14   Immantled in ambrosial dark,
15   To drink the cooler air, and mark
16 The landscape winking through the heat:

17 O sound to rout the brood of cares,
18   The sweep of scythe in morning dew,
19   The gust that round the garden flew,
20 And tumbled half the mellowing pears!

21 O bliss, when all in circle drawn
22   About him, heart and ear were fed
23   To hear him, as he lay and read
24 The Tuscan poets on the lawn:

25 Or in the all-golden afternoon
26   A guest, or happy sister, sung,
27   Or here she brought the harp and flung
28 A ballad to the brightening moon:

29 Nor less it pleased in livelier moods,
30   Beyond the bounding hill to stray,
31   And break the livelong summer day
32 With banquet in the distant woods;

33 Whereat we glanced from theme to theme,
34   Discussed the books to love or hate,
35   Or touched the changes of the state,
36 Or threaded some Socratic dream;

37 But if I praised the busy town,
38   He loved to rail against it still,
39   For 'ground in yonder social mill
40 We rub each other's angles down,

41 'And merge' he said 'in form and gloss
42   The picturesque of man and man.'
43   We talked: the stream beneath us ran,
44 The wine-flask lying couched in moss,

45   Or cooled within the glooming wave;
46   And last, returning from afar,
47   Before the crimson-circled star
48   Had fallen into her father's grave,*

49   And brushing ankle-deep in flowers,
50   We heard behind the woodbine veil
51   The milk that bubbled in the pail,
52   And buzzings of the honied hours.

XC.

1   He tasted love with half his mind,
2   Nor ever drank the inviolate spring
3   Where nighest heaven, who first could fling
4   This bitter seed among mankind;

5   That could the dead, whose dying eyes
6   Were closed with wail, resume their life,
7   They would but find in child and wife
8   An iron welcome when they rise:

9   'Twas well, indeed, when warm with wine,
10   To pledge them with a kindly tear,
11   To talk them o'er, to wish them here,
12   To count their memories half divine;

13   But if they came who past away,
14   Behold their brides in other hands;
15   The hard heir strides about their lands,
16   And will not yield them for a day.

17   Yea, though their sons were none of these,
18   Not less the yet-loved sire would make
19   Confusion worse than death, and shake
20   The pillars of domestic peace.

21   Ah dear, but come thou back to me:
22   Whatever change the years have wrought,
23   I find not yet one lonely thought
24   That cries against my wish for thee.

---

48 Before Venus, the evening star, had dipt into the sunset. The planets, according to Laplace, were evolved from the sun.

XCI.

1 When rosy plumelets tuft the larch,
2   And rarely pipes the mounted thrush;
3   Or underneath the barren bush
4 Flits by the sea-blue bird of March;

5 Come, wear the form by which I know
6   Thy spirit in time among thy peers;
7   The hope of unaccomplished years
8 Be large and lucid round thy brow.

9 When summer's hourly-mellowing change
10   May breathe, with many roses sweet,
11   Upon the thousand waves of wheat,
12 That ripple round the lonely grange;

13 Come: not in watches of the night,
14   But where the sunbeam broodeth warm,
15   Come, beauteous in thine after form,
16 And like a finer light in light.

XCII.

1 If any vision should reveal
2   Thy likeness, I might count it vain
3   As but the canker of the brain;
4 Yea, though it spake and made appeal

5 To chances where our lots were cast
6   Together in the days behind,
7   I might but say, I hear a wind
8 Of memory murmuring the past.

9 Yea, though it spake and bared to view
10   A fact within the coming year;
11   And though the months, revolving near,
12 Should prove the phantom-warning true,

13 They might not seem thy prophecies,
14   But spiritual presentiments,
15   And such refraction of events
16 As often rises ere they rise.

The mourner prays to feel his dead friend's presence.
See: 'Losing Touch'.

XCIII.

1   I shall not see thee. Dare I say
2   No spirit ever brake the band
3   That stays him from the native land
4   Where first he walked when claspt in clay?

5   No visual shade of some one lost,
6   But he, the Spirit himself, may come
7   Where all the nerve of sense is numb;
8   Spirit to Spirit, Ghost to Ghost.

9   O, therefore from thy sightless range
10   With gods in unconjectured bliss,
11   O, from the distance of the abyss
12 Of tenfold-complicated change,

13 Descend, and touch, and enter; hear
14   The wish too strong for words to name;
15   That in this blindness of the frame
16 My Ghost may feel that thine is near.

XCIV.

1   How pure at heart and sound in head,
2   With what divine affections bold
3   Should be the man whose thought would hold
4   An hour's communion with the dead.

5   In vain shalt thou, or any, call
6   The spirits from their golden day,
7   Except, like them, thou too canst say,
8   My spirit is at peace with all.

9   They haunt the silence of the breast,*
10   Imaginations calm and fair,
11   The memory like a cloudless air,
12 The conscience as a sea at rest:

13 But when the heart is full of din,
14   And doubt beside the portal waits,
15   They can but listen at the gates,
16 And hear the household jar within.

---

9 This was what I felt.

XCV.

1 By night we lingered on the lawn,
2   For underfoot the herb was dry;
3   And genial warmth; and o'er the sky
4 The silvery haze of summer drawn;

5 And calm that let the tapers burn
6   Unwavering: not a cricket chirred:
7   The brook alone far-off was heard,*
8 And on the board the fluttering urn:

9 And bats went round in fragrant skies,
10   And wheeled or lit the filmy shapes
11   That haunt the dusk, with ermine capes
12 And woolly breasts and beaded eyes*

13 While now we sang old songs that pealed
14   From knoll to knoll, where, couched at ease,
15   The white kine glimmered, and the trees
16 Laid their dark arms about the field.

17 But when those others, one by one,
18   Withdrew themselves from me and night,
19   And in the house light after light
20 Went out, and I was all alone,

21 A hunger seized my heart; I read
22   Of that glad year which once had been,
23   In those fallen leaves which kept their green,
24 The noble letters of the dead:

25 And strangely on the silence broke
26   The silent-speaking words, and strange
27   Was love's dumb cry defying change
28 To test his worth; and strangely spoke

29 The faith, the vigour, bold to dwell
30   On doubts that drive the coward back,
31   And keen through wordy snares to track
32 Suggestion to her inmost cell.

The mourner reads letters, written by his dead friend.
See: 'Lost for Words' and 'Losing Touch'.

---

7 It was a marvellously still night and I asked my brother Charles to listen to the brook, which we had never heard so far off before.
12 The ermine or perhaps the puss-moth.

33   So word by word, and line by line,
34   The dead man touched me from the past,
35   And all at once it seemed at last
36   The living soul was flashed on mine,

37   And mine in this was wound, and whirled
38   About empyreal heights of thought,
39   And came on that which is, and caught
40   The deep pulsations of the world,

41   Æonian music measuring out
42   The steps of Time – the shocks of Chance –
43   The blows of Death. At length my trance*
44   Was cancelled, stricken through with doubt.

45   Vague words! but ah, how hard to frame
46   In matter-moulded forms of speech,
47   Or even for intellect to reach
48   Through memory that which I became:

49   Till now the doubtful dusk revealed
50   The knolls once more where, couched at ease,
51   The white kine glimmered, and the trees
52   Laid their dark arms about the field:

53   And sucked from out the distant gloom
54   A breeze began to tremble o'er
55   The large leaves of the sycamore,
56   And fluctuate all the still perfume,

57   And gathering freshlier overhead,
58   Rocked the full-foliaged elms, and swung
59   The heavy-folded rose, and flung
60   The lilies to and fro, and said

61   'The dawn, the dawn,' and died away;
62   And East and West, without a breath,
63   Mixt their dim lights, like life and death,
64   To broaden into boundless day.

---

43 The trance came to an end in a moment of critical doubt, but the doubt was dispelled by the glory of the 'boundless day'.

XCVI.

1　You say, but with no touch of scorn,
2　　Sweet-hearted, you, whose light-blue eyes
3　　Are tender over drowning flies,
4　You tell me, doubt is Devil-born.

5　I know not: one indeed I knew
6　　In many a subtle question versed,
7　　Who touched a jarring lyre at first,
8　But ever strove to make it true:

9　Perplext in faith, but pure in deeds,
10　　At last he beat his music out.
11　　There lives more faith in honest doubt,
12　Believe me, than in half the creeds.

13　He fought his doubts and gathered strength,
14　　He would not make his judgment blind,
15　　He faced the spectres of the mind
16　And laid them: thus he came at length

17　To find a stronger faith his own;
18　　And Power was with him in the night,
19　　Which makes the darkness and the light,
20　And dwells not in the light alone,

21　But in the darkness and the cloud,
22　　As over Sinaï's peaks of old,
23　　While Israel made their gods of gold,
24　Although the trumpet blew so loud.

XCVII.

1　My love has talked with rocks and trees;
2　　He finds on misty mountain-ground
3　　His own vast shadow glory-crowned;*
4　He sees himself in all he sees.

5　Two partners of a married life –
6　　I looked on these and thought of thee
7　　In vastness and in mystery,
8　And of my spirit as of a wife.

Considering the gulf that separates him from his friend, the mourner compares himself with the wife of a great scientist. See: 'Lost for Words'.

3 Like the spectre of the Brocken.

9   These two-they dwelt with eye on eye,
10   Their hearts of old have beat in tune,
11   Their meetings made December June
12   Their every parting was to die.

13   Their love has never past away;
14   The days she never can forget
15   Are earnest that he loves her yet,
16   Whate'er the faithless people say.

17   Her life is lone, he sits apart,
18   He loves her yet, she will not weep,
19   Though rapt in matters dark and deep
20   He seems to slight her simple heart.

21   He thrids the labyrinth of the mind,
22   He reads the secret of the star,
23   He seems so near and yet so far,
24   He looks so cold: she thinks him kind.

25   She keeps the gift of years before,
26   A withered violet is her bliss:
27   She knows not what his greatness is,
28   For that, for all, she loves him more.

29   For him she plays, to him she sings
30   Of early faith and plighted vows;
31   She knows but matters of the house,
32   And he, he knows a thousand things.

33   Her faith is fixt and cannot move,
34   She darkly feels him great and wise,
35   She dwells on him with faithful eyes,
36   'I cannot understand: I love.'

                XCVIII.
1   You leave us:* you will see the Rhine,
2   And those fair hills I sailed below,
3   When I was there with him; and go
4   By summer belts of wheat and vine

---

1 'You' is imaginary.

5	To where he breathed his latest breath,
6	That City. All her splendour seems
7	No livelier than the wisp that gleams
8	On Lethe in the eyes of Death.

9	Let her great Danube rolling fair
10	Enwind her isles, unmarked of me:
11	I have not seen, I will not see
12	Vienna; rather dream that there,

13	A treble darkness, Evil haunts
14	The birth, the bridal; friend from friend
15	Is oftener parted, fathers bend
16	Above more graves, a thousand wants

17	Gnarr* at the heels of men, and prey
18	By each cold hearth, and sadness flings
19	Her shadow on the blaze of kings:
20	And yet myself have heard him say,

21	That not in any mother town
22	With statelier progress to and fro
23	The double tides of chariots flow
24	By park and suburb under brown

25	Of lustier leaves; nor more content,
26	He told me, lives in any crowd,
27	When all is gay with lamps, and loud
28	With sport and song, in booth and tent,

29	Imperial halls, or open plain;
30	And wheels the circled dance, and breaks
31	The rocket molten into flakes
32	Of crimson or in emerald rain.

XCIX.

1	Risest thou thus, dim dawn, again,
2	So loud with voices of the birds,
3	So thick with lowings of the herds,
4	Day, when I lost the flower of men;

17 Snarl.

5   Who tremblest through thy darkling red
6   On yon swollen brook that bubbles fast
7   By meadows breathing of the past,
8   And woodlands holy to the dead;

9   Who murmurest in the foliaged eaves
10   A song that slights the coming care,
11   And Autumn laying here and there
12   A fiery finger on the leaves;

13   Who wakenest with thy balmy breath
14   To myriads on the genial earth,
15   Memories of bridal, or of birth,
16   And unto myriads more, of death.

17   O wheresoever those may be,
18   Betwixt the slumber of the poles,*
19   To-day they count as kindred souls;
20   They know me not, but mourn with me.

C.

1   I climb the hill:* from end to end
2   Of all the landscape underneath,
3   I find no place that does not breathe
4   Some gracious memory of my friend;

5   No gray old grange, or lonely fold,
6   Or low morass and whispering reed,
7   Or simple stile from mead to mead,
8   Or sheepwalk up the windy wold;

9   Nor hoary knoll of ash and haw
10   That hears the latest linnet trill,
11   Nor quarry trenched along the hill
12   And haunted by the wrangling daw;

13   Nor runlet tinkling from the rock;*
14   Nor pastoral rivulet that swerves
15   To left and right through meadowy curves,
16   That feed the mothers of the flock;

18 The ends of the axis of the earth, which move so slowly that they seem not to move, but slumber.
1 Hill above Somersby.
13 The rock is Holywell, which is a wooded ravine, commonly called there 'the Glen'.

17   But each has pleased a kindred eye,
18   And each reflects a kindlier day;
19   And, leaving these, to pass away
20   I think once more he seems to die.

CI.

1   Unwatched , the garden bough shall sway,
2   The tender blossom flutter down,
3   Unloved, that beech will gather brown,
4   This maple burn itself away;

5   Unloved, the sun-flower, shining fair,
6   Ray round with flames her disk of seed,
7   And many a rose-carnation feed
8   With summer spice the humming air;

9   Unloved, by many a sandy bar,
10   The brook shall babble down the plain,
11   At noon or when the lesser wain
12   Is twisting round the polar star;

13   Uncared for, gird the windy grove,
14   And flood the haunts of hern and crake;
15   Or into silver arrows break
16   The sailing moon in creek and cove;

17   Till from the garden and the wild
18   A fresh association blow,
19   And year by year the landscape grow
20   Familiar to the stranger's child;

21   As year by year the labourer tills
22   His wonted glebe, or lops the glades;
23   And year by year our memory fades
24   From all the circle of the hills.

CII.

1   We leave the well-belovèd place
2   Where first we gazed upon the sky;
3   The roofs, that heard our earliest cry,
4   Will shelter one of stranger race.

5   We go, but ere we go from home,
6   As down the garden-walks I move,
7   Two spirits of a diverse love*
8   Contend for loving masterdom.

9   One whispers, 'Here thy boyhood sung
10   Long since its matin song, and heard
11   The low love-language of the bird
12   In native hazels tassel-hung.'

13   The other answers, 'Yea, but here
14   Thy feet have strayed in after hours
15   With thy lost friend among the bowers,
16   And this hath made them trebly dear.'

17   These two have striven half the day,
18   And each prefers his separate claim,
19   Poor rivals in a losing game,
20   That will not yield each other way.

21   I turn to go: my feet are set
22   To leave the pleasant fields and farms;
23   They mix in one another's arms
24   To one pure image of regret.

              CIII.
1   On that last night before we went
2   From out the doors where I was bred,
3   I dreamed a vision of the dead,
4   Which left my after-morn content.

5   Methought I dwelt within a hall,
6   And maidens with me:* distant hills
7   From hidden summits fed with rills
8   A river* sliding by the wall.

9   The hall with harp and carol rang.
10   They sang of what is wise and good
11   And graceful. In the centre stood
12   A statue veiled, to which they sang;

7 First, the love of the native place; second, this enhanced by the memory of A. H. H.

6 They are the muses, poetry, arts – all that made life beautiful here, which we hope will pass with us beyond the grave.

8 Life.

13 And which, though veiled, was known to me,
14   The shape of him I loved, and love
15   For ever: then flew in a dove
16 And brought a summons from the sea:*

17 And when they learnt that I must go
18   They wept and wailed, but led the way
19   To where a little shallop lay
20 At anchor in the flood below;

21 And on by many a level mead,
22   And shadowing bluff that made the banks,
23   We glided winding under ranks
24 Of iris, and the golden reed;

25 And still as vaster grew the shore
26   And rolled the floods in grander space,
27   The maidens gathered strength and grace
28 And presence, lordlier than before;

29 And I myself, who sat apart
30   And watched them, waxed in every limb;
31   I felt the thews of Anakim,
32 The pulses of a Titan's heart;

33 As one would sing the death of war,
34   And one would chant the history
35   Of that great race, which is to be,
36 And one the shaping of a star;

37 Until the forward-creeping tides
38   Began to foam, and we to draw
39   From deep to deep, to where we saw
40 A great ship lift her shining sides.

41 The man we loved was there on deck,
42   But thrice as large as man he bent
43   To greet us. Up the side I went,
44 And fell in silence on his neck:

45 Whereat those maidens with one mind
46   Bewailed their lot; I did them wrong:

16 Eternity.

47   'We served thee here,' they said, 'so long,
48   And wilt thou leave us now behind?'

49   So rapt I was, they could not win
50   An answer from my lips, but he
51   Replying, 'Enter likewise ye
52   And go with us:' they entered in.

53   And while the wind began to sweep
54   A music out of sheet and shroud,
55   We steered her toward a crimson cloud
56   That landlike slept along the deep.

CIV.

1   The time draws near the birth of Christ;
2   The moon is hid, the night is still;
3   A single church below the hill*
4   Is pealing, folded in the mist.

5   A single peal of bells below,
6   That wakens at this hour of rest
7   A single murmur in the breast,
8   That these are not the bells I know.

9   Like strangers' voices here they sound,
10   In lands where not a memory strays,
11   Nor landmark breathes of other days,
12 But all is new unhallowed ground.

The following three sections describe the third Christmas.
See: 'Cycle and Ritual'.

CV.

1   To-night ungathered let us leave
2   This laurel, let this holly stand:
3   We live within the stranger's land,
4   And strangely falls our Christmas-eve.

5   Our father's dust is left alone
6   And silent under other snows:
7   There in due time the woodbine blows,
8   The violet comes, but we are gone.

9   No more shall wayward grief abuse
10   The genial hour with mask and mime;

3 Waltham Abbey church.

11   For change of place, like growth of time,
12   Has broke the bond of dying use.

13   Let cares that petty shadows cast,
14   By which our lives are chiefly proved,
15   A little spare the night I loved,
16   And hold it solemn to the past.

17   But let no footstep beat the floor,
18   Nor bowl of wassail mantle warm;
19   For who would keep an ancient form
20   Through which the spirit breathes no more?

21   Be neither song, nor game, nor feast;
22   Nor harp be touched, nor flute be blown;
23   No dance, no motion, save alone
24   What lightens in the lucid east

25   Of rising worlds by yonder wood.*
26   Long sleeps the summer in the seed;
27   Run out your measured arcs, and lead
28   The closing cycle rich in good.

      CVI.
1   Ring out, wild bells, to the wild sky,
2   The flying cloud, the frosty light:
3   The year is dying in the night;
4   Ring out, wild bells, and let him die.

5   Ring out the old, ring in the new,
6   Ring, happy bells, across the snow:
7   The year is going, let him go;
8   Ring out the false, ring in the true.

9   Ring out the grief that saps the mind,
10   For those that here we see no more;
11   Ring out the feud of rich and poor,
12   Ring in redress to all mankind.

13   Ring out a slowly dying cause,
14   And ancient forms of party strife;

---

25 The scintillating motion of the stars that rise.

15   Ring in the nobler modes of life,
16   With sweeter manners, purer laws.

17   Ring out the want, the care, the sin,
18   The faithless coldness of the times;
19   Ring out, ring out my mournful rhymes,
20   But ring the fuller minstrel in.

21   Ring out false pride in place and blood,
22   The civic slander and the spite;
23   Ring in the love of truth and right,
24   Ring in the common love of good.

25   Ring out old shapes of foul disease;
26   Ring out the narrowing lust of gold;
27   Ring out the thousand wars of old,
28   Ring in the thousand years of peace.

29   Ring in the valiant man and free,
30   The larger heart, the kindlier hand;
31   Ring out the darkness of the land,
32   Ring in the Christ that is to be.

              CVII.   Marks Arthur's birthday.
1   It is the day when he was born,*   See: 'Cycle and Ritual'.
2   A bitter day that early sank
3   Behind a purple-frosty bank
4   Of vapour, leaving night forlorn.

5   The time admits not flowers or leaves
6   To deck the banquet. Fiercely flies
7   The blast of North and East, and ice
8   Makes daggers at the sharpened eaves,

9   And bristles all the brakes and thorns
10   To yon hard crescent, as she hangs
11   Above the wood which grides* and clangs
12   Its leafless ribs and iron horns

13   Together, in the drifts that pass
14   To darken on the rolling brine

1 February 1, 1811, in Bedford Place, London.
11 Grates.

15   That breaks the coast. But fetch the wine,
16   Arrange the board and brim the glass;

17   Bring in great logs and let them lie,
18   To make a solid core of heat;
19   Be cheerful-minded, talk and treat
20   Of all things even as he were by;

21   We keep the day. With festal cheer,
22   With books and music, surely we
23   Will drink to him, whate'er he be,
24   And sing the songs he loved to hear.

CVIII.

1   I will not shut me from my kind,*
2   And, lest I stiffen into stone,
3   I will not eat my heart alone,
4   Nor feed with sighs a passing wind:

5   What profit lies in barren faith,
6   And vacant yearning, though with might
7   To scale the heaven's highest height,
8   Or dive below the wells of Death?

9   What find I in the highest place,
10   But mine own phantom chanting hymns?
11   And on the depths of death there swims
12   The reflex of a human face.

13   I'll rather take what fruit may be
14   Of sorrow under human skies:
15   'Tis held that sorrow makes us wise,
16   Whatever wisdom sleep with thee.

CIX.

1   Heart-affluence in discursive talk
2   From household fountains never dry;
3   The critic clearness of an eye,
4   That saw through all the Muses' walk;

---

1 Grief shall not make me a hermit, and I will not indulge in vacant yearnings and barren aspirations; it is useless trying to find him in the other worlds – I find nothing but the reflections of myself: I had better learn the lesson sorrow teaches.

5   Seraphic intellect and force
6   To seize and throw the doubts of man;
7   Impassioned logic, which outran
8   The hearer in its fiery course;

9   High nature amorous of the good,
10   But touched with no ascetic gloom;
11   And passion pure in snowy bloom
12   Through all the years of April blood;

13   A love of freedom rarely felt,
14   Of freedom in her regal seat
15   Of England; not the schoolboy heat,
16   The blind hysterics of the Celt;

17   And manhood fused with female grace
18   In such a sort, the child would twine
19   A trustful hand, unasked, in thine,
20   And find his comfort in thy face;

21   All these have been, and thee mine eyes
22   Have looked on: if they looked in vain,
23   My shame is greater who remain,
24   Nor let thy wisdom make me wise.*

        CX.
1   Thy converse drew us with delight,
2   The men of rathe and riper years:
3   The feeble soul, a haunt of fears,
4   Forgot his weakness in thy sight.

5   On thee the loyal-hearted hung,
6   The proud was half disarmed of pride,
7   Nor cared the serpent at thy side
8   To flicker with his double tongue.

9   The stern were mild when thou wert by,
10   The flippant put himself to school
11   And heard thee, and the brazen fool
12   Was softened, and he knew not why;

24 If I do not let . . .

13   While I, thy nearest, sat apart,
14   And felt thy triumph was as mine;
15   And loved them more, that they were thine,
16   The graceful tact, the Christian art;

17   Nor mine the sweetness or the skill,
18   But mine the love that will not tire,
19   And, born of love, the vague desire
20   That spurs an imitative will.

      CXI.
1   The churl in spirit, up or down
2   Along the scale of ranks, through all,
3   To him who grasps a golden ball,
4   By blood a king, at heart a clown;

5   The churl in spirit, howe'er he veil
6   His want in forms for fashion's sake,
7   Will let his coltish nature break
8   At seasons through the gilded pale:

9   For who can always act? but he,
10   To whom a thousand memories call,
11   Not being less but more than all
12   The gentleness he seemed to be,

13   Best seemed the thing he was, and joined
14   Each office of the social hour
15   To noble manners, as the flower
16   And native growth of noble mind;

17   Nor ever narrowness or spite,
18   Or villain fancy fleeting by,
19   Drew in the expression of an eye,
20   Where God and Nature met in light;

21   And thus he bore without abuse
22   The grand old name of gentleman,*
23   Defamed by every charlatan,
24   And soiled with all ignoble use.

---

22 From Italian *ciarlatano*, a mountebank; hence the accent on the last syllable.

CXII.

1   High wisdom holds my wisdom less,
2   That I, who gaze with temperate eyes
3   On glorious insufficiencies,*
4   Set light by narrower perfectness.

5   But thou, that fillest all the room
6   Of all my love, art reason why
7   I seem to cast a careless eye
8   On souls, the lesser lords of doom.*

9   For what wert thou? some novel power
10   Sprang up for ever at a touch,
11   And hope could never hope too much,
12   In watching thee from hour to hour,

13   Large elements in order brought,
14   And tracts of calm from tempest made,
15   And world-wide fluctuation swayed
16   In vassal tides that followed thought.

CXIII.

1   'Tis held that sorrow makes us wise;
2   Yet how much wisdom sleeps with thee
3   Which not alone had guided me,
4   But served the seasons that may rise;

5   For can I doubt, who knew thee keen
6   In intellect, with force and skill
7   To strive, to fashion, to fulfil –
8   I doubt not what thou wouldst have been:

9   A life in civic action warm,
10   A soul on highest mission sent,
11   A potent voice of Parliament,
12   A pillar steadfast in the storm,

13   Should licensed boldness gather force,
14   Becoming, when the time has birth,
15   A lever to uplift the earth
16   And roll it in another course,

---

3 Unaccomplished greatness such as Arthur Hallam's.
8 Those that have free-will, but less intellect.

17   With thousand shocks that come and go,
18   With agonies, with energies,
19   With overthrowings, and with cries.
20   And undulations to and fro.

        CXIV.
1   Who loves not Knowledge? Who shall rail
2   Against her beauty? May she mix
3   With men and prosper! Who shall fix
4   Her pillars?* Let her work prevail.

5   But on her forehead sits a fire:
6   She sets her forward countenance
7   And leaps into the future chance,
8   Submitting all things to desire.

9   Half-grown as yet, a child, and vain –
10   She cannot fight the fear of death.
11   What is she, cut from love and faith,
12   But some wild Pallas from the brain

13   Of Demons? fiery-hot to burst
14   All barriers in her onward race
15   For power. Let her know her place;
16   She is the second, not the first.

17   A higher hand must make her mild,
18   If all be not in vain; and guide
19   Her footsteps, moving side by side
20   With wisdom, like the younger child:

21   For she is earthly of the mind,
22   But Wisdom heavenly of the soul.
23   O, friend, who camest to thy goal
24   So early, leaving me behind,

25   I would the great world grew like thee,
26   Who grewest not alone in power
27   And knowledge, but by year and hour
28   In reverence and in charity.

---

4 'Wisdom hath builded her house, she hath hewn out her seven pillars' (Proverbs, 9: 1).

CXV.

1   Now fades the last long streak of snow,
2   Now burgeons every maze of quick
3   About the flowering squares, and thick
4   By ashen roots the violets blow.

5   Now rings the woodland loud and long,
6   The distance takes a lovelier hue,
7   And drowned in yonder living blue
8   The lark becomes a sightless song.

9   Now dance the lights on lawn and lea,
10   The flocks are whiter down the vale,
11   And milkier every milky sail
12 On winding stream or distant sea;

13 Where now the seamew pipes, or dives
14   In yonder greening gleam, and fly
15   The happy birds, that change their sky
16 To build and brood; that live their lives

17 From land to land; and in my breast
18   Spring wakens too; and my regret
19   Becomes an April violet,
20 And buds and blossoms like the rest.

CXVI.

1   Is it, then, regret for buried time
2   That keenlier in sweet April wakes,
3   And meets the year, and gives and takes
4   The colours of the crescent prime?*

5   Not all: the songs, the stirring air,
6   The life re-orient out of dust,
7   Cry through the sense to hearten trust
8   In that which made the world so fair.

9   Not all regret: the face will shine
10   Upon me, while I muse alone;
11   And that dear voice, I once have known,
12 Still speak to me of me and mine:

4 Growing spring.

13 Yet less of sorrow lives in me
14   For days of happy commune dead;
15   Less yearning for the friendship fled,
16 Than some strong bond which is to be.

CXVII.

1 O days and hours, your work is this
2   To hold me from my proper place,
3   A little while from his embrace,
4 For fuller gain of after bliss:

5 That out of distance might ensue
6   Desire of nearness doubly sweet;
7   And unto meeting when we meet,
8 Delight a hundredfold accrue,

9 For every grain of sand that runs,
10   And every span of shade that steals,*
11   And every kiss of toothéd wheels,*
12 And all the courses of the suns.

CXVIII.

1 Contemplate all this work of Time,
2   The giant labouring in his youth;
3   Nor dream of human love and truth,
4 As dying Nature's earth and lime;

5 But trust that those we call the dead
6   Are breathers of an ampler day
7   For ever nobler ends. They say,
8 The solid earth whereon we tread

9 In tracts of fluent heat began,
10   And grew to seeming-random forms,
11   The seeming prey of cyclic storms,
12 Till at the last arose the man;

13 Who throve and branched from clime to clime,
14   The herald of a higher race,
15   And of himself in higher place,
16 If so he type this work of time

10 The sun-dial.
12 The clock.

17   Within himself, from more to more;
18   Or, crowned with attributes of woe
19   Like glories, move his course, and show
20   That life is not as idle ore,

21   But iron dug from central gloom,
22   And heated hot with burning fears,
23   And dipt in baths of hissing tears,
24   And battered with the shocks of doom

25   To shape and use. Arise and fly
26   The reeling Faun, the sensual feast;
27   Move upward, working out the beast,
28   And let the ape and tiger die.

CXIX.

1   Doors , where my heart was used to beat
2   So quickly, not as one that weeps
3   I come once more; the city sleeps;
4   I smell the meadow in the street;

5   I hear a chirp of birds; I see
6   Betwixt the black fronts long-withdrawn
7   A light-blue lane of early dawn,
8   And think of early days and thee,

9   And bless thee, for thy lips are bland,
10   And bright the friendship of thine eye;
11   And in my thoughts with scarce a sigh
12   I take the pressure of thine hand.

CXX.

1   I trust I have not wasted breath:
2   I think we are not wholly brain,
3   Magnetic mockeries; not in vain,
4   Like Paul with beasts,* I fought with Death;

5   Not only cunning casts in clay:
6   Let Science prove we are, and then
7   What matters Science unto men,
8   At least to me? I would not stay.

---

4 'If after the manner of men I have fought with beasts at Ephesus, what advantageth me, if the dead rise not? Let us eat and drink; for tomorrow we die' (1 Corinthians 15: 32).

9   Let him, the wiser man who springs
10   Hereafter, up from childhood shape
11   His action like the greater ape,
12   But I was *born* to other things.

CXXI.

1   Sad Hesper o'er the buried sun
2   And ready, thou, to die with him,
3   Thou watchest all things ever dim
4   And dimmer, and a glory done:

5   The team is loosened from the wain,
6   The boat is drawn upon the shore;
7   Thou listenest to the closing door,
8   And life is darkened in the brain.

9   Bright Phosphor, fresher for the night,
10   By thee the world's great work is heard
11   Beginning, and the wakeful bird;
12   Behind thee comes the greater light:

13   The market boat is on the stream,
14   And voices hail it from the brink;
15   Thou hear'st the village hammer clink,
16   And see'st the moving of the team.

17   Sweet Hesper-Phosphor, double name*
18   For what is one, the first, the last,
19   Thou, like my present and my past,
20   Thy place is changed; thou art the same.

CXXII.

1   Oh, wast thou with me, dearest, then,
2   While I rose up against my doom,
3   And yearned to burst the folded gloom,
4   To bare the eternal Heavens again,

5   To feel once more, in placid awe,
6   The strong imagination roll
7   A sphere of stars about my soul,
8   In all her motion one with law;

The mourner wonders whether his friend has been with him as he has begun to recover from his grief. See: 'Cycle and Ritual'.

17 Death and sorrow brighten into death and hope.

9   If thou wert with me, and the grave
10   Divide us not, be with me now,
11   And enter in at breast and brow,
12   Till all my blood, a fuller wave,

13   Be quickened with a livelier breath,
14   And like an inconsiderate boy,
15   As in the former flash of joy,
16   I slip the thoughts of life and death;

17   And all the breeze of Fancy blows,
18   And every dew-drop paints a bow,*
19   The wizard lightnings deeply glow,
20   And every thought breaks out a rose.

CXXIII.

1   There rolls the deep where grew the tree.
2   O earth, what changes hast thou seen!
3   There where the long street roars, hath been
4   The stillness of the central sea.*

Considers the changes wrought on the earth's surface by evolution. See: 'Profit and Loss'.

5   The hills are shadows, and they flow
6   From form to form, and nothing stands;
7   They melt like mist, the solid lands,
8   Like clouds they shape themselves and go.

9   But in my spirit will I dwell,
10   And dream my dream, and hold it true;
11   For though my lips may breathe adieu,
12   I cannot think the thing farewell.

CXXIV.

1   That which we dare invoke to bless;
2   Our dearest faith; our ghastliest doubt;
3   He, They, One, All; within, without;
4   The Power in darkness whom we guess;

Describes a renewal of faith. See: 'Lost for Words'.

5   I found Him not in world or sun,
6   Or eagle's wing, or insect's eye;
7   Nor through the questions men may try,
8   The petty cobwebs we have spun:

18 Every dew-drop turns into a miniature rainbow.
4 Balloonists say that even in a storm the middle of the sea is noiseless.

9   If e'er when faith had fallen asleep,
10   I heard a voice 'believe no more'
11   And heard an ever-breaking shore
12   That tumbled in the Godless deep;

13   A warmth within the breast would melt
14   The freezing reason's colder part,
15   And like a man in wrath the heart
16   Stood up and answered 'I have felt.'

17   No, like a child in doubt and fear:
18   But that blind clamour made me wise;
19   Then was I as a child that cries,
20   But, crying, knows his father near;

21   And what I am beheld again
22   What is, and no man understands;
23   And out of darkness came the hands
24   That reach through nature, moulding men.

CXXV.

1   Whatever I have said or sung,
2   Some bitter notes my harp would give,
3   Yea, though there often seemed to live
4   A contradiction on the tongue,

5   Yet Hope had never lost her youth;
6   She did but look through dimmer eyes;
7   Or Love but played with gracious lies,
8   Because he felt so fixed in truth:

9   And if the song were full of care,
10   He breathed the spirit of the song;
11   And if the words were sweet and strong
12   He set his royal signet there;

13   Abiding with me till I sail
14   To seek thee on the mystic deeps,
15   And this electric force, that keeps
16   A thousand pulses dancing, fail.

CXXVI.

1   Love is and was my Lord and King,
2   And in his presence I attend

3   To hear the tidings of my friend,
4   Which every hour his couriers bring.

5   Love is and was my King and Lord,
6   And will be, though as yet I keep
7   Within his court on earth, and sleep
8   Encompassed by his faithful guard,

9   And hear at times a sentinel
10   Who moves about from place to place,
11   And whispers to the worlds of space,
12   In the deep night, that all is well.

CXXVII.

1   And all is well, though faith and form
2   Be sundered in the night of fear;
3   Well roars the storm to those that hear
4   A deeper voice across the storm,

5   Proclaiming social truth shall spread,
6   And justice, ev'n though thrice again
7   The red fool-fury of the Seine
8   Should pile her barricades with dead.

9   But ill for him that wears a crown,
10   And him, the lazar, in his rags:
11   They tremble, the sustaining crags;
12   The spires of ice are toppled down,

13   And molten up, and roar in flood;
14   The fortress crashes from on high,
15   The brute earth lightens to the sky,
16   And the great Æon sinks in blood,

17   And compassed by the fires of Hell;
18   While thou, dear spirit, happy star,
19   O'erlook'st the tumult from afar,
20   And smilest, knowing all is well.

CXXVIII.

1   The love that rose on stronger wings,
2   Unpalsied when he met with Death,
3   Is comrade of the lesser faith
4   That sees the course of human things.

These two sections express the faith that, in spite of the violent changes that pattern human experience, history works towards an end that is ordained by God.
See: 'Profit and Loss'.

5   No doubt vast eddies in the flood
6   Of onward time shall yet be made,
7   And thronèd races may degrade;
8   Yet O ye mysteries of good,

9   Wild Hours that fly with Hope and Fear,
10   If all your office had to do
11   With old results that look like new;
12   If this were all your mission here,

13   To draw, to sheathe a useless sword,
14   To fool the crowd with glorious lies,
15   To cleave a creed in sects and cries,
16   To change the bearing of a word,

17   To shift an arbitrary power,
18   To cramp the student at his desk,
19   To make old bareness picturesque
20   And tuft with grass a feudal tower;

21   Why then my scorn might well descend
22   On you and yours. I see in part
23   That all, as in some piece of art,
24   Is toil cöoperant to an end.

CXXIX.
1   Dear friend, far off, my lost desire,
2   So far, so near in woe and weal;
3   O loved the most, when most I feel
4   There is a lower and a higher;

5   Known and unknown; human, divine;
6   Sweet human hand and lips and eye;
7   Dear heavenly friend that canst not die,
8   Mine, mine, for ever, ever mine;

9   Strange friend, past, present, and to be;
10   Loved deeplier, darklier understood;
11   Behold, I dream a dream of good,
12   And mingle all the world with thee.

CXXX.
1   Thy voice is on the rolling air;
2   I hear thee where the waters run;

3   Thou standest in the rising sun,
4   And in the setting thou art fair.

5   What art thou then? I cannot guess;
6   But though I seem in star and flower
7   To feel thee some diffusive power,
8   I do not therefore love thee less:

9   My love involves the love before;
10   My love is vaster passion now;
11   Though mixed with God and Nature thou,
12 I seem to love thee more and more.

13 Far off thou art, but ever nigh;
14   I have thee still, and I rejoice;
15   I prosper, circled with thy voice;
16 I shall not lose thee though I die.

CXXXI.

1   O living will that shalt endure
2   When all that seems shall suffer shock,
3   Rise in the spiritual rock,
4   Flow through our deeds and make them pure,

5   That we may lift from out of dust
6   A voice as unto him that hears,
7   A cry above the conquered years
8   To one that with us works, and trust,

9   With faith that comes of self-control,
10   The truths that never can be proved
11   Until we close with all we loved,
12 And all we flow from, soul in soul.

Epilogue*

1   O true and tried, so well and long,
2   Demand not thou a marriage lay;
3   In that it is thy marriage day
4   Is music more than any song.

Addresses the will of God and looks with faith towards the future.
See: 'Lost for Words'.

Describes the marriage of Tennyson's sister, Cecilia, to his friend, Edmund Lushington.
See: 'Lost for Words' and 'Profit and Loss'.

Epilogue The marriage of Edmund Lushington and Cecilia Tennyson, October 10, 1842.

5   Nor have I felt so much of bliss
6   Since first he told me that he loved
7   A daughter of our house; nor proved
8   Since that dark day a day like this;

9   Though I since then have numbered o'er
10   Some thrice three years: they went and came,
11   Remade the blood and changed the frame,
12   And yet is love not less, but more;

13   No longer caring to embalm
14   In dying songs a dead regret,
15   But like a statue solid-set,
16   And moulded in colossal calm.

17   Regret is dead, but love is more
18   Than in the summers that are flown,
19   For I myself with these have grown
20   To something greater than before;

21   Which makes appear the songs I made
22   As echoes out of weaker times,
23   As half but idle brawling rhymes,
24   The sport of random sun and shade.

25   But where is she, the bridal flower,
26   That must be made a wife ere noon?
27   She enters, glowing like the moon
28   Of Eden on its bridal bower:

29   On me she bends her blissful eyes
30   And then on thee; they meet thy look
31   And brighten like the star that shook
32   Betwixt the palms of paradise.

33   O when her life was yet in bud,
34   He too foretold the perfect rose.
35   For thee she grew, for thee she grows
36   For ever, and as fair as good.

37   And thou art worthy; full of power;
38   As gentle; liberal-minded, great,
39   Consistent; wearing all that weight
40   Of learning lightly like a flower.

41   But now set out: the noon is near,
42   And I must give away the bride;
43   She fears not, or with thee beside
44   And me behind her, will not fear.

45   For I that danced her on my knee,
46   That watched her on her nurse's arm,
47   That shielded all her life from harm
48   At last must part with her to thee;

49   Now waiting to be made a wife,
50   Her feet, my darling, on the dead
51   Their pensive tablets round her head,
52   And the most living words of life

53   Breathed in her ear. The ring is on,
54   The 'wilt thou' answered, and again
55   The 'wilt thou' asked, till out of twain
56   Her sweet 'I will' has made you one.

57   Now sign your names, which shall be read,
58   Mute symbols of a joyful morn,
59   By village eyes as yet unborn;
60   The names are signed, and overhead

61   Begins the clash and clang that tells
62   The joy to every wandering breeze;
63   The blind wall rocks, and on the trees
64   The dead leaf trembles to the bells.

65   O happy hour, and happier hours
66   Await them. Many a merry face
67   Salutes them – maidens of the place,
68   That pelt us in the porch with flowers.

69   O happy hour, behold the bride
70   With him to whom her hand I gave.
71   They leave the porch, they pass the grave
72   That has to-day its sunny side.

73   To-day the grave is bright for me,
74   For them the light of life increased,
75   Who stay to share the morning feast,
76   Who rest tonight beside the sea.

77 Let all my genial spirits advance
78   To meet and greet a whiter sun;
79   My drooping memory will not shun
80 The foaming grape of eastern France.

81 It circles round, and fancy plays,
82   And hearts are warmed and faces bloom,
83   As drinking health to bride and groom
84 We wish them store of happy days.

85 Nor count me all to blame if I
86   Conjecture of a stiller guest,
87   Perchance, perchance, among the rest,
88 And, though in silence, wishing joy.

89 But they must go, the time draws on,
90   And those white-favoured horses wait;
91   They rise, but linger; it is late;
92 Farewell, we kiss, and they are gone.

93 A shade falls on us like the dark
94   From little cloudlets on the grass,
95   But sweeps away as out we pass
96 To range the woods, to roam the park,

97 Discussing how their courtship grew,
98   And talk of others that are wed,
99   And how she looked, and what he said,
100 And back we come at fall of dew.

101 Again the feast, the speech, the glee,
102   The shade of passing thought, the wealth
103   Of words and wit, the double health,
104 The crowning cup, the three-times-three,

105 And last the dance; – till I retire:
106   Dumb is that tower which spake so loud,
107   And high in heaven the streaming cloud,
108 And on the downs a rising fire:

109 And rise, O moon, from yonder down,
110   Till over down and over dale
111   All night the shining vapour sail
112 And pass the silent-lighted town,

113 The white-faced halls, the glancing rills,
114   And catch at every mountain head,
115   And o'er the friths that branch and spread
116 Their sleeping silver thro' the hills;

117 And touch with shade the bridal doors,
118   With tender gloom the roof, the wall;
119   And breaking let the splendour fall
120 To spangle all the happy shores

121 By which they rest, and ocean sounds,
122   And, star and system rolling past,
123   A soul shall draw from out the vast
124 And strike his being into bounds,

125 And, moved thro' life of lower phase,
126   Result in man, be born and think,
127   And act and love, a closer link
128 Betwixt us and the crowning race

129 Of those that, eye to eye, shall look
130   On knowledge; under whose command
131   Is Earth and Earth's, and in their hand
132 Is Nature like an open book;

133 No longer half-akin to brute,
134   For all we thought and loved and did,
135   And hoped, and suffered, is but seed
136 Of what in them is flower and fruit;

137 Whereof the man, that with me trod
138   This planet, was a noble type
139   Appearing ere the times were ripe,
140 That friend of mine who lives in God,

141 That God, which ever lives and loves,
142   One God, one law, one element,
143   And one far-off divine event,
144 To which the whole creation moves.

Note

1. This approach is, in part, suggested by J. H. Buckley's reading of *In Memoriam* in which he identifies dark, light, water and the hand as four key images on which the structure of *In Memoriam* depends (Buckley 1960: 112).

Chapter 3
The Guide

Lost for Words: Prologue, II, V, VI, VIII, XIII, XVI, XX, XXI, XXXII, XL, LII, LIV, LVI, LX, XCV, XCVII, CXXIV, CXXXI, Epilogue

In Memoriam is centrally concerned with the limits of linguistic expression. As we have seen, in section V, Tennyson's mourner bleakly reflects that poetic composition is useful because the rhythm that it generates numbs his grief. The implication of this line is clear: measured language is good for little else; it is no use as an accurate or adequate description of the mourner's own feelings, or of the friend that he has lost. This failure of language in the face of grief is a familiar convention of mourning. Faced with the grief of a bereaved friend, we might well resort to phrases such as 'I am more sorry than I can say' or 'I know there is nothing I can say' or 'nothing I can say will bring them back.' These kinds of non-utterance both fulfil the social need for speech and also acknowledge that death is an event that defeats speech. Of course, to say that one is lost for words is a way of indicating the extremity of one's response to almost any situation. I might be rendered speechless with rage, or love someone more than words can say. Again, these expressions are linguistic conventions. They are ways of saying 'I am very angry' or 'I love you very much.' They are therefore less interesting for the quality of emotion that they (fail to) express than for what they, like Tennyson's stanza about measured language, say about words. These phrases, embedded in our social discourse, define the limits of language and accept that words are an imperfect way of communicating. This fact is unlikely to be a cause for concern on a daily basis (in fact, it relieves us of the responsibility of saying exactly what we mean), but a poem is more likely to be aware of and frustrated by the inadequacy of words because they are the medium or material it uses to create art. If poetry is, as Coleridge's definition has it, 'the best words in the best order' (Coleridge [1835] 1990, XIV, I, 90), then what happens when there is no right word, but only words that are wrong or half-right? *In Memoriam* is filled with articulate distress about its own inarticulacy. The defining paradox of *In Memoriam* is that it writes at length about the impossibility of writing. This first section of the Reading Guide will focus on some of the sections in which the mourner voices his doubts about language, trace the movement of the poem towards a renewed faith in words and introduce some of the religious and philosophical ideas that inform Tennyson's linguistic anxiety.

'What words are these have fallen from me?'

The first stanza of section V sums up the elegist's ambivalence about his work:

> I sometimes hold it half a sin
> To put in words the grief I feel
> For words, like nature, half reveal
> And half conceal the soul within.
> (V, 1–4)

The sense of this stanza is fairly straightforward: the mourner feels that writing about his grief is almost sinful because words disguise or mask reality as much as they communicate it (this lack of faith in language is reflected in the repeated use of 'half', which suggests that the mourner is so uncertain of language that he is unable to commit himself to any definite statement). But as well as communicating and performing ambivalence, these four lines also allude to two philosophical traditions concerning the origin and work of language. The first of these has to do with language and the 'sin' that the mourner refers to in line 1; the second is concerned with the relationship between language, nature and the soul, which Tennyson sketches in lines 3 and 4.

It may not be immediately apparent why the mourner associates failed language with sin. Perhaps he feels that the injustice his poem does to his friend's memory amounts to a sort of crime (what Proust describes in *Remembrance of Things Past* as 'posthumous infidelity' (Proust 1981 III: 940)). However, Tennyson's use of the word 'sin' suggests that the crime he half-commits is against God rather than Hallam. The association of language and sin is not made by Tennyson alone. It has a long tradition in Christian religious philosophy and has to do with a post-lapsarian understanding of the world. Post-lapsarian means 'after the fall' and it is a term that refers to humankind's fall from grace, which is described in the Old Testament book of Genesis. One of the things that is understood to characterise the fallen-ness of humanity is language. As humanity becomes separated from God, words are cut adrift from the things that they name. Genesis describes pre-lapsarian language as one in which words are perfectly fitted to the things they name: 'And out of the ground the Lord God formed every beast of the field and every fowl of the air, and brought them unto Adam to see what he would call them; and whatsoever Adam called every living creature, that was the name thereof' (Genesis 2: 19). As Stanley Fish puts it,

> Adam's knowledge is infused into him by God and the names he imposes are accurate, intensively and extensively [. . .] The loss of perfect language is, more than anything else, the sign of the Fall since, in Eden, speech is an outward manifestation of the inner paradise. (Fish 1998: 114)

Contemporary literary theory also recognises a separation between words and their meanings, which they frame in secular terms, identifying a troubling disconnect between the 'signifier' (the word) and the 'signified' (the thing it describes). This means that language is never absolute or universal, but is always subjective and shifting, affected by the social, historical and cultural context in which it is used. We cannot look to language for complete truth or knowledge. Without these burdens of responsibility, some theorists argue, language gains its freedom. The ambiguity of language is the source of its creative potential and opens words up to interpretation. However, unable to rely on our ability to know the world through language, our grip on a shared reality is loosened. This is the give-and-take of deconstructionist theory, which is discussed in complex detail in the work of critics such as Roland Barthes and Jacques Derrida. Derrida has written about how death opens up the unbridgeable gap between the name (signifier) and the dead object (the signified) in a way that might be helpful when considering Tennyson's self-consciously post-lapsarian elegy. Derrida argues that, when a person dies, all that survives is their name and that this survival is the ultimate proof of the 'alienability' of language: its separateness from the things or people it describes. When we call a person or a thing by its name we pre-empt, anticipate or rehearse their death: 'in calling or naming someone while he is alive, we know that his name can survive him and *already survives him* [. . .] the name begins during his life to get along without him speaking and bearing his death each time it is pronounced' (Derrida 2001: 49). This means that a name (or word), always inadequate, in the event of death becomes both more inadequate and more important, because the person to whom it belonged is no longer around to speak for themselves. Therefore, in mourning, language becomes more crucial and more elusive. As Derrida puts it, mourning has 'to fail, to fail *well*' (144).

A good, or thorough, failure is an apt description of *In Memoriam* and Derrida's work on mourning shares some of Tennyson's concerns. In the first lines of section 2, for example, the elegist considers 'the stones / That name the underlying dead', figuring the gap between name and person as one of physical depth. However, although mourning presents Derrida and Tennyson with a common linguistic problem, the implications of that problem remain very different. For Derrida, writing as an atheist Jew in post-war Europe, language has, to use his famous phrase, 'always already' failed. It is a closed system that can never get beyond itself. Names have never been 'internally and exclusively accurate' and there is no possibility of a world in which language works better. For Tennyson, the chasm that exists between word and world symbolises the chasm that exists between God and sinful humanity. The Christian tradition insists that humankind was not created in this state of alienation and professes faith in a time when 'the Word was with God and the Word was God' (John 1: 1) and hope for a time when word and world will be reunited. When Derrida names things and people, he rehearses their death; when Adam names the animals in Eden, he performs an act of creation. In *In Memoriam*, the broken relationship with God, symbolised by Tennyson's broken or sinful language, is experienced afresh by the loss of Hallam. As Sinfield has it, 'the life together of Hallam and the poet had all the beauty, freshness and innocence of the garden of Eden – and as with Eden [. . .] it was the entry of death into the poet's pre-lapsarian world which marked its end' (Sinfield 1971: 65). It is from this second Fall – experienced as a loss of poetic and religious faith – that the elegist struggles to recover over the course of the poem.

The great epic of the Fall is Milton's *Paradise Lost*, which retells the story of Genesis over twelve books. Milton's version focuses in detail on the character of Satan, himself a fallen (or rebel) angel, who tempts Eve to sin. An epic must have a hero, and readers of *Paradise Lost* frequently assign that role to Satan, who seems to embody a heroic individualism that might be compared with Ulysses or Achilles. A reading of this kind recasts the Fall in a positive light, seeing what Milton describes in the poem's opening lines as 'man's first disobedience' as a revolutionary act against the despotic authority of God. According to this reading, sin becomes a word to describe an act that tests the limits imposed on humanity, challenges received wisdom and asserts that no knowledge (not even the knowledge of good and evil) is out of bounds. Sin is scientific investigation, geographical exploration, artistic creativity. This reading held great appeal for Romantic writers who lived through a time of revolution in Europe and political unrest in Britain. Their works express their support of radical political change and their fascination with the possibilities and changes of human invention (or imagination), the hero as over-reacher. In his Preface to *Prometheus Unbound*, for example, Shelley writes that Satan has 'courage, and majesty, and firm and patient opposition to omnipotent force' (Shelley 1970: 205).[1] Tennyson was born just a few decades after these poets, as the memory of revolution was beginning to recede. As a young poet, Tennyson was greatly influenced by the Romantics and so, although the fallen-ness equates to Tennyson's experience of grief and his relationship to the language of elegy, there is, at the same time, a sense in which *In Memoriam* clings jealously to the half-sin that it commits, drawing out the period of mourning across the poem's length, exploring its transgressive, creative possibilities.

Behind the Veil

The second two lines of section V point towards a second philosophical framework that Tennyson employs in *In Memoriam*'s struggle for language. By comparing words to the natural world that conceals as much as it reveals of its inner soul, Tennyson adopts a Platonic world view. Plato was an Ancient Greek philosopher, the pupil of Socrates, who argued that reality was made up of essential forms which were beyond the everyday experience and comprehension of humankind. Plato's famous illustration of this philosophy, included in his work, *The Republic* (380 BC), compares human beings to prisoners, chained to one another in a cave, looking at shadows cast by an artificial light, which show the outlines of objects being moved around by unseen beings outside the cave.[2] The shadows both conceal and reveal this reality. Like human experience of the world, the shadows bear some relationship to the objects that cast them, but the effect they give is both partial and misleading. Tennyson's stanza suggests that words behave like Platonic shadows, secondary representations or echoes of truth, that mediate it into the sensible or literate world, but incur a crucial loss in the act of translation. This idea returns a few lines later when the mourner resolves to wrap himself in words, which he says will behave like 'weeds' (mourning dress) or 'coarsest clothes against the cold'. Like Plato's shadows, clothes both conceal the body of the wearer and reveal the shape or 'outline' of the body they conceal. The mourner implies that the words of his elegy are coarse, so that the outline of grief that they offer is likely to be bulky, ill-fitting and crude.

Tennyson writes that the thing that words both conceal and reveal is the soul. This refers to another, related aspect of Platonic philosophy, which explores the relationship between the soul and the body. Platonic philosophy argues that the soul and not the body is the location of a person's true self, or identity. Rather like the shadows on the cave wall, or the clothing of words worn by Tennyson's mourner, the body is merely the outward manifestation of the inner reality of any individual. Plato illustrates this idea when he tells the story of Socrates' death, recording a conversation between Socrates and one of his followers:

'How shall we bury you?' asked Crito. 'However you like,' Socrates said [. . .] 'When I drink the poison I shall no longer remain here with you, but will go away to some kind of happiness of the blessed. You must cheer up and say you are burying my body.' (Plato 1993: 182)

This anecdote identifies death as the moment when soul and body are revealed to be separate; the corpse, the soul's outer casing, becomes an object of small concern that can be disposed of without too much fuss. This has particular relevance for *In Memoriam*, which, as we will see in the next chapter, bemoans and worries about the loss of Hallam's body. In section V, Tennyson forges a connection between bodies and words, writing that words conceal and reveal the soul in the same way that, according to Platonic philosophy, the body reveals and conceals the soul. By stressing the corporeality or materiality of poetic language, Tennyson again emphasises that he is ill equipped to deal with the mourned object, who is, by definition, no longer of the body.

This Platonic understanding of poetic language also comes to Tennyson via Romanticism. Shelley, the Romantic poet most associated with Platonism, employs the image of the cave in an allegorical image of poetic creativity, describing the cave as 'the still cave of the witch Poesy', in which the mind seeks 'in the shadows that pass by / Ghosts of all things that are' ('Mont Blanc', 43–5). As we saw in *Adonais*, Shelley employs a second Platonic image – the veil – to achieve consolation at the conclusion of his elegy. A veil is another thing that both reveals and conceals, and, as in *Adonais*, Shelley's poetry often talks about lifting or going beyond the veil in order to express his desire to get to the truth of things. Whereas, for Tennyson, this veil is composed of language, for Shelley at the end of *Adonais* poetic language is employed to penetrate the veil. In other poems Shelley tests his poetic faith even further. Whereas in *Adonais* Shelley declares that Keats's soul will penetrate the innermost veil of heaven, in 'Mont Blanc', looking on the sublime Alpine landscape, he wonders if the veil has been lifted before the eye of his imagination: 'Has some unknown omnipotence unfurled / The veil of life and death?' ('Mont Blanc', 52–3). These kinds of Romantic possibilities seem to be shut down by Tennyson's mourner when his question, 'what hope of answer or redress?', receives what sounds like the fading echo of a reply: 'Behind the veil, behind the veil' (LVI, 27–8). The speaker of *In Memoriam*, cut off from God and sceptical of any natural order or law, understands language to be part of a world in which he can perceive scant evidence of connection to a wider truth.

In the Prologue to *In Memoriam*, which, as we have seen, draws the poem into a circle, revealing the redemptive consolatory path that the elegy haltingly follows, Tennyson employs a kind of Platonic Christianity, writing about the 'little systems' (of knowledge or, perhaps, of language) that are 'but broken lights' of God (Prologue, 17–19). The following stanzas go on to talk about the impossibility of knowledge through sight, 'for knowledge is of what we see' (22), and to profess faith in a connection between the limited knowledge of body and mind and God's truth, which is again figured as illumination: 'a beam in darkness'. The mourner calls for the beam of human knowledge to grow, asserting confidence in the possibility of human progress, and looks forward to the point when 'mind and soul, according well / May make one music as before'. Here again we see Tennyson's Christian Platonism at work. 'Mind and soul' alludes to the Platonic idea of mind / body dualism, while the idea that mind and soul might eventually return to a state of original harmony locates the poem firmly within the Christian framework of Fall and Redemption. Reunited, mind and soul are imagined making 'one music', a meta-poetic reference that figures the redemption of humankind as a harmonious composition, or perfect poem.

In the following stanzas the mourner asks God to forgive 'what seemed my sin in me' (33). This line pre-empts the reference to the elegy's 'half sin', identifying sin, grief and poetry closely with one another. Something that 'seemed' a sin is, by implication, something that has been revealed not to be a sin and so, even when asking for forgiveness, the speaker suggests that forgiveness is unnecessary or that it has somehow already occurred through the redemptive work of the poem. *In Memoriam* is very interested in how things 'seem'. If something only seems to be the case, there is every chance that it is not as it seems. When, for example, in section II, the mourner writes that, as he gazes on the yew tree whose roots make contact with the buried bodies of the dead, 'I seem to fail from out my blood / And grow incorporate into thee' (II, 15–16), the word 'seem' indicates to the reader that the mourner is deluded or is indulging in a bleak fantasy.

In section VIII, the same note of doubt is introduced when the mourner again tries to justify his failed attempts to write. He employs an extended simile that compares his grief to the grief of a 'happy lover' who goes to visit his beloved and finds out that she has gone away. He imagines the lover wandering along paths down which he used to walk with his love and finding a flower 'beat with rain and wind / Which once she fostered up with care' (VIII, 15–16). He compares this flower to his poem – 'this poor flower of poesy' (a piece of wordplay that turns Tennyson's collection of lyrics into a posy of flowers) – suggesting that in Hallam's absence, his words begin to fail, but still survive. Or at least, 'so *seems* it in my deep regret' (17, my emphasis). 'Seems' connects the simile with the thing it illustrates, making the simile appear untrustworthy. His poem seems like a flower, but is it? Perhaps it is a flower that has already died. By introducing a sense of doubt about his simile, Tennyson acts out the doubtful or fading poetry that he describes.

Tears of a widower

If *In Memoriam* is (or seems) like a flower, then the mourner is like a lover. This comparison between the mourner's friendship with his 'lost Arthur' and the heterosexual relationship between a man and a woman points to a second aspect of *In Memoriam*'s struggle for language. Critics differ widely in the way they define the sexuality of Tennyson's and Hallam's relationship.[3] To describe it as a close friendship hardly does justice to the passionate desire expressed throughout *In Memoriam*. However, to apply the label 'homosexual' to the relationship implies a physical sexuality of which there is no evidence. Part of the problem is one of language. As Alan Sinfield has discussed in his studies of representations of sexuality in the nineteenth century, the words that we now use to describe sexuality do not simply provide labels for a set of pre-existing, fixed sexual identities (Sinfield 1994: 11). Words such as 'heterosexual', 'homosexual', 'bisexual', 'gay' and 'straight' also construct or contribute to a modern understanding of sexual identity, making sex central to the way the modern self is defined. Sinfield argues that, in the nineteenth century, sex did not enter into questions of identity in the same way.

This difference between Victorian and modern articulations of sexual identity means that it is difficult to gain an accurate understanding of Tennyson's relationship with Hallam and cautions against an autobiographical reading of *In Memoriam* that seeks out a suppressed homosexuality that we – with our modern, post-Freudian understanding of sexuality – feel must lurk behind it. By placing the language of homosexuality in its historical context, Sinfield suggests that *In Memoriam*, by failing to define its sexuality (refusing to speak its name), makes room for multiplicity and ambiguity, and escapes the controlling power of public discourse. This ambiguity is achieved by the similes in sections VI, VIII, XIII, XXXII, XL, LX and XCVII that compare the mourner's grief to the grief of a widow or widower, or compare the separation between the mourner and his dead friend as the separation of an uneven love match, in which the woman cannot match the man's social status or intelligence. In each case, the 'as', 'like' or 'seems' that signposts the simile creates a connection and a distance between its two halves, implying both sameness and difference. When the mourner writes that his grief seems like the grief of a man for a woman who has gone away on a long journey, the word 'seems' makes clear that this image of heterosexual love does not quite capture the nature of the relationship between mourner and friend. In section XIII, the mourner confidently describes his tears, which fall 'like' the tears of a 'widower' (XIII, 1). The mourner's tears are 'like', but not the same as, the tears of a bereaved husband. A 'widower' is a word borrowed from a heterosexual discourse that names those relationships and identities that it recognises as legitimate. By using the name 'widower' as an inadequate stand-in for his own identity, the mourner points out that there is no such name for what he is. His relationship with his friend, both in life and in death, evades the grasp of language.

Feminist criticism has coined the term 'homosocial' to get beyond the question of sexuality, arguing that same-sex relationships are most fruitfully understood in socio-political terms and demonstrating how the close bonds that men form with other men are a means of maintaining patriarchal power, a means by which, as Eve Sedgwick puts it, '"men promot[e] the interests of men"' (Sedgwick 1985: 4). Reading *In Memoriam* from this perspective, it becomes interesting to think about how women – particularly Tennyson's sister Emily, who was engaged to Hallam when he died – are represented within the poem. If heterosexual relationships are employed by Tennyson as a way of both describing and not describing his relationship with Hallam, then Emily's place within the poem becomes problematic. Similes such as the one in section VIII lead the reader to think of Tennyson's bereaved sister, but the simile seems to elbow her out of the way so that it is Tennyson and not Emily that is 'widowed'. Tennyson's sister is curiously absent from *In Memoriam*. Some similes appear to be written with Emily in mind. Section LX, for example, compares the mourner's love to the love 'of some poor girl whose heart is set / On one whose rank exceeds her own' (LX, 3–4), an accurate description of the barriers that prevented Emily and Hallam's engagement. But even in this case, the image is merely the means of illustrating the relationship between mourner and friend, which remains the poem's exclusive focus. By repeatedly figuring himself as a woman, Tennyson effectively denies the possibility of feminine agency within the poem. The images of femininity that Tennyson employs are passive, silent and intellectually weak. In section VI, the girl waiting for her love to return from the sea is a 'meek, unconscious dove'; the eyes of Lazarus's sister are 'homes of silent prayer' (XXXII, 1); and in section XCVII, Tennyson compares himself, separated from Hallam, who has gone on ahead of him in death, to the wife of a great scientist: 'She knows but matters of the house, / And he, he knows a thousand things' (XCVII, 30–1). Although, in each case, the mourner identifies himself with these women, his similes rely for their meaning on a patriarchal power structure that silences and subjugates women. Whereas *In Memoriam* maintains a fruitfully ambiguous sexual identity, it reinforces categories of gender, defining itself throughout as a masculine elegy.[4]

Living words of life

As the Prologue promises, *In Memoriam*'s sinful language works towards its own redemption. As the mourner gradually moves out of his state of grief towards a tentative recovery, his language becomes less fraught with doubt and questions posed in earlier sections are resolved. Section XVI asks, 'what words are these have fall'n from me?' (XVI, 1), a question which suggests that the mourner exerts no conscious control over his elegy. He does not speak the words; they fall from his mouth or his pen, unwilled. He barely recognises the poem as his own and refuses responsibility for what he has written. Questioning the changeful nature of his sorrow, which he sometimes experiences as 'calm despair', sometimes as 'wild unrest', he again offers a special metaphor to suggest the separation between his written expressions of grief and that grief's reality: 'doth she only *seem* to take / The touch of change in calm or storm / But knows no more of transient form / In her deep self, than some dead lake' (XVI, 5–8). Like the stones in section II, that 'name the underlying dead', the surface of the lake reveals nothing of its depths. Each of these similes locates language on the surface, marking or masking a deeper, unreadable truth. This motif returns again in section XX, when the mourner compares his 'lighter moods', which gain comfort from his words, with 'other griefs within' (11) that find no outward or surface expression. Whereas shallow feeling is easily articulated, deep grief is best expressed by an absence of language, in silence.[5]

In the following sections these doubts about the value and responsibility of the elegy return, but here they are put into the mouths of other speakers so that the elegist is forced to defend his work. These stanzas represent a brief return to the pastoral mode and therefore allude to those earlier works that have greater faith in the consolations of poetry and nature. Again, the distance that separates the dead body from the living is emphasised: 'I sing to him that rests below' (XXI, 1); but, whereas in section II the speaker 'gazes' at the tree that grows beside the gravestones, on this occasion he takes 'the grasses of the grave / And makes them pipes whereon to blow' (XXI, 3–4), so that the music or song of his poetry achieves a physical, natural connection with the resting place of the friend he mourns. The voices that critique this pastoral scene sound strikingly modern. They accuse him of 'weakness' (8), of courting public approval and of wasting his poetry on private grief, when it should be used to address a national cause. Wearing the mask of the pastoral elegist, the mourner is able to voice a defence of his poem: 'I do but sing because I must / And pipe but as the linnets sing' (XXI, 23–4). He continues to insist that he is not responsible for his poetry, but rather than expressing dismay at words that have 'fallen' from his pen unbidden, here he implies that poetry comes naturally to him and that his grief is part of the natural cycle of life and death.

Section LII again interrogates the relationship between depth and surface, language and meaning. Here again, the lyric constitutes a dialogue between two voices, but it is the mourner who has relapsed into expressions of self-doubt: 'My words are only words, and moved / Upon the topmost froth of thought' (LII, 3–4). As the poet's doubts return, so do those images associated with doubt in earlier sections. 'Topmost froth' suggests the white foam that appears on the crest of a wave and so recalls the lake in section XVI that communicates nothing of its depths. In this section, words are imperfect acts of love rather than grief, and the mourner is answered by the Spirit of true love who instructs him, '"blame not thou thy plaintive song"' (LII, 5). In each of these self-reflexive dialogues the last word is given to the voice that speaks in defence of the elegy, so that each marks a temporary moment of renewed faith in the illusory and fragile surfaces of language.

Although the mourner resolves to sing rather than to keep silent, he continues to insist on his lack of control over his broken language. One of the poem's most famous stanzas offers a powerful image of poetry as spontaneous, senseless noise: 'So runs my dream: but what am I? / An infant crying in the night / An infant crying for the light: / And with no language but a cry' (LIV, 17–20). 'Infant' derives from the Latin 'infans', which means 'unable to speak', so it is a word that defines childishness in part by a lack of language. In these terms, the poet is indeed an infant: he is unable to speak his grief. Like the 'wild and wandering cry' described in the Prologue, the cry of the child is the non- / pre-linguistic sound of basic human (or even animal) need, distress or desire. This bleak metaphor describes a moment of intense self-doubt in which the mourner appears to stumble backwards, undoing the progress he has made. However, it also allows for the possibility that progress will begin again. The stanza recalls Paul's letter to the Corinthians: 'When I was a child, I spake as a child, I understood as a child, I thought as a child: but when I became a man, I put away childish things. For now we see through a glass, darkly: but then face to face' (1 Corinthians 13: 11–12). Writing in the confidence of his faith, Paul's letter employs childhood as a metaphor for development. Likewise, Tennyson's image contains the same, albeit unspoken, promise of articulate adulthood. The image of the crying child returns towards the end of the elegy, a repetition that enables the reader to register that development: 'Then was I as a child that cries, / But crying knows its father near' (CXXIV, 17–20). This time, the metaphor is employed in the past tense, implying that the speaker has moved beyond his infantile state and is able to reflect back on it using poetic language. At this point of mature reflection the speaker is able to conclude that even his most senseless cries formed part of his progress. The metaphor is rewritten, demonstrating the elegy's changing relationship with its own language.

The final section of *In Memoriam* looks forward to a time 'when all that seems shall suffer shock' (CXXXI, 2), describing death, or the end of the world, as a moment of visual revelation, when the illusions created by the way the world 'seems' through the eyes of fallen humanity is destroyed. The final use of the word 'seems' deliberately recalls the way things so often 'seem' to the mourner over the course of his poem so that redemption is described as the achievement of perfect poetic vision and language. The mourner also offers a last cry: 'That we may lift from out of dust / A voice as unto him that hears, / A cry above the conquered years / To one that with us works' (CXXXI, 5–8). As the mourner draws his elegy to a close, his cry is no longer the wild inarticulate cry of a child; it is transformed into the cry of a communal voice that speaks to God, confident in the faith that it will be heard.

In the Epilogue, the private, fallen language of grief gives way to the public, social language of a wedding ceremony. The Epilogue describes the marriage of Tennyson's sister Cecilia to his friend, Edmund Lushington. It follows the redemptive pattern of pastoral elegy, ending with the promise of new life by imagining the child that will result from the marriage. By concluding his poem with a wedding rather than, for example, the coming of spring or the break of day after night, *In Memoriam* frames the cycle of death and new life in social rather than in natural terms, so that social laws and customs are lent a kind of natural force.

The Epilogue is long and the wedding is recounted in some detail, but the mourner begins this section by writing that he will not write: 'Demand thou not a marriage lay; / In that it is thy marriage day / Is music more than any song' (Epilogue, 2–4). If what follows is not a marriage song, then what is it? With what kind of language does *In Memoriam* conclude? *In Memoriam* uses the Epilogue to look for an answer to this question and to experiment with the possibilities of post-elegiac language. The speaker rejects the poetry of mourning, 'No longer caring to embalm / In dying songs a dead regret' (Epilogue, 13) and describing 'the songs I made' as 'echoes out of weaker times' (Epilogue, 22). Heard as 'dying songs' and as 'echoes', the elegy is experienced as if at a distance, so that the speaker suggests that he has travelled far beyond his grieving self.

He continues in this gently dismissive mood: 'As half but idle brawling rhymes / The sport of random sun and shade' (Epilogue, 23–4) – descriptions that are themselves faint echoes of the 'half a sin' and 'touch of change in calm and storm' described in the poem's opening sections. The speaker still entertains the same doubts about the value of his words, but although these doubts remain, there is now less at stake and he breaks off, almost mid-thought, to ask, 'But where is she, the bridal flower [. . .]?' (Epilogue, 25). The elegy is snapped shut and the speaker is brought back to the present just as his sister enters the room, 'glowing like the moon / Of Eden on its bridal bower' (Epilogue, 28–9). Describing the new beginning of marriage in pre-lapsarian terms, the speaker suggests that his sister's wedding is redemptive. It rescues poet and poem from their fallen state and allows for the possibility of a renewed faith in God and in language.

This faith is reinforced by the marriage ceremony, which is described as an exchange of words that have the power to bind two people together: 'And the most living words of life / Breathed in her ear. The ring is on, / The "Wilt thou" answered, and again / The "wilt thou" asked, till out of twain / Her sweet "I Will" has made you one' (Epilogue, 54–6).This exchange is what J. L. Austin, in his series of published lectures, *How To Do Things With Words*, describes as 'performative' (Austin 1976). Performative language is language that does what it says so that speech constitutes action. A promise is performative because to say 'I promise' is the same as the act of promising. Likewise, spoken in a marriage ceremony, 'I will' is performative because the marriage is achieved through that utterance ('Her sweet "I will" has made you one'). Performative language, therefore, is language at its most powerful and direct. It acts, rather than describing action, removing the gap that separates word and meaning. To recognise the performative is to acknowledge that words are not 'only words', as Tennyson's mourner so often insists, but that they carry authority. Austin emphasises that performative language only works within a framework of established social conventions, offering the wedding ceremony as an example: 'For (Christian) marrying, it is essential that I should not be already married with a wife living, sane and undivorced [Austin was writing at a time when the laws governing marriage and divorce were much stricter than they are today] and so on. Without this framework, performative language is a mockery: like marriage to a monkey' (Austin 1976: 8–9). To employ performative language is therefore to acknowledge and participate in society. By recording the marriage vows, the Epilogue achieves a transition from the alienated language of grief, to the language of religious and social contract.

In Memoriam concludes with resurrection, at the expense of, as well as by means of, the poetic language of elegy. Whereas Adonais and Lycidas are both brought back to life by the poems that mourn their deaths, the Epilogue to *In Memoriam* silences its own song in order to make way for a new kind of language, the 'living words of life' that marry his sister to his friend. 'Living words of life' is itself a strikingly unpoetic phrase, a tautology that implies that the descriptive language of poetry has exhausted itself. The description of the wedding celebration continues to emphasise the close relationship between language and social custom. The mourner lists 'the feast, the speech, the glee' and describes 'the wealth of words and wit' before he departs alone into a landscape that is characterised by silence; the bell-tower is 'dumb' and the town is 'silent-lighted' (Epilogue, 101–12). In this final, wordless setting, the moon rises, recalling the 'moon of Eden' described a few lines earlier, while the mourner imagines the birth of his as-yet unconceived nephew or niece who will be a 'closer link / Betwixt us and the crowning race' (Epilogue, 127–8). The mourner expresses his faith in the progress of humanity towards God with an image of pre-lapsarian literacy: 'Of those that, eye to eye, shall look / On knowledge; under whose command is Nature like an open book' (Epilogue, 129–32). Whereas in section V, words, 'like nature', concealed as much as they revealed, here the simile shifts so that nature is compared to the written word, which can be read and perfectly understood. The union of man, God, language and nature that the Epilogue promises, is a return to the Eden described in Genesis where the gap between name and thing, perception and truth, man and God is closed.

Losing Touch: I, II, III, VII, X, XIV, XVIII, XXX, XXXVI, XLIV, XLV, LXIV, LXIX, LXXX, LXXXIV, LXXXV, XCIII, XCV

'These touching lines'

A second core motif which this Guide seeks to draw to the reader's attention is that of touch. Many of the early reviews of *In Memoriam* remark on the poem's capacity to touch its readership. The reviewer for *The Examiner* writes that the poem is 'as beautiful as touching' and that, when reading *In Memoriam*, 'every chord of the human heart is touched in turn' (Forster 1850: 357). *The Athenaeum* describes the 'touching and graceful modesty' with which 'the heart's experience is so touchingly chronicled' (Marston 1850: 629). In *Tait's Edinburgh Magazine*, Franklin Lushington enthusiastically asserts that *In Memoriam* is 'one of the most touching and exquisite monuments ever raised to a departed friend' (Lushington 1850: 499), and the *Memoir* records the misguided conviction of an anonymous reviewer that 'these touching lines evidently come from the full heart of the widow of a military man' (*Memoir* I: 298). These references to the touching quality of *In Memoriam*, which are offered as tokens of praise, indicate the reviewers' shared participation in a particular aesthetic discourse whereby a piece of literature is judged on its ability to elicit an emotional response from its readership. This understanding of how literature works, or what literature (and other forms of artistic production) ought to do, is familiar and still has currency today. As readers, gallery and cinema-goers, or music lovers, we are still likely to express our appreciation of a particular poem, painting, film or song in terms of the way it works on our feelings. We might describe it as 'affecting' or 'moving' (an adjective which suggests itself as a more emphatic version of 'touching'; to be moved is to be touched with some force), or claim particular attachment to works that we feel we 'relate to' or 'sympathise with', or that strike an emotional chord with us. The roots of these kinds of value judgements can be traced back to the cultural and philosophical traditions of sentiment and sensibility that developed alongside the Empiricist philosophy of Hume and Locke in the eighteenth century, and this section of the Reading Guide aims to explore *In Memoriam*'s engagement with these traditions and the discourses that they generated. The reviewers' repeated use of the language of touch also echoes *In Memoriam*'s own tactile vocabulary. *In Memoriam* is a touching poem that is obsessed with touch, haunted by Arthur Hallam's absent, disembodied or remembered hands. Focusing on those moments in the poem when hands 'reach', 'clasp', 'grasp', 'catch', 'tremble', 'weave', 'stretch', 'break', 'grasp', 'grapple', 'clap', 'strike', 'hold' and – again and again – 'touch', it is possible to appreciate how the feeling body that Tennyson's elegy mourns is central to an understanding of what it means to be touched by *In Memoriam*.

'Touch' is a word that belongs in the realm of the physical and the material. As a noun it denotes one of the five physical senses; as a verb it describes the act of one physical / material body coming into contact with another. Therefore, if we use the word 'touch' to describe the way something has affected us emotionally, we are likely to understand ourselves to be speaking figuratively. If I describe an actor's performance as 'touching', I am unlikely to be talking about his physical manhandling of members of the cast or audience. The *Oxford English Dictionary* (*OED*) records examples of 'touch' being used to describe emotional affect that date back almost as far as the earliest recorded use of 'touch' in the English language. This suggests that the difference between physical touch and emotional touch is not as great – or as straightforward – as it seems, and that to express the communication of the emotions in terms of touch is to acknowledge emotional experience as something material, to locate it within the feeling body.

One way to think about the materiality of emotional experience is to think about the way the body registers emotion through a quickened heart beat, through tears or through a blush. These bodily manifestations of feeling are sometimes referred to as affective responses, or the language of affect. Modern psychological theory still argues about whether the body's affective response to an encounter or event occurs before or as the result of mental processes so that emotion 'happens' in the mind and is then communicated to the body.[6] In the eighteenth and nineteenth centuries the experience of bodily affect was understood as evidence of the body's ability to respond directly to the world around it. This way of knowing and interacting with the world through the body was one of the founding ideas of the discourses of sentiment and sensibility, which revolutionised the way literature was written and understood in Britain and throughout Europe in the mid to late eighteenth century.

This new focus on sentiment and sensibility was influenced by the work of philosophy, which developed new ideas about human nature and the way humans relate to one another and to the world around them. John Locke's Empiricist treatise, the *Essay Concerning Human Understanding* (1690), argues that the self is a product of the world it encounters, that the mind begins as a blank slate (*tabula rasa*) and that its ideas and understanding are formed as the result of sense impressions of its environment. Taught by the senses, the mind is subordinate to them, so that knowledge – of the self as well as of the world – is entirely material.[7] Worried by the implications of Locke's materialism, which called into question an understanding of the human self as innately moral, philosophers such as Hume and Shaftsbury suggested that, rather than being entirely blank, the human mind was created with an ability to distinguish good from evil. However, this model retains an emphasis on bodily experience because it claims that moral judgement is *felt* before it is understood. If anything, these modifications of Locke's theory therefore extend the power of the feeling body, giving it the capacity to judge as well as to know.

Sentiment and sensibility are terms that describe this capacity. The culture, or 'cult', of sensibility placed great value on human feeling so that acute emotional receptiveness, manifested through the weeping, sighing, swooning, blushing body, was understood as the mark of refined, moral and intelligent character. Literature contributed to this cult in a number of ways. The sentimental novel told the stories of men and women of feeling who embodied the sentimental ideal, providing examples for its readership to follow and inviting the reader to experience and exhibit emotional / bodily responses in sympathy with the novel's fictional characters. Likewise, readers of poetry now looked for evidence of the fine sensibility of the poet in his or her verses and expected to be moved by what they read. The Romantic formulation of poetry as 'the spontaneous overflow of powerful feeling recollected in tranquillity' (Wordsworth [1800] 1991) developed out of the sentimental tradition, and early Romantic poets such as Wordsworth and Coleridge engage directly with the Empiricist philosophy and sentimental discourse. In one short lyric Wordsworth writes, 'My heart leaps up when I behold a rainbow in the sky' (Wordsworth [1807] 1982), recording the joy he experiences in nature in terms of an immediate bodily response. As well as describing this sentimental response, poetry now sought to elicit a like response in its readership, asserting a new confidence in its own importance for the development of human subjectivity, understanding and knowledge.

As Jerome McGann demonstrates in his detailed exploration of the poetics of sensibility, the elegiac tradition also took a sentimental turn during this period (McGann 1996: 29). Thomas Gray's *Elegy Written in a Country Churchyard* (1751) reflects on the sentimental reaction effected by the inscriptions carved on a collection of gravestones:

> Yet ev'n these bones from insult to protect
> Some frail memorial still erected nigh,
> With uncouth rhimes and shapeless sculpture deck'd,
> Implores the passing tribute of a sigh.
> (Gray 1969: 77–80)

Here poetry stands in for the body of the deceased and of other mourners, causing a sympathetic response on their behalf. The simple words of the epitaph work on the sensible body of the poet, which replies with a release of breath, a sentimental response that precedes language. It is interesting that the 'rhimes' that Gray reads on the gravestones and the sculptures that he sees are 'uncouth' and 'shapeless'. By drawing attention to their lack of artistic accomplishment, Gray suggests that poetry should not be valued for its skill, but for the quality of the sentiment that produced it. Gray's elegy forms an important part of *In Memoriam*'s sentimental inheritance. When the first reviews of *In Memoriam* say that it is a 'touching poem', they respond to the elegy on its own terms, indicating their knowledge and sympathetic understanding of the cultural discourse that the elegy invokes.

'Empty hands'

However, throughout *In Memoriam*, Tennyson's mourner repeatedly experiences what Angela Leighton describes as the 'trouble of touch' (Leighton 2007: 70), describing an inability to touch and be touched that indicates a sensibility imprisoned by its own materiality. A similar crisis is more briefly evoked in 'Break, Break, Break', a short lyric by Tennyson, written around the time of Hallam's death and published in 1842:

> Break, break, break,
>   On thy cold gray stones, O Sea!
> And I would that my tongue could utter
>   The thoughts that arise in me.
> (1–4)

'Break, break, break' is a poem that describes the failure of sympathy. Out of touch with the vanished hand of a loved one, the speaker is unable to establish any meaningful connection with anything else. The simile that the lyric fails to draw is that the speaker is like the cold grey stones against which the sea beats. The repeated, rhythmic invocation to the sea to 'break' might be read as the expression of the speaker's own desire to be broken down, or violently moved by the experience of loss. Instead, the speaker remains untouched by the natural scene he describes (his heart is not broken, nor does it leap up like Wordsworth's), or by the affective rhythms of his own lyric, which are experienced as hollow, meaningless and without compensation. The same, of course, cannot be said for the reader, who is moved, or touched, by the speaker's affective crisis.

The tactile images and figures of speech that pervade *In Memoriam* from the outset suggest a materialist world view plunged into a crisis by the physical absence of the dead man's body. As Buckley puts it, 'the hand comes to represent the material body that defines and isolates the individual and pulses with the only sort of life he can immediately understand' (Buckley 1960: 114). The first section begins with just such a figure of speech: 'I *held* it truth with him who sings' (I, 1, my italics), a common turn of phrase that nevertheless suggests the physical apprehension of truth or knowledge. Tennyson encourages this literal reading by developing the conceit in the following stanzas:

> But who shall so forecast the years
>   And find in loss a gain to match?
>   Or reach a hand through time to catch
> The far-off interest of tears?
>   (I, 5–8)

Truths that can be held are physical, immediate and earthbound and so the promise of future comfort is impossible to grasp. Limited within present sensation the mourner can only resolve to 'let love clasp grief' (I, 9), to cling bodily to the only impression he has left of the friend he has lost. Rather than reaching through time, his hands can only 'beat the ground' (I, 12), an image of poetic composition that identifies it as a crudely physical act.

From this materialist perspective, the 'Old Yew' that grows by the graveside in section II is an ideal mourner. It 'graspest at the stones / That name the underlying dead' (II, 1–2), a model of enduring grief, 'untouched' (12) by the changing seasons. The speaker dwells on the yew:

> And gazing on thee, sullen tree,
>   Sick for thy stubborn hardihood,
>   I seem to fail from out my blood
> And grow incorporate into thee.
>   (II, 13–16)

These lines recall (or perhaps parody) Romantic descriptions of the sensible self's sympathetic union with the natural world ('My heart leaps up when I behold a rainbow in the sky'). The mourner's apprehension of the tree via the physical gaze leads to an experience of corporeal union that is a surrogate for reunion with his friend. This return to the empirical certainties of the natural world is also the theme of section III. The sorrow to which the mourner clings speaks to him, offering a bleak image of a purely material universe in which nature is represented as a 'phantom', 'A hollow form with empty hands' (III, 12). Listening to the 'sweet and bitter' voice of Sorrow, the mourner asks whether he should accept or reject the vision of nature that she describes: 'Embrace her as my natural good; / Or crush her, like a vice of blood, / Upon the threshold of the mind' (III, 14–16). Again this mental struggle is represented in manual terms. The mourner may either 'embrace' or 'crush' Sorrow's philosophy; thought is still located within the body.

Throughout the first half of *In Memoriam* the mourner continues to experience his loss in physical terms: 'the attempt to recover the body of Hallam [. . .] involves him in a long, tormented drama of touch' (Leighton 2007: 69). The part of Hallam's body that is most often remembered and regretted is his hand, which both represents and creates the bond of friendship. The hand also writes and so Tennyson's focus on Hallam's hands also invites the reader to think about the way that writing, or poetry, might relate to, or stand in for the body. A short poem by John Keats, composed around 1819 and published in 1892, in which the poet reflects on the relationship between hand and text, provides a helpful way into Tennyson's tactile poetics:

This living hand, now warm and capable
Of earnest grasping, would, if it were cold
And in the icy silence of the tomb,
So haunt thy days and chill thy dreaming nights
That thou wouldst wish thine own heart dry of blood
So in my veins red life might stream again,
And thou be conscience-calm'd – see here it is
I hold it towards you.

(Keats [1819] 1972: 700)

In this unsettling lyric fragment the text attempts literally to touch the reader. The hand that writes the poem preserves itself in the act of composition so that, regardless of the fact that by the time the poem was published, Keats had been dead for nearly seventy years, when the poem is read, the hand lives. It performs the haunting that it promises, insisting both on the intimate connection between written word and writing body, and on the ability of words to act like, or in place of, bodies. The speaker of *In Memoriam* desires to be haunted rather than to haunt. By continually dwelling on the dead and absent hands of his friend, he invites comparison with the living hand that holds the pen.

Without the physical contact of hand in hand, the mourner's isolation in grief is absolute. In section VII, the mourner returns to the 'dark house' where his friend used to live, stands at the door, but turns away without going in:

Dark house, by which once more I stand
  Here in the long unlovely street,
  Doors, where my heart was used to beat
So quickly, waiting for a hand.

A hand that can be clasped no more –
                          (VII, 1–5)

The description mingles hand and heart. Standing at the doors of the house, he remembers, not his hand beating the door, but his heart beating in antici- pation of the friendly handshake he would receive when the door was opened. By slipping from heart to hand in this way, Tennyson again invokes a sen- timental, materialist discourse, suggesting an intimate connection between physical sense and emotional sensibility so that the heart is almost trans- formed into a hand that beats and is touched. But at the word 'hand' the spell of memory is broken and the mourner is forced to recognise himself as an iso- lated figure within a bleak cityscape, where 'ghastly through the drizzling rain / On the bald streets breaks the blank day' (VII, 9–12). The hard alliteration of 'bald', 'break' and 'blank' emphasises the materiality of poetic language as it beats within the body of the reader.

In the 'fair ship' lyrics, some of the earliest composed by Tennyson, the mourner's anticipation of the ship carrying 'my lost Arthur's loved remains' (again note that it is the remains, i.e. the body, that is described as an object of love here) is experienced through the senses:

I hear the noise about thy keel;
  I hear the bell struck in the night:
  I see the cabin-window bright;
I see the sailor at the wheel.
                  (X, 1–4)

The repetition of 'I hear', 'I hear', 'I see', 'I see' creates a list of sense impres- sions felt in the mourner's imagination that express his desire for the safe return of Hallam's body. Its return is prefaced by a series of reunions between other bodies. The ship brings 'the sailor to his wife', 'travelled men from vanished lands' and 'letters unto trembling hands' (X, 5–7). This last image again encourages a reading of word as body. The trembling hand, an image familiar to readers of the sentimental body, responds to the touch of the letter as if it were the living body that it both represents and guarantees. In contrast, Hallam's body is figured as a physical absence, obscure and invisible: 'thy dark freight, a vanished life' (X, 8). The mourner reflects that his hankering after the remains of his friend is therefore an 'idle dream', but it maintains its hold over him and the section concludes with the haunting image of a body lost at sea: 'hands so often clasped in mine, / Should toss and tangle with the shells' (X, 19–20). Isolated from its human context, the familiar hand is made strange, transformed into a specimen of marine biology, a ghoulish sea anemone or a piece of flotsam.

Canto XIV is the stuff of more sustained fantasy. Continuing to address himself to the ship that bears Arthur's body, the mourner imagines hearing the news that it has 'touched the land' (XIV, 2), a touch which prefaces the arrival, not of dead, but of living hands, 'beckoning unto those they know' (XIV, 8) and the return of his friend. He considers how he would respond if 'The man I held as half-divine; / Should strike a sudden hand in mine' (XIV, 10–11) and concludes, 'I should not feel it to be strange' (XIV, 20). Because grief has been experienced thus far as a physical absence or loss, the mourner is easily able to imagine reunion. Arthur's death is conflated with his journey overseas and so his return seems entirely plausible. However, this happy scene rests on a flimsy construction of 'if's, 'should's and 'and's. It is a hasty list of possibilities, driven by the speaker's desire, but undermined by the conditional mood, which betrays the immateriality of the imagined scene. When the ship does finally arrive, in canto XVIII, vital hand does not clasp vital hand; instead, Arthur's head is borne by the 'pure hands' of those that make up the funeral procession, an image that emphasises the passive vulnerability of the corpse and its new relationship with the living.

'Lame hands of faith'

The materialism that dominates *In Memoriam*'s understanding and articulation of bereavement in its early sections, making the mourner's separation from his lost friend so absolute, begins to lose its hold as time passes, allowing for the possibility of a kind of touch that might extend beyond the grave. A. C. Bradley writes that 'the process of change [in *In Memoriam*] consists largely in the conquest of the soul over its bondage to sense' (Bradley 1901: 42). This change begins during the first of three Christmases that chart the poem's cyclical progress, as the mourner's sensible hands join those of his family in a solemn performance of the customary festivities: 'With trembling fingers did we weave / The holly round the Christmas hearth' (XXX, 1–2). 'Hand-in-hand' (XXX, 11), the group sit in silence and then sing 'A merry song we sang with him / Last year' (XXX, 15–16), so that community, or fellow-feeling, is established through the joining of hands and voices, a tentative suggestion of the touching properties of poetry. Far from the work of the poet alone, however, this awakening of sentiment is established as the work of

Christian faith within a domestic, familial setting that ends with a prayer for the intervention of God's touch in the approaching dawn: 'O Father, touch the east, and light / The light that shone when Hope was born' (XXX, 31–2).

Christian discourse offers the mourner a way of conceiving and articulating touch that is both physical and metaphysical. Section XXXVI talks about the story of the Gospel, 'truth embodied in a tale' (7), so that the truth of God, which is beyond language, is bodied forth both in New Testament narrative and in the living body of Christ. Words stand for and act like the bodies they describe, sharing the divine agency of the incarnation: 'And so the Word had breath, and wrought / With human hands the creed of creeds' (XXXVI, 9–10). Here Tennyson adapts the words of John 1: 14: 'And the word became flesh and dwelt among us.' The change from 'flesh to breath' demands the reader's attention. 'Breath', which implies speech as well as life, is, perhaps, a more literal rendering of the incarnated word and so Tennyson's rephrasing of the famous words from John's Gospel makes an emphatic connection between human body, divine power and language. The works of God, word and body are so closely related in these lines that the 'human hands' that wrought the 'creed of creeds' are almost, but not quite, the human hands that *wrote* the creed of creeds. This reading is encouraged by the following stanza, which describes the power of the embodied word to reach men from all walks of life: 'Which he may read that binds the sheaf, / Or builds the house, or digs the grave' (XXXVI, 13–14). These three manual labourers will read and understand the Gospel because, the stanza implies, it is also a piece of manual work, wrought / written by human hands like theirs.

As *In Memoriam* works towards its faltering recovery of faith ('I stretch lame hands of faith' (LV, 17)), it expresses hope that the touch of friendship will be renewed beyond the grave. Section XL concludes, 'But thou and I have shaken hands / Till growing winters lay me low' (XL, 29–30), lines that echo section VII: 'A hand that can be clasped no more'; however, rather than breaking off to consider the isolated figure of the mourner guiltily creeping to the house where he knows he will not find his friend, these lines run on into the possibility of another meeting. The mourner also allows himself to hope that the memory of touch that haunts him might likewise haunt his friend. He wonders if some remnant of his dead friend's sensing self remains intact, receptive to the memory of a touch that is both 'dim' and 'dreamy' but that the mourner prays will yield a response. Like the imagined reunion of mourner and friend in section XIV, these lines are written in the conditional mood, but whereas the first reunion is described using the future unreal conditional ('if . . . should'), which emphasises the impossibility of Arthur's return, the second is described using the future real conditional ('if . . . then'), which contains the hope of renewed connection.

The mourner attempts to reason out this hope in the following section, using the image of a child who gains self-consciousness, or a sense of identity via a touch that, like so many of the instances of touch in *In Memoriam*, prefaces separation (Ricks's notes to the poem inform us that this image was borrowed from an essay by Hallam, entitled 'On Sympathy', which Hallam presented at a meeting of the Apostles and which was subsequently published in the *Remains*). Touch, again associated with speech, the means by which the child establishes his identity in relation to the world around him, is a strangely isolating act, understood as a meeting of physical boundaries that confirms difference or otherness rather than achieving connection. The body is a 'frame' that 'binds' the individual within himself until 'the second birth of death' (XLV, 11 and 16). The tentative hope that the mourner may be remembered and recognised by his dead friend, which is offered by the analogy of birth and death, gives way to the image of the isolated living body in which the speaker remains trapped.

The question of posthumous reunion returns in section LXIV, via an extended metaphor that again describes life in terms of a sequence of manual tasks and experiences. The mourner's separation from his friend is compared with the separation of childhood companions in adulthood, as one pursues a successful political career, leaving the other to live out a rural existence in the place of their birth. The mourner imagines that, in spite of their separate lives, each retains a memory of their earlier life together. This metaphor is a more straightforward expression of the hope and anxiety surrounding the permanence of the mourner's separation from his friend described in XL and XLI, a concern that presses on the poem throughout. Like the 'baby new to earth and sky', the two friends establish their identity through different kinds of touch. One 'grasps', 'grapples', 'clutches' and 'moulds' (LXIV, 5–10); the other 'reaps the labour of his hands' (LXIV, 26). Although the work the two men do and the status they achieve is markedly different, the way their work is described emphasises their shared, bodily humanity, inferring connection even as it talks about separation and establishing grounds for a continued and significant bond between them. The metaphor also works to make the separation of the living from the dead more surmountable, reducing it to a matter of physical distance that might easily be bridged.

Just as body and embodied language extend their reach beyond the isolating limits that separate life and death in *In Memoriam*, so the mourner begins to imagine a reciprocal touch, reaching back towards him. Section LXIX describes a dream in which the poet / mourner sees himself as a Christ figure. The elegy itself is reimagined as a crown of thorns, which the mourner binds around his own head, an act of self-martyrdom that invites scorn from a public who, like the detractors in section XXI, voice the poet's own doubts about the value and purpose of his elegy. However, in his dream, the poet finds 'an angel of the night' who 'reached the glory of a hand, / That seemed to touch it into leaf' (LXIX, 17–18). The transformative touch of the angel who might be Hallam, an agent of God, or both, enlivens crown of thorns or verses, so that they are transformed into a symbol of the new birth of spring. This dream of recovery, which alludes to the resurrection of pastoral elegy (a resurrection achieved here through the direct intervention of touch rather than via the natural cycle of the seasons), is invoked repeatedly throughout the second half of the poem. Section LXXX concludes with a desire that Hallam might 'Reach out dead hands and comfort me' (LXXX, 16), and section LXXXIV looks forward to the time when God will 'reach us out the shining hand, / And take us as a single soul' (LXXXIV, 43–4). The power of this touch is not always benevolent. The poet describes an anniversary of his friend's death as a 'Day, marked as with some hideous crime, / When the dark hand struck down through time, / And cancelled nature's best' (LXXII, 18–19), and in section LXXXV Hallam's death is described in more gently euphemistic terms: 'God's finger touched him, and he slept' (LXXXV, 20). However, even these descriptions of Hallam's death, which imagine God's will as embodied act, comprehending spiritual belief in physical terms, break down the barriers that determine the poet's isolation from his friend in the earlier sections of the poem.

The mourner's desire for a reciprocal touch achieves its fullest and most confident expression in sections XCIII and XCV. The touch that the mourner despairs of, alludes to and dreams about throughout *In Memoriam* is commanded and then received. In XCIII the poet asks the spirit of his friend to visit him while he sleeps, describing slumber as the temporary death of the sensing body, 'where all the nerve of sense is numb'. The mourner accepts, 'I shall not see thee,' that he will not encounter a 'visual shade of someone lost', and describes the place where his friend's spirit now lives as 'thy sightless range'. He does not desire to see his friend, but to be touched by him, requesting that he

> Descend, and touch, and enter; hear
>   The wish too strong for words to name;
>   That in the blindness of the frame
> My ghost may feel that thine is near.
>   (XCIII, 13–16)

Here again, sight, or blindness, represents the limitation of physical senses, whereas touch is imagined exceeding or penetrating the frame of the body, sensed by the spirit / ghost of the mourner. The recognition of one spirit by another, one ghost by another, returns the elegy to the conventions of sentiment, describing a fellow-feeling that transcends death. The other sense that is invoked is hearing, which responds to wishes rather than words. In the same way that touch extends beyond the material contact of one body with another, hearing is described as receptive to something beyond language. The lines establish a connection between the limits of the body and the limits of language, and present a powerful challenge to both. At the same time the words of the poem draw attention to themselves as things that are both seen and heard. 'Hear' might be heard as 'here' ('Descend, and touch, and enter here'), even as it is seen or read as 'hear'. Hearing and the immediate presence implied by 'here' are thereby mapped on to one another, suggesting something of the touching properties of poetry and so promising the sympathetic connection for which the mourner longs.

This promise is fulfilled in the next section but one, when 'word by word, and line by line, / The dead man touched me from the past' (XCV, 33–4), a reunion of souls that is achieved through the reading of letters. Again this occurs as night, when the mourner is alone and the world is dark, but it is encircled by a richly sensed experience of the natural world around him. No longer cut off from the natural world, the mourner is gathered into its 'dark arms', in a relationship of renewed sympathy with nature that perhaps enables him to feel the touch of his friend.

Profit and Loss: IV, X, XIII, XX, XXXV, XLII, XLVI, LII, LIV, LV, LVI, LVIII, LXI, LXII, LXXX, LXXXI, LXXXII, CVII, CVIII, CXXIII, CXXVII, CXXVIII, Epilogue

An Idle King

In 1833 Tennyson composed a series of poems that dramatised the voices of four characters from classical mythology and religious history: 'Tithonus', a man who wished for immortality but failed to ask for eternal youth and so was doomed to live out an eternal life of increasing decrepitude; 'Tiresias', the blind prophet; 'St Simeon Stylites', who achieved sainthood by living out his old age on the top of a high column; and 'Ulysses', the warrior hero of Homer's *Odyssey*, who is imagined after his return home from his epic voyage, a bored and ageing ruler. These poems yield interesting readings in the context of Hallam's death. Through the mouths of these old men, Tennyson, aged only twenty-four, communicates his grief in terms of an intense world-weariness and a sense of having been left behind. As Tennyson himself put it, in a conversation with his friend James Knowles: 'There is more about myself in "Ulysses", which was written under the sense of loss and that all had gone by, but that still life must be fought out to the end. It was more written with the feeling of his loss upon me than many poems in *In Memoriam*' (in Ricks 1989: 113). With these remarks in mind, it is worth noting that the opening lines of 'Ulysses' are concerned, not with loss, but with profit (or lack of it):

> It little profits that an idle king,
> By this still hearth, among these barren crags,
> Matched with an aged wife, I mete and dole
> Unequal laws unto a savage race,
> That hoard, and sleep, and feed, and know not me.
>
> ('Ulysses', 1–5)

Ulysses reflects on how best to spend his declining years and concludes that his current occupation is likely to yield 'little profit'. He describes his life as an economic transaction, whereby the spending or investing of himself ought to yield payment.[8] However, as Herbert Tucker puts it, 'the outstanding feature of Ulysses' tally sheet is that the quantities fail to tally. The books are out of balance' (Tucker 1988: 213). The ageing king understands his domestic reign over Ithaca as an unwilling involvement in an unfamiliar and unsatisfactory economic system. Describing himself as idle within a barren landscape, he suggests that a natural economy in which labour yields harvest has been replaced by a less reciprocal economic exchange in which he spends himself in the work of legislation and his race give him nothing in return. Instead, they 'hoard' – an unprofitable economic activity that is related to the idle consumption of eating and sleeping.

The image of a hoarded life returns a few lines later:

> Life piled on life
> Were all too little, and of one to me
> Little remains: but every hour is saved
> From the eternal silence, something more,
> A bringer of new things; and vile it were
> For some three suns to store and hoard myself
>
> (24–9)

Ulysses' decision to set off on one final voyage is again described as the choice of one economy over another. A model of stagnant accumulation ('life piled on life') is rejected in favour of a model of transaction where the 'little' that remains promises more. As many critics of the poem have pointed out, Ulysses never makes this final transaction. The poem ends with an expression of resolve 'to strive, to seek, to find and not to yield', but with no definite action. We are therefore led to question whether Ulysses' speech is no more than idle rhetoric and whether Tennyson's acknowledgement that 'life must be fought out to the end' is, in fact, overwhelmed by his sense of loss. This section of the Reading Guide aims to consider those moments in *In*

Memoriam when the speaker, like Ulysses, has to choose between hoarding and spending. It will discuss the relationship between mourning and economics by looking at Freudian theories of mourning and it will think about the way the poem engages with the different models of change and exchange that were introduced by the discoveries of Victorian natural science.

The Work of Mourning

The economic vocabulary employed by Ulysses returns in *In Memoriam* in two sections that express doubt in the work / worth of elegy. In section XXXV, the speaker holds an imaginary conversation with Love and asks whether it is worth trying to keep his love for his friend alive in the knowledge that, in the end, everything will be forgotten. The conversation ends with a feeling of resignation – 'O me, what profits it to put / An idle case?' (XXXV, 17–18) – and the speaker reflects that it is impossible to love fully with death always in mind. In section CVIII, the same words are used in an expression of more sustained resolve. Echoing Ulysses' vocabulary, the mourner adopts a similar economic position. He rejects an isolated and introspective state, which he describes in terms of eating, feeding and harvesting, invoking the economy of agriculture and describing a series of fruitless or uncertain investments that he decides to exchange for the 'fruit [. . .] of sorrow under human skies' (CVIII, 14). The choice he makes here is not between mourning and not mourning but between two different kinds of mourning: one more economically sound (fruitful or profitable) than the other. However, as with so many of the moments of resolve and revelation that punctuate *In Memoriam*, and like the unfulfilled resolve of Ulysses at the end of his monologue, the investment that Tennyson's speaker appears determined to make in this section is repeatedly held back. We cannot trust the strength of mind that seems to be communicated in the repeated 'will' at the beginning of this section and might begin to suspect that the speaker is trying to convince himself, as well as us, of his purpose.

The economic choice that is presented to Ulysses and to Tennyson's mourner enables us to relate Tennyson's experience and expression of grief to an essay by Freud, the founder of psychoanalytic theory, called 'On Mourning and Melancholia' (1917). In his essay, Freud compares two different but connected psychological states: mourning, which he describes as 'normal [. . .], commonly the reaction to the loss of a beloved person', and melancholia, which he describes as a 'narcissistic mental disorder' that 'appears in the place of mourning' (Freud 2005: 203). One of the ways that Freud describes the difference between these two states is through the language of economics. He talks about mourning as a kind of psychological 'work'. The person who has experienced a bereavement or loss must work to acknowledge that the lost person or object no longer exists, cut her connection to that person or object, and turn back to or reconnect with reality. Freud writes that even the 'normal' process or work of mourning 'is carried out piecemeal at great expenditure of time and investment of energy' (205). He uses the language of expense and investment to explain mourning as the means by which a loss might be regained.

In the case of melancholia, mourning does not 'work'; or, to be more precise, work is carried out, but it is the wrong work and so no profit is achieved. Freud argues that the reason for this is that the loss that has caused this psychological reaction is unknown or somehow less certain. Freud writes that this might happen if someone has not died, but has been lost to the mourner in another way, 'as, for example, in the case of an abandoned bride' (205) (an example that might make us think again about the pairs of separated lovers that Tennyson's mourner compares himself to throughout *In Memoriam*). Because the mourner is unable to identify his loss as a distinct object or solid fact, he cannot achieve separation from it and so the work of mourning turns inward, becoming a kind of loss of self and, in Freud's words, 'drawing investment energies to itself from all sides' (212). In his essay, Freud mentions Hamlet, a literary figure who provides a good example of a melancholic subject. Hamlet's father is dead, but because of the circumstances of his death, Hamlet is unable to mourn successfully and he is trapped in a torpor of indecision and inaction. One of Hamlet's best-known soliloquies begins by suggesting economic failure: 'How weary, stale, flat and *unprofitable* / Seem to me all the uses of this world' (I, ii, 133–4, emphasis mine). Hamlet's psychological state isolates him from the day-to-day world. He hoards himself away from it, shuts himself from his subjects, spending emotional energy but profiting nothing. To return to 'Ulysses' and *In Memoriam*, the unprofitable idleness and hoarding described by Ulysses, or the elegist's solitary eating of his own heart and 'vacant yearning' can also be understood as descriptions of a melancholic state. Both speakers are caught up in an economy of melancholy, where the exchange of death for life cannot be transacted.

In the case of 'Ulysses', the currency that Ulysses must hoard or invest is his own life. His speech makes a persuasive argument about how he should spend his declining years. Similarly, in *In Memoriam* the speaker repeatedly tries and fails to invest in the routines and rituals of the world around him (for more on these rituals see the following section, 'Cycle and Ritual'). However, in both poems the speakers also comment on the economic work of their own words. The self-absorbed voice of the poetic subject can be regarded as a melancholic investment (hoarding or eating one's own heart) that prevents profitable transaction. According to this reading, which chimes with W. H. Auden's famous comment that 'there was little about melancholia that [Tennyson] didn't know; and little else that he did' (Auden 1973: 222), a working, fruitful economy only begins at the point when the poem ends. On the other hand, we might think about each poem as a text that carries out the work of mourning, gradually reaping the 'fruit [. . .] of sorrow'.

Idle Tears

Tennyson dwells on the meaning of tears in a short lyric, which was published as part of his long narrative poem, *The Princess* (1847):

> Tears, idle tears, I know not what they mean,
> Tears from the depths of some divine despair
> Rise in the heart and gather to the eyes,
> In looking on the happy Autumn-fields,
> And thinking of the days that are no more.
> ('Tears, Idle Tears', 1–5)

Idle tears, like Ulysses the idle king, might be identified as figures of melancholy.[9] Their meaning is unknown and they serve no known purpose, constituting emotional investment without profit. They are not caused by a specific loss or bereavement, but by thinking about the past while experiencing the beauty of the present. The lyric employs images of dawn and dusk, in which night and day, death and life, past and present occupy the same space. However, whereas Ulysses is unhappy in the idle half-life of Ithaca and strives to move onwards, the speaker of 'Tears, Idle Tears' seems to enjoy the melancholy experience he describes. If Ulysses seeks to escape from his melancholia, then the voice of this later lyric indulges in it, creating something that is both 'sad' and 'sweet' and which the reader is invited to enjoy. The perverse enjoyment of idleness explored in 'Tears, Idle Tears' is helpful to bear in mind when thinking about work and idleness, profit and loss, mourning and melancholia in *In Memoriam*. The elegist attempts to carry out the work of mourning, but he is also attracted to melancholia's idle tears.

Peter Sacks argues that *In Memoriam* is balanced between these two impulses, reflecting 'an attitude that we recognise as melancholia' while at the same time representing 'a successful work of mourning' (Sacks 1985: 169). He encourages us to think about the form of the poem in terms of an economy of melancholy, arguing that the length of the poem, its 'fragmentary hoarding of self-encircling but incomplete eddies or wreaths of song' (183), represents the way the mourner 'accumulates rather than lets go' (168). From this perspective the mourner becomes a kind of miser, and the elegy might be compared to a growing pile of gold hidden under the mattress. However,

Herbert Tucker suggests that it would be more accurate to think of the accumulative form of *In Memoriam* in capitalist terms, so that the poem is more like money placed in a bank, which accrues interest by carrying out work of its own over the passing of time. Tucker writes: 'the therapeutic magic of *In Memoriam* – which in the broadest terms converts the debt burden of "loss" into "gain" – [is] a miracle of emotional capitalism' (Tucker 1988: 392). He quotes from section I of the poem, which adds the vocabulary of finance to that of song and touch. The mourner asks, 'But who shall so forecast the years / And find in loss a gain to match?', expressing his scepticism that the loss of Hallam might be recouped in the distant future. The hands that the mourner attempts to imagine reaching through time attempt to catch 'the far-off *interest* of tears' (I, 8, emphasis mine). The mourner, like Ulysses, thinks that his books are out of balance. He sees no prospect of compensation for the loss of Hallam and, at the opening of the poem, expresses doubt in a capitalist model of investment where interest is paid 'for the forbearance of debt' (*OED*). Seeing no prospect of profit from his tears, the mourner considers them to be a poor investment and turns away from the natural or conventional expressions of grief (what Freud might describe as the 'normal affect of mourning' (203)).

However, tears and weeping are referred to repeatedly throughout *In Memoriam*. Often the shedding of tears is associated with poetic composition; both are outward signs of an inner grief. For the elegist, both tears and words represent a currency of uncertain value. In section XX, the mourner describes two different kinds of grief:

> My lighter moods are like to these
>   That out of words a comfort win;
>   But there are other griefs within,
> And tears that at their fountain freeze;
>   (XX, 9–12)

He suggests that his less intense periods of mourning do serve an economic function – words win, or earn comfort – but that the grief that is felt most deeply does not. Unable to express itself using tears or words, this grief remains unspent (we might describe his tears, anachronistically, as frozen assets) and so the capitalist marketplace of mourning cannot work. In section IV, he desires that these frozen tears should be allowed to flow: 'Break, thou deep vase of chilling tears, / That grief has shaken into frost!' (IV, 11–12); but in section LVIII, the mourner's muse asks 'Wherefore grieve / Thy brethren with a fruitless tear?' (LVIII, 9–10), suggesting that tears are a wasteful or meaningless expense. The fluctuating value placed on tears and the other expressions of grief that are associated with them – namely, poetry – points towards the mourner's own uncertainty about the kind of mourning-work he carries out.

Idleness is also an idea that tempts and troubles the mourner, who often accuses himself of idle action. In section X, idleness is again associated with the conventions of mourning. The speaker confesses his belief that it is better for Hallam's body to be buried in native soil than to perish at sea. He describes this belief as an 'idle dream' caused by 'habit' (X, 9), but nevertheless desires Hallam's body to be returned safely to England. He is accused of fretting '"like an idle girl"' (LII, 13); describes his love as 'an idle tale' (LXII, 3) and, in the Epilogue, writes that, looking back, his elegiac lyrics appear 'As echoes out of weaker times, / As half but idle brawling rhymes, / The sport of random sun and shade' (Epilogue, 22–4). In order to bring the poem to an end, the mourner discredits the work carried out over the course of its 131 lyric sections. His ability finally to put an end to the idleness that he accuses himself of throughout the elegy demonstrates change or recovery and therefore suggests that his words and tears were not so idle after all. As Peter Sacks suggests, the difference between mourning and melancholia, hoarding and spending in *In Memoriam* is not straightforward and the poem represents a paradoxical economy in which idleness performs a kind of work.

What hope of answer or redress?

In Memoriam not only employs economic language to describe the individual psychology of mourning. It also talks about the mourned object as a loss that must be repaid. At different points in the poem Hallam is compared to money or economic produce. The mourner watches the approaching sails of the ship that carries Arthur's body 'as though they brought but merchants' bales' (XIII, 19), allowing the reader to think about Hallam as an object of economic exchange. He describes aspects of Hallam's character in financial terms, making references to Hallam's 'ransomed reason' (LXI, 2) and his 'heart-affluence' (the riches of his heart) (CIX, 1); and in a section addressed to Charles Tennyson, he compares his relationship with his brother to his relationship with Hallam by talking about himself and Hallam as different kinds of currency. In each of these examples, Hallam's death becomes a measurable, material payment made to nature and to God, and so the mourner looks to both religion and natural science to find compensation.

As we saw earlier in this Reading Guide, when the mourner cries out 'What hope of answer, or redress?', the reply comes, 'Behind the veil, behind the veil' (LVI, 27–8). The mourner wants an answer, an explanation for Hallam's death, but he also wants redress, or compensation. The suggestion made here is that repayment will be made in the afterlife, so that, in crude terms, loss on earth is exchanged for heavenly gain. *In Memoriam* struggles towards this hope. In section XLII, the speaker finds comfort in the thought that he may later reap the reward of his loss by feeding on the fruits of Hallam's greater experience. Hallam, by now a 'lord of large experience' will 'train / To riper growth' the 'mind and will' (XLII, 7–8) of his less experienced friend. He imagines the joy he will find in 'reaping' the truths that Hallam has learned. This is one of many occasions when Tennyson employs the vocabulary of agricultural economy to talk about religious faith. A few sections later, it is not Hallam's lost future, but Hallam and Tennyson's shared past that is imagined ripening to fruition in 'that deep dawn behind the tomb' (XLVI, 6). There, the past 'bloom[s]' into an eternal landscape. By talking about the relationship between past and future in these terms, the mourner begins to transform his loss into something natural, so that Hallam's sudden death, which is initially recognised as an untimely and unnatural rupture, becomes part of the economic cycles of sowing and harvesting.

Sections LXXX to LXXXII return to these meditations on loss and gain, this time combining images of agricultural economy with a vocabulary that is more directly financial. In section LXXX the mourner describes a 'vague desire' that the situation be reversed and that he had died first, instead of Hallam. Hallam, whom the speaker considers to be superior to him in every other way, is now also described as the ideal mourner, providing an example for the speaker to follow:

> I make a picture in the brain;
>   I hear the sentence that he speaks;
>   He bears the burthen of the weeks
> But turns his burthen into gain.
>
> His credit thus shall set me free;
>   And, influence-rich to soothe and save,
>   Unused example from the grave
> Reach out dead hands to comfort me.
>   (LXXX, 15–16)

The economic work going on in these stanzas is twofold. Firstly, Hallam is imagined turning the burden of his grief into gain. He does this through speech and therefore provides a model not only for an effective economic system of mourning but also for the role of words – and, by extension, poetry – in that system. Hallam is described as both the mourner and the poet that Tennyson is trying to be. Secondly, the example of Hallam is itself shown to have economic value. The speaker refers to Hallam's 'credit', a word that means both 'good name, reputation, honour' (*OED*) and that which 'enables a person or body of persons to be trusted with goods or money in expectation of future payment' (*OED*). This double meaning allows us to read Hallam's death in capitalist terms. Because Hallam died early, the example of his life is 'unused' and therefore exists as credit. The speaker hopes that the unused riches of Hallam's influence might now be cashed in.

Section LXXXI pursues a different line of thought, complaining that, by taking Arthur early, Death has prevented the mourner's love for his friend from fulfilling its potential. In this instance Hallam's sudden death seems at first to disrupt rather than to participate in the natural economy of agriculture. Love is compared to a plant or crop, harvested before it was 'mature in ear' (LXXXI, 4), when it still had 'hope of richer store' (5). However, Death, who is given the last word, demonstrates a better knowledge of agriculture and explains, '"My sudden frost was sudden gain, / And gave all ripeness to the grain, / It might have drawn from after-heat"' (LXXXI, 10–12). Again, the circumstances of Hallam's death find a parallel in nature that rebalances the books of loss and gain so that, in section LXXXII, the speaker is content that 'transplanted human worth / Will bloom to profit otherwhere' (LXXXII, 11–12).

Tennyson places particular emphasis on the periods of inactivity that punctuate the agricultural year. Harvest is the result of 'fruitful hours of *still* increase', a 'wealthy *peace*' (XLVI, 10 and 11), and the mourner is advised to '*Abide*: thy wealth is gathered in, / When Time hath sundered shell from pearl' (LII, 15–16). According to this economic model, waiting is a sort of work. The remaining years of Tennyson's life, and particularly the three years of grief that *In Memoriam* charts, accrue value that will be reaped or gathered in the future. This is the theme of sections CXVII and CXVIII, which consider the 'work of Time' (CXVIII, 1). The 'days and hours' that separate the mourner from his friend work to achieve 'fuller gain of after bliss' (CXVII, 4). 'Distance' creates 'desire of nearness doubly sweet', (CXVII, 6) so that the delight that they will experience when they meet again will 'a hundredfold accrue' (CXVII, 8).

Tennyson's use of numerical calculations in these stanzas – 'doubly', 'a hundredfold' – demonstrates how time is measured and evaluated like a kind of commodity or currency with which the mourner stakes his claim on the future. With this in mind, the description of 'measured language' in section V gains new significance. The measures of the elegy's metrical patterns do not just mark time; they also keep count. Each stanza gives a material weight to the time of loss, so that the mourner can demonstrate just how much he is owed. In the Epilogue, time is enumerated again:

> Though I since then have numbered o'er
>   Some thrice three years: they went and came,

> Remade the blood and changed the frame,
> And yet is love not less, but more
>   (Epilogue, 9–12)

Between the end of the final section and the beginning of the Epilogue, three years have become nine and the work carried out during the time that the preceding stanzas record has trebled. At the wedding of his sister the mourner begins to experience the fruits of his labour. There is a sense of repayment here – of gain made for loss suffered – but there is also a sense of gain beyond calculation. The mourner's precise 'thrice three' receives 'more', a quantity that is not and cannot be measured. The Epilogue is full of the language of increase: 'regret is dead, but love is more' (Epilogue, 17); the mourner has 'grown' to 'something greater' (Epilogue, 20); his sister is a rose that 'grew' and 'grows' for her husband (Epilogue, 35–6); and the wedding celebration is a 'wealth / Of words and wit'. These wealthy words suggest, finally, the possibility of a new kind of economy, one that is invoked again in the Preface when the speaker declares, 'Let knowledge grow from more to more, / But more of reverence in us dwell' (Prologue, 25–6). 'More' leads to 'more' and yet 'more', an incalculable profit that comes from God.

Idle Ore

Christopher Ricks's notes to the poem draw attention to the similarity between the Prologue's expectation that more knowledge will lead to more reverence and the following sentence from *Vestiges of the Natural History of Creation* by Robert Chambers: 'The acquisition of this knowledge is consequently an available means of our growing in a genuine reverence for him [God]' (233). Chambers's *Vestiges* (1844) was one of two influential forerunners to *On the Origin of Species* by Charles Darwin (1859). The other was *The Principles of Geology* by Charles Lyell, published in 1833–4. The theories set out in these publications differ significantly, both from one another and from Darwin's theory of evolution, but both presented a huge challenge to a Judeo-Christian understanding of a God-created universe. Lyell used evidence of rock formations and fossils to demonstrate the massive geological changes that had shaped the earth and its species over time. Chambers set out a theory of transmutation, arguing that all living species (including humans) developed from earlier, less sophisticated forms. Tennyson read both Lyell and Chambers in the years between Hallam's death and the publication of *In Memoriam*, but he was unwilling to admit that his poem was directly influenced by these controversial theories, claiming that the sections that deal with evolutionary theory were composed before the publication of Chambers's

Vestiges. However, the poem's 'honest doubt' is often caused by observations of the natural world which call the certain returns of faith into question.

As we have seen, Christian faith provides a benevolent image of a natural world, where 'not a worm is cloven in vain' (LIV, 9); but in sections LV and LVI, this economy is called into question when Nature is shown to be a careless and haphazard book-keeper. The mourner complains that, although Nature seems to ensure the survival of whole species, 'she' is 'careless of the single life' (LV, 11). This failure to account for individuals is also recognised in Chambers, who suggests that nature operates through an economy of chance, which disrupts a balanced give-and-take that makes sacrifice meaningful. In the broader scheme of things, the individual is not counted and therefore does not count / matter.

The mourner's doubts become more insistent in the following section, as the extent of Nature's carelessness increases. Drawing on Lyell's contention that 'species cannot be immortal, but must perish, one after the other, like the individuals which compose them' (1835: iii, 155), Tennyson imagines an abrupt interruption from Nature herself, who declares the full measure of her indifference, crying, '"A thousand types are gone: / I care for nothing, all shall go"' (LVI, 3–4). 'A thousand', 'nothing' and 'all' are quantities that lend uncompromising extremes of scale to the ravages of evolution, making the mourner's single loss appear absolutely insignificant. With the stakes raised in this way, Hallam becomes a metonym (a part that represents a greater whole) for the human race – 'Man, her last work, who seemed so fair' (LVI, 9) – and his death prefigures human extinction. Hallam's significance is not increased by this comparison; instead, the destruction of the race seems to matter as much or as little as the end of a single life. 'Blown about the desert dust / Or sealed within the iron hills' (19–20), humanity appears flimsy and insubstantial compared to the weight and force of the natural world.

However, Lyell's geological theory does not entirely support this nihilistic interpretation of nature. *Principles* argues that geological change works towards an eventual good; that 'the general tendency of subterranean movements, when their effects are considered for a sufficient lapse of ages, is eminently beneficial' (ii, 290). From this perspective, nature is not 'red in tooth and claw', an agent of uncalculating destruction; she is a careful investor, working towards long-term stability and profit. In fact, as Isobel Armstrong points out, Lyell talks about the systems that govern geological change as an 'economy', whereby damage always leads to repair (Armstrong 1993: 254).

It is this perspective that the mourner adopts in the closing sections of *In Memoriam*. In section CXVIII, he compares Hallam's death with the creation of the human race rather than its extinction. The second stanza trusts that 'those we call the dead / Are breathers of an ampler day' (CXVIII, 5–6) and connects this belief to a description of earth's origins in which man rises out of 'seeming-random forms' and 'cyclic storms'. This development is again described using the vocabulary of incalculable increase as man grows 'from more to more' (CXVIII, 17). Humanity is 'not idle ore', but iron that has been mined and manufactured into something useful. Tennyson combines images of evolutionary change with images of human industry so that the creation of the world is compared to the work of miner and blacksmith and its violence is reinterpreted as the productive violence of industrial labour. In these terms, Hallam's death becomes, paradoxically, a work of creation: a profitable rupture that works towards the greater good.

In sections CXXIII and CXXVII to CXXVIII, the connection between rupture and creation is developed in ways that encourage the reader to consider the work of the poet himself. The mourner looks out on a landscape and sees its apparently solid forms as a series of ongoing fluctuations. Trees have been exchanged for seas and seas for streets; hills 'flow / From form to form' and 'melt like mist'; and the 'solid lands' are 'like clouds' (CXXII, 5–8). The mourner still cannot bring himself to let his friend become part of this change, but he no longer regards it with the terror that dominates his earlier contemplation of nature. He accepts that 'all is well, though faith and form / Be sundered in the night of fear' (CXXVII, 1–2), implying that even Hallam's death is part of that 'all'. Tennyson's repeated reference to 'form' implies a connection between geology and poetry. In the first section of this Guide, I described *In Memoriam* as a series of fragments that make up a complete whole. In the context of the natural economies with which the poem engages, this formal tension between fragmentation and wholeness might be read as an echo or performance of the violent economy of evolutionary science. According to this reading, the breaks and shifts that constitute the poem's uncertain movement are part of its wider work and contribute, in Lyell's words, to a 'stable system'. Tennyson concludes section CXVIII with a self-reflexive simile that endorses this reading. The mourner reflects that 'all, as in some piece of art, / Is toil cöoperant to an end' (CXVIII, 23–4). Nature and art (or poetry) carry out similar work: each toils bit by bit towards promised completion.

Cycle and Ritual: IX, XVII, XVIII, XXVIII, XXX, XLIII, XLV, XLVII, LI, LXI, LXXVII, LXXVIII, LXXXV, LXXXVI, LXXXIX, CIV, CV, CVI, CVII, CXXII

By the end of *In Memoriam*, the speaker has come to terms with the economic give-and-take of evolutionary progress. Nevertheless, *In Memoriam* itself does not so much *evolve* as *revolve*. It rolls towards its conclusion, turning forward, round and back in a series of cycles that carry mourner and reader onwards through time and also turn and return to the scenes of the past. Reading the poem, our attention is constantly drawn to the fact that time is passing, but the passage of time is often marked by moments of repetition that draw us back to where we started. The three years of mourning that the poem charts could be represented as a straight line – year one, year two, year three; but they could equally be drawn as a circle that is traced three times, like the hands moving round a clock face – a year, another year, another year. This paradoxical tension between repetition and change, circle and line, means that the poem is able to incorporate the past into the present and the future, ensuring the preservation of Hallam's memory. The backwards and onwards movement of time is naturalised, ritualised and formalised by the elegy, enabling the mourner to be reincorporated into the everyday world from which his grief has separated him.

Three Examples: From Lucy to Prufrock

Before considering the images and forms of cycle and ritual in *In Memoriam*, it is worth looking at the way three other poems address this temporal paradox. The first is a poem by William Wordsworth:

> A slumber did my spirit seal
> I had no human fears
> She seemed a thing that could not feel
> The touch of earthly years
>
> No movement has she now, no force
> She neither hears nor sees
> Rolled round in earth's diurnal course
> With rocks and stones and trees.
> (Wordsworth [1800] 1991: 154)

This short lyric is one of a series known as the 'Lucy Poems', written by Wordsworth about the death of a young woman. The first stanza, written in the past tense, describes the speaker's love for Lucy as a kind of sleep that lulls him into the belief that the woman is immune to the passing of time. The second stanza, written in the present tense, informs the reader that Lucy is now dead and describes her insensible body lying in the ground. In one sense, therefore, the change that occurs between stanzas one and two is sudden and shocking. The poem describes a movement from life to death, immortality to mortality, sleep to wakefulness. However, the tone, language and form of the poem strangely fail to register that shock. The death itself is not described; occurring in the space between the two stanzas, it is passed over or enveloped by the poem as the lines of iambic tetrameter and trimeter move seamlessly from the first to the second stanza. The rhythm drives time forward, but because the metrical pattern of the two stanzas is identical, time is also represented as repetition and return. The difference between 'now' and 'then' is both described and refused. This formal work echoes the images employed by the lyric voice, which imagines the dead woman incorporated into the natural revolutions of the earth so that life and death, like day and night, become part of the same repetitive process.

Two poems by the modernist poet T. S. Eliot regard cycle and ritual differently. *The Waste Land*, Eliot's best-known work, begins at the return of spring:

> April is the cruellest month, breeding
> Lilacs out of the dead land, mixing
> Memory and desire, stirring
> Dull roots with spring rain.
>   (Eliot 2004: 61)

These lines are just a small part of a much longer poem, but it is possible to think about this opening sentence in isolation. Whereas, in Wordsworth's lyric, poetic form is presented as natural or organic – it rolls with and like the rolling course of day into night – Eliot's poem is presented as an artificial construct, under attack from the forces of nature. In Wordsworth's lyric, the diurnal (daily) cycle works with the form of the poem in its incorporation of the dead woman. Here, the cycle of months, seasons and years causes 'cruel' disturbance. The kind of work performed by the passing of time is similar in both poems. April 'breeds', 'mixes' and 'stirs', in much the same way that Wordsworth's diurnal course 'rolls'; each verb describes an act of combination, suggesting the blurring of distinct boundaries. But this blurring works *against* the form of Eliot's poem. 'Breeding', 'mixing' and 'stirring' all disrupt the separation of one poetic line from another so that each unit of sense runs over two lines, causing an overlapping effect that appears to dissolve the formal limits of the text. It is as if the poet and his poem have become a victim of the rolling seasons. The return of April makes it impossible to separate line from line and impossible to separate past from present and future or death from life.

In one final example – again from Eliot – the cycles of passing time appear less unsettling and more mundane:

> For I have known them all already, known them all –
> Have known the evenings, mornings, afternoons,

> I have measured out my life with coffee spoons;
> I know the voices dying with a dying fall
>   (Eliot 2004: 16)

These lines are taken from 'The Love Song of J. Alfred Prufrock', a dramatic monologue in which the speaker repeatedly fails to declare his love or even to identify a love-object. In this case, time's repetitions are not the repetitions of nature, but the repetitions of domestic ritual. The 'evenings', 'mornings' and 'afternoons' are not earth's diurnal course, but a sequence of hot drinks, taken at the same time each day. The form of the poem remains undisturbed. The beat of the lines maintains a regular rhythm and each line contains a unit of sense. However, there is no organic or formal harmony. Instead, ritualised or formalised time appears stale and empty, and the speaker's experience of time becomes a symptom of his malaise. These three examples, which illustrate the powerful unity of poetic, natural and temporal cycles in the face of death, experience natural time as a painful and intrusive force over which it fails to exert formal control, or experience time through the superficial forms of everyday life, provide some insight into the different ways that *In Memoriam* shapes and is shaped by time.

'Wheels of Being'

To take the Wordsworthian example first, one of the images that *In Memoriam* keeps returning to is that of the circle.[10] Like Wordsworth's lyric, in which day rolls round into night, *In Memoriam* employs circles and circular movement to represent the natural rhythm of creation. Tennyson is decidedly concerned with 'creation' rather than Wordsworth's more straightforward 'earth'. Harmonious nature is always closely related to Christian faith. In the Prologue, the speaker reaffirms his faith in God the creator, declaring,

> Thine are these orbs of light and shade
>   Thou madest Life in man and brute;
>   Thou madest Death; and lo, thy foot
> Is on the skull which thou hast made.
>   (Prologue, 5–8)

As images of creation, the sun and moon combine circular shape with cyclical movement and these circles and cycles provide a model for understanding the relationship between life and death in lines 6 and 7, so that death is to life what night is to day. Having established that this kind of circular space and time symbolises the created universe, Tennyson repeatedly describes different kinds of movement as cyclical, each time giving tacit emphasis to his Christian belief. From the description of the baby who presses his palm 'Against the *circle* of the breast' (XLV, 3, emphasis mine) and, as he matures, 'rounds he to a separate mind' (XLV, 9) to the description of the 'rolling hours' (LI, 14) and the 'wheels of Being' (L, 4), circles imply form and movement ordained by God.

In sections IX to XVII cyclical motion is again invoked in prayer as the mourner looks for the return of the 'fair ship' that carries Arthur's 'loved remains'. The mourner addresses the heavens, asking them to 'sphere all your lights around, above' (IX, 13) and imagines the boat moving 'through circles of the bounding sky' (XVII, 5–6). Here, too, thoughts of the cycle of death and life are not far from the mourner's mind and the sleep of the heavens and the winds provides a simile for Arthur's own sleep: three sleeps that will each end with waking. These implications are made explicit in section XLIII, which considers that 'If Sleep and Death be truly one' (XLIII, I), then 'that still garden of the souls / In many a figured leaf enrolls / The total world since life began' (XLIII, 10–12). Heaven, described as a garden in which souls grow like plants, is both divine and natural. The metaphor of the 'figured leaf' which '*enrolls*' the world, in the same way that Wordsworth's Lucy is 'rolled round' with the rest of the earth, suggests a close relationship between natural and supernatural forms, so that it might be possible to see the pattern of the next world in this one.

As the poem progresses, the life beyond the grave is frequently imagined in terms of rounds and cycles. Section XLVII, one of a number of lyrics that struggle with the possibility that the mourner and his friend will not recognise one another when they meet in heaven, employs an image that again echoes Wordsworth's Lucy poem. Two sections earlier, as we have seen, Tennyson describes growing up as a process through which an individual 'rounds' to 'a separate mind'. Considering the next phase of development, from life on earth to life in death, Tennyson reverses this image:

> That each, who seems a separate whole,
>   Should move his rounds, and fusing all
>   The skirts of self again, should fall
> Remerging in the general Soul
>   (XLVII, 1–4)

In the same way that Lucy's self is given over to the earth, the separate self-hood of adult identity is surrendered in death and the individual 'fuses' the skirts (or edges) of himself with a greater whole. Whereas Wordsworth's speaker appears to accept this incorporation, Tennyson's mourner expresses a tentative faith that 'Eternal form shall still divide / The eternal soul from all beside' (6–7), so that he and his Arthur will still be able to make one another out after death. However, there is a strange tension here between the idea of a 'general Soul' and an 'eternal soul'. Hallam's soul is both eternally separate from and part of a general whole. The difficulty involved in comprehending this idea is reflected in the fact that the mourner is forced to use the word 'soul' twice, so that it becomes a word or thing that has to accommodate two opposite concepts (this relation between separateness and wholeness might bring us back to the separation and wholeness of *In Memoriam* itself. I will return to the relationship between cycle and poetic form at the end of this section).

Returning to the same concerns in section LXI and LXII, the speaker jealously imagines his friend making conversation with 'the circle of the wise' (LXI, 3) and travelling 'unto vaster motions' than himself, describing 'The circuits of thine orbit round / A higher height, a deeper deep' (LXIII, 10–12). Again, the speaker is very aware of his exclusion from these cycles and tries to remember himself to his friend. The same image is repeated once more in section LXXXV, the longest section in the poem, which signals a measure of recovery by describing the experience of new friendship (the 'you' addressed by the speaker may be either Edmund Lushington, whose marriage to Tennyson's sister Cecilia is described in the Epilogue, or Emily Sellwood, whom Tennyson himself married in 1850). This section reflects back on the earlier periods of grief, evaluating thoughts expressed in the elegy's previous stanzas. It describes

> The great Intelligences fair
> > That range above our mortal state,
> > In circle round the blessed gate
> Received and gave him welcome there
>
> And led him through the blissful climes,
> > And showed him in the fountain fresh
> > All knowledge that the sons of flesh
> Shall gather in the cycled times.
> > > > (LXXXV, 21–8)

The shift into the simple past tense – quite rare in *In Memoriam* – that characterises this section; and the use of the simple future in the last line quoted above ('Shall gather') means that the poem performs, or works in harmony with 'the cycled times' it describes, rolling from past to future and thereby drawing mourner and Arthur together.

The following stanza, which begins, 'But I remained, whose hopes were dim' (LXXXV, 29), sums up the sense of desertion expressed in so much of the first half of the elegy, but even this description of deep despair hints at the divine cycle that moves the mourner closer to his lost love. The next stanza, which is made up of a series of exclamations, each describing Arthur in more and more rhapsodic terms, provides a visual pun or clue that hints towards the shape of things to come:

> O friendship, equal-poised control,
>   O heart, with kindliest motion warm,
>   O sacred essence, other form,
> O solemn ghost, O crownèd soul!
>   (LXXXV, 33–6)

Each description of Arthur's memory begins with an 'O', a wordless sound that communicates both desire and regret. On the printed page, these sounds appear as a series of circles that might represent the natural and heavenly cycles that form a significant part of the reflections and imaginings of this section. Looking and listening to the stanza again, we begin to notice that the stanza is made up of a pattern of o's; 'poised control', 'motion', 'other form', 'solemn ghost' and 'crownèd soul' are all words with circles at their centres and these circles might symbolise a connection between written language, created nature and the deeper movement of life beyond the grave. Although Hallam is described as an 'other form', a phrase that suggests that he has become different from or alien to the speaker, the shapes that form themselves on the page imply the possibility of a link between the forms of this world and the next.

From this point, the poem repeatedly invokes this natural / supernatural motion in order to comfort and reassure. In the following section, the 'ambrosial air' that follows rainfall 'rollest' from the 'gloom' of evening, over 'brake and bloom' (note, again, all those o's), down through 'the round of space' and towards the speaker, fanning his brows, blowing the fever from his cheek, and filling his body in a way that makes him part of its natural rolling movement (LXXXVI, 1–10). A couple of sections later, the word 'ambrosial' is used again, this time to describe the darkness that 'immantled' (clothed or enveloped) Arthur, as he read poetry on the lawn at Tennyson's family home in Somersby. The idyllic scene described in this section also contains a sequence of exclamatory O's, but the tone has shifted slightly, from desire and regret to happy recollection. Arthur is described coming from 'the dust and din and steam of town' to a pastoral retreat, which brings him 'joy' and those he meets there (Tennyson and his siblings), 'bliss' (LXXXIX, 13 and 21). Here, the O's are more directly echoed in the sounds that encircle family and friends as they sit together in the natural environment. The family group is drawn into a circle with Arthur at its centre (21) and they listen to the 'sweep of scythe' (a long arced blade that is wielded with a circular sweep of the arm) and a gust of wind that flies 'round' the garden. This memory leads on to a second, in which the two friends walk and converse together, returning 'Before the crimson-circled star / Had fallen into her father's grave' (LXXXIX, 47–8). Human and heavenly activity mirror one another in their harmonious geometry.

In section CXXII, as *In Memoriam* draws to a close, the earthly and heavenly circles that have shaped the elegy's faith, both in God and in the possibility of reunion between living and dead, are internalised by the speaker so that they become directly involved in the poetic process. Perhaps recalling the touch of the 'dead man' that he experienced in section XCV, the speaker remembers a desire, felt in the presence of his friend's ghost,

> To feel once more, in placid awe,
>   The strong imagination roll
>   A sphere of stars about my soul,
> In all her motion one with law;
>   (CXXII, 5–8)

Here, the imagination 'rolls', adopting the kind of movement that the poem has described throughout as both divine and natural. In this way it can be understood as 'one with law'. In other words, the imagination works with, rather than against, the created order of the universe. The speaker refers to 'The strong imagination' (rather than 'my strong imagination'), which works in or on the soul of the speaker, while the speaker himself remains 'placid'. The imagination described here is therefore not (or not just) the imagination of the speaker, but the divine imagination working within him. At this moment God becomes a poet and the circles and cycles that have rolled forth from God's imagination become a poem.

The description of creator-poet employed in section CXXII invites the reader to think about the place of *In Memoriam* itself within the divine order that links heaven to earth and promises an ongoing connection between the mourner and his dead friend. At the beginning of this section I said that *In Memoriam* might be understood as a circle traced three times. This reading is suggested by the way time is measured in the poem, through a return to significant festivals and anniversaries (more on this below), but it is also implied in the *In Memoriam* stanza, which moves forward by circling round and back on itself. To take that same stanza from section CXXII as an example, it is possible to see the 'roll' of the imagination and the 'sphere' of stars reflected in the rhyme scheme of the lines that describe them. The ABBA lines, which refuse or halt the onward momentum of rhyming couplets (ABAB), are often read as a pattern that expresses the mourner's unwillingness or inability to progress: a rhyme scheme that represents stasis (see Chapter 1). However, if we interpret this doubling back as a circle, the stanza becomes an organic form that rolls and rounds in imitation of the motion of the created universe. The poem's separate fragments are brought together to form a general whole because of the pattern of movement that they share, a pattern that finds its origins in created nature.

In the Epilogue the speaker imagines the conception of a new niece or nephew, son or daughter of his newly married sister and her husband. The moment of conception occurs when, 'star and system rolling past, / A soul shall draw from out the vast / And strike its being into bounds' (Epilogue, 122–4). The beginning of the life-cycle is therefore understood in much the same terms as the end of the life-cycle. The 'separate whole' that was imagined 'remerging with the general Soul' in section XLVII, is here seen at its initial point of separation. It is not so much a compensation for death – a new life given in return for the life that has been lost – as a reinterpretation of death as just one point in a perpetual cycle.

The Ritual of the Dead

However, as with so many sets of images in *In Memoriam*, this interpretation of the poem as an organic cycle that incorporates both speaker and mourner is not the whole story. The natural circles that the poem draws are marked by a repetitive sequence of human rituals that mediate between the individual and the social, the human, divine and natural. At times, these rituals are valuable and meaningful; at others they are hollow and comfortless, resembling the empty domestic rituals that have measured out the life of Eliot's Prufrock. Catherine Bell, in her important study of the theory of ritual, provides some definitions that work as a useful starting point for a reading of *In Memoriam*'s repetitive performances. One of the first things she establishes about ritual is that it is action; it will 'act out, express or perform' ideas or concepts (Bell 1993: 19). Furthermore, Bell observes that it is often understood as 'particularly *thoughtless* action – routinized, habitual, obsessive or mimetic – and therefore the purely formal, secondary and mere physical expression of logically prior ideas' (19). In other words, by taking an idea and turning it into an action and then by repeating that action so that it becomes a habit or routine, ritual becomes separate from the ideas that they are supposed to express.

Bell also writes that 'ritual is the means by which individual perception and behaviour are socially appropriated or conditioned' (20). Ritual is not a natural or spontaneous action (crying or laughing, for example); it is the kind of action that we learn and that identifies us as part of a particular social group. To return to the example of Prufrock's coffee spoons, drinking coffee is not necessarily a ritual. I might drink coffee at any time of day if I were tired or cold. But it becomes a ritual when it is repeated at the same time each day and performed not as an individual response to thirst or fatigue, but out of habit and as part of a social custom. As a ritual, drinking coffee, particularly using a specific kind of cutlery to do so, becomes a way of identifying an individual as part of a particular social class (Prufrock's coffee spoons identify him as a member of the bourgeois gentility that Eliot's poem aims to poke fun at). Finally, Bell talks about the relationship between ritual and time, arguing that ritual challenges a linear understanding of time through its series of identical, repetitive performances that collapse different points in time together.

Rituals – repetitive, formal performances that emphasise action more than thought and the social more than the individual and that understand time as static rather than progressive – are referred to throughout *In Memoriam*. Also, in an important sense, *In Memoriam* is itself a kind of ritual; but I turn first to the rituals it describes. The first is the ritual of burial, described in section XVIII. Reading this section, it is important to remember that Tennyson did not attend Hallam's burial; nor did he visit Hallam's grave until after the publication of *In Memoriam*. These facts do not call into question the sincerity of Tennyson's grief or the authenticity of these stanzas, but they do suggest that when Tennyson imagines a burial, he is speaking with a voice that is not straightforwardly personal. It is perhaps easier to see what I mean by this if we look at the first stanza of the section:

> 'Tis well; 'tis something; we may stand
>   Where he in English earth is laid,
>   And from his ashes may be made
> The violet of his native land.
>
> (XVIII, 1–4)

Here, like in Wordsworth's 'Song', a dead body is incorporated into the earth. However, the emphasis this time is not on nature, but on nation; the mourner draws consolation from the fact that his friend will be posthumously repatriated. By emphasising their shared Englishness, the speaker draws on a sense of identity that is social rather than personal. The use of the plural first-person pronoun ('we') also suggests a shift away from the individual intimacy of the lyric 'I', towards a more communal, public voice. Writing about social, religious ritual, the mourner speaks with the voice of the nation. He repeats an invocation to his fellow-mourners, using the poem as a force for social cohesion and collective experience by calling them to 'come [. . .] and hear the ritual of the dead' (XVIII, 12).

However, in the next two stanzas the communal voice breaks down into an expression of grief that is deeply personal:

> Ah yet, even yet, if this might be,
>   I, falling on his faithful heart,

> Would breathing through his lips impart
> The life that almost dies in me;
>   (XVIII, 13–16)

The spontaneous, exclamatory 'Ah' interrupts the measured solemnity of the previous stanza, suggesting that the speaker cannot sustain the public voice of ritual. The speaker's desire to breathe life into his friend's corpse is a macabre assault on the restraint of the funeral rites and has no place in the social forms of ritual action. By placing the social, public voice of ritual alongside the private voice of grief in this way, this section communicates *In Memoriam*'s ambivalence about ritualised action and speech.

The next occasion for ritual action in the poem is the first of three Christmases. The speaker's relationship with this ritual celebration is expressed through his ambivalent response to the communal voice of Christian worship. As Christmas draws near, the mourner listens as the 'Christmas bells from hill to hill / Answer each other in the mist' (XXVIII, 3–4). The ringing of church bells – a Christian ritual – is understood to be a cohesive force, drawing separate villages together into a single community that speak the same language. The mourner hears these 'four voices', which exert a strange power over him, overcoming his suicidal despair by speaking to his memory: 'But they my troubled spirit rule, / For they controlled me when a boy' (XXVIII, 17–18). In the same way that ritual sound unites different geographical places, it unites different temporal moments, bringing the past into the present so that the changes and losses that have occurred with the passing of time momentarily lose their force. It is possible to detect a note of resentment in the speaker's voice as he gives himself over to ritual and memory. The verbs 'controlled' and 'rule' imply that the speaker is unable to resist the strength of ritualised memory that is exerted against his will. Christian ritual elicits a conditioned response that is at odds with individual experience. The last line describes the 'merry merry bells of Yule', employing repetition in such a way that makes the Yuletide merriment sound troublingly insistent.

At first, the rituals of Christmas are at odds with the sombre mood of the family, but as they join hands in a circle and sing together the mood shifts. The 'merry song' they sing, like the 'merry bells', does not express how they are feeling, but the ritualised act of singing effects a change:

> Then echo-like our voices rang;
>   We sung, though every eye was dim,
>   A merry song we sang with him
> Last year: impetuously we sang
>   (XXX, 13–16)

This stanza reflects and performs the work of ritual. The family sing the song they 'sang with him' (Arthur) the previous Christmas, and although the repeated song draws attention to the painful difference between present and past, the echo-rhymes collapse the two moments into one. The first two lines of the stanza describe the Christmas just past; the second two describe the previous year. The difference between the two is indicated by a shift in the verb, from 'sung' to 'sang'. However, rhymes and half-rhymes bind the two pairs of lines together, from 'rang' to 'sung' to 'song' to 'sang' to 'sang', and the line between immediate past and more distant past blurs.

When they sing a second time, the words of their song are reported in the poem so that poem and song become one. In this way the poem itself becomes a ritual performance and the isolated, sceptical voice of elegy is drawn into the communal expressions of religious faith. The speech marks that indicate the beginning and end of reported speech still maintain some separation between elegy and hymn, but because the hymn is transposed into the *In Memoriam* stanza, this difference appears negligible. The song ends in the penultimate stanza of section XXX, but its theme and tone persist in the final stanza so that the elegy appears to identify with and continue the ritual work of Christian song.

In Memoriam continues to perform the repetitions of ritual in its description of the second Christmas. Section LXXVIII begins with a stanza almost identical to the opening stanza of section XXX:

> With trembling fingers did we weave
> The holly round the Christmas hearth;
> A rainy cloud possessed the earth,
> And sadly fell our Christmas-eve. (XXX, 1–4)

> Again at Christmas did we weave,
> The holly round the Christmas hearth
> The silent snow possessed the earth,
> And calmly fell our Christmas-eve. (LXXVIII, 1–4)

Apart from the first line, which acknowledges repetition, only the weather and the mood have undergone slight alterations, shifting from rain to 'silent snow' and from sadness to calm. This repetition of language, syntax and end-rhyme means that we experience the stanza as routine or habit: the ritualised description of ritual. Whereas in section XXX, the games and songs of Christmas celebration neither express nor conceal the grief of the Tennyson family, this second Christmas passes without 'token of distress' (XXX, 13). Both Christmases mark and mourn loss, but the first Christmas mourns a lost friendship and the second Christmas marks a lost grief, asking 'O sorrow, then can sorrow wane? / O grief, can grief be changed to less?' (XXX, 15–16).

The paradox of this double loss is expressed in the next line: 'O last regret, regret can die!'(XXX, 17). The end of sorrow is not a cause for celebration, but the occasion for new sorrow and a second bereavement. In this sense, the unchanging rituals of Christmas serve to highlight unwelcome change. However, in another sense, they represent a deeper continuity that overwrites change. Responding to his own regretful exclamation, the mourner concludes his second Christmas with an image of natural and spiritual continuity: 'No – mixt with all this mystic frame, / Her deep relations are the same, / But with long use her tears are dry' (XXX, 18–20).

The final Christmas occurs in a new location, a change that disrupts habitual custom and causes the mourner to reassess the form and function of ritual practice once again. The call and response of the bells described in section XXVIII are replaced by 'a single peal' that sounds 'like strangers' voices' (CIV, 9) in the unfamiliar landscape; the holly is left 'ungathered' (CV, 1) and Christmas games are not played. The poem holds echoes of its ritualised form. The final line of the first stanza repeats the refrain of the previous two: 'And strangely fell our Christmas-eve'; but 'eve' rhymes with 'leave' rather than 'weave' so that the action of making the wreath is replaced by an injunction not to act. Like the tears that are described as having dried 'through long use' in section LXXVII, the 'dying use' of family ritual comes to an end: 'For who would keep the ancient form / Through which the spirit breathes no more?' (CV, 19–20). This question has implications for more than just the ancient forms of the Christian festival. It can also be asked of the elegy itself, the form of which, though not ancient, has certainly been well used by this, its 105th section. Therefore, when the speaker asked that there be 'neither song, nor game, nor feast; / Nor harp be touched, nor flute be blown' (CV, 21–2), we sense that the poem might likewise soon fall silent.

In the following section the speaker listens again to the unfamiliar bells that he describes in CIV and finds new meaning there. They peal through section CVI, renouncing the 'old forms', 'mournful rhymes' and 'old shapes' of elegy, and announcing a new poetry, 'the fuller minstrel', which forms part of an optimistic vision of the future. But this optimism is short-lived. In one of the poem's most striking juxtapositions, the following section leaps forward two months to 'the day when he was born' (CVII, 1); this time, 'he' is not Christ, but Arthur. This anniversary is represented as a fractured echo of the preceding Christmases. The pattern of the stanza that begins sections XXX, LXXVIII and CVI returns as a trace in lines 5 to 8, which rhymes 'leaves' with 'eaves' rather than 'leave' and 'eve', creating different meanings out of the same sounds. Whereas the third Christmas is observed in silence, song is still used to mark Arthur's birthday. The speaker expresses a determined resolve to 'keep the day': 'surely we / Will drink to him' (22–3). This is not a question, but it looks like one and perhaps indicates the speaker's embarrassment at falling back on the habits of ritual so soon after the bold declarations of the previous section. It communicates a self-conscious awareness that poet and poem are unable to practise what they preach. The tension that exists between sections CVI and CVII, between the renunciation and the preservation of ritual, therefore dramatises the struggle that takes place throughout *In Memoriam* between different forms of faith and different kinds of poetry, a struggle that, despite the poem's best intentions, is never quite resolved.

Notes

1. For a comprehensive exploration of the reception of *Paradise Lost* in the early nineteenth century, see Lucy Newlyn (2001), *Paradise Lost and the Romantic Reader*.
2. For a lucid discussion of the fable of the cave and its place in Platonic philosophy, see David Ross (1953), pp. 69–77.
3. A good summary of the arguments on both sides of the question is provided by Ricks (1989: 205–12) and Sinfield (1986: 128–9). See also Jeff Nunokawa's essay, '*In Memoriam* and the Extinction of the Homosexual', reproduced in Stott (1996).
4. The best feminist reading of *In Memoriam* is *Alfred Lord Tennyson* by Marion Shaw (1988), which explores representations of love and marriage in Tennyson's poetry.
5. T. S. Eliot, in the essay which is included in part in the 'Contexts and Reception' section of the Guide, provides a different perspective on this set of images, writing that the 'surface' of Tennyson's poetry is 'intimate with its depths' (Eliot [1936] 1999: 338).
6. See, for example, R. S. Lazarus (1982), 'Thoughts on the Relations between Emotions and Cognition', *American Physiologist*, 37 (10), pp. 1019–24.
7. Donald S. Hair's reading of *In Memoriam* provides a detailed discussion of the relationship between Locke's philosophy and *In Memoriam*'s faith (Hair 1991: 102–16). Another relevant and illuminating perspective is provided by Isobel Armstrong's chapter, 'The Collapse of Object and Subject in *In Memoriam*' (Armstrong 1982: 172–206), which looks at Tennyson's poem in the context of Idealist philosophy.
8. The discussion of Tennyson's use of economic images in this section is heavily indebted to Iain Kee Vaughan, whose doctoral thesis, *Wordsworth's Economic Spirit* (2009), explores the relationship between early nineteenth-century theories of economics and the poetry of William Wordsworth.
9. One of the best readings of the melancholia of 'Tears, Idle Tears' and *In Memoriam* is provided by Gerhard Joseph in the first chapter of *Tennyson and the Text* (Joseph 1992: 9–24).
10. *In Memoriam*'s circle imagery is also addressed by Sinfield as part of his discussion of the way language works in *In Memoriam* (Sinfield 1971: 146–56).

Chapter 4

Contexts and Reception

This section brings together extracts from a range of primary material that offers a sense of the literary, philosophical and print-cultural context of *In Memoriam*'s composition, publication and afterlife. In each case, an extract from an essay, article or review is accompanied by an introduction that links it to Tennyson's poem. The section begins with a review of Tennyson's first volume of poetry written by Hallam himself, originally published in the *Englishman's Magazine* and later included in the *Remains in Verse and Prose of Arthur Henry Hallam*, published by Arthur's father, Henry, in 1834. This is followed by part of Henry Hallam's memoir of his son and an account of the funeral. I also include an extract from Hallam Tennyson's *Memoir* of his father, which includes Tennyson's own remarks about *In Memoriam* and a draft section that was not included in the final published version of the poem. Extracts from Charles Lyell's *Principles of Geology* and Robert Chambers's *Vestiges of the Natural History of Creation* are included to provide a starting point for explorations of the scientific context of *In Memoriam*'s composition (see also the 'Profit and Loss' section of the Reading Guide). The second half of the section focuses on material published in response to *In Memoriam*, beginning with some contemporary reviews and ending with an essay by T. S. Eliot, which demonstrates how *In Memoriam*'s identity and reputation were shaped by its readership.

Compositional Contexts

Arthur Henry Hallam, Review of *Poems, Chiefly Lyrical*

Hallam's review of Tennyson's first volume of poetry, one of the most influential early essays on Tennyson, was published in the *Englishman's Magazine* in August 1831. The full title of the review, 'On Some of the Characteristics of Modern Poetry and on the Lyrical Poems of Alfred Tennyson', indicates that Hallam's review aimed to use Tennyson to define the role of poetry in the early 1830s, a period that is now recognised as a time of transition between the Romantic and Victorian eras. In the extract printed below, Hallam talks about the relationship between poetry and national culture, arguing that 'modern poetry', often characterised by a spirit of disillusionment and melancholy, exists at the edge of British cultural life and is written in opposition to the national mood. He suggests that a mark of a poet's quality is his lack of mainstream cultural appeal and he paints a picture of the poet as visionary outsider. This picture is heavily influenced by Hallam's love of the Romantics – particularly Shelley – but it also relates closely to the poetic identity Tennyson fashions for himself in his early work and that he continues to develop in *In Memoriam*. Because Tennyson and Hallam were close friends when Hallam wrote this review, it is fair to assume that his definition of the modern poet is also, to some extent, Tennyson's, and this essay can be related to the anxious discussion of the purpose and efficacy of poetry that takes place throughout *In Memoriam*.

But the age in which we live comes late in our national progress. That first raciness and juvenile vigour of literature, when nature 'wantoned as in her prime, and played at her will her virgin fancies' is gone never to return. Since that day we have undergone a period of degradation. 'Every handicraftsman has worn the mask of poesy.' It would be tedious to repeat the tale so often related of the French contagion and the heresies of the Popian school. With the close of last century came an era of reaction, an era of painful struggle to bring our over-civilised condition of thought into union with the fresh productive spirit that brightened the morning of our literature. But repentance is unlike innocence: the laborious endeavour to restore has more complicated methods of action than the freedom of untainted nature. Those different powers of poetic disposition, the energies of Sensitive, of Reflective, of Passionate Emotion, which in former times were intermingled, and derived from mutual support an extensive empire over the feelings of men, were now restrained within separate spheres of agency. The whole system no longer worked harmoniously, and by intrinsic harmony acquired external freedom; but there arose a violent and unusual action in the several component functions, each for itself, all striving to reproduce the regular power which the whole had once enjoyed. Hence the melancholy which so evidently characterises the spirit of modern poetry; hence that return of the mind upon itself and the habit of seeking relief in idiosyncrasies rather than community of interest. In the old times the poetic impulse went along with the general impulse of the nation; in these it is a reaction against it, a check acting for conservation against a propulsion towards change. We have indeed seen it urged in some of our fashionable publications, that the diffusion of poetry must be in the direct ration of the diffusion of machinery, because a highly civilised people must have new objects of interest. But this notable argument forgets that against this *objective* amelioration may be set the decrease of *subjective* power, arising from a prevalence of social activity, and a continual absorption of higher feelings into the palpable interests of ordinary life. The French Revolution may be a finer theme than the war of Troy, but it does not so evidently follow that Homer is to find his superior. Our inference, therefore, from this change in the relative position of the artist to the rest of the community is, that modern poetry in proportion to its depth and truth is likely to have little immediate authority over public opinion. Admirers it will have; sects consequently it will form; and these strong undercurrents will in time sensibly affect the principle stream. Art herself, less manifestly glorious than in her periods of undisputed supremacy, retains her essential prerogatives, and forgets not to raise up chosen spirits who may minister to her state and vindicate her title. (Hallam 1831: 619–20)

Henry Hallam's Memoir

Remains in Verse and Prose by Arthur Henry Hallam is an important contextual document, not only because it provides evidence of Hallam's early promise, but also because it offers a range of other accounts of Hallam and responses to his death. It includes a letter from his close friend at Eton, William Ewart Gladstone, and others written by members of the Cambridge Apostles who went on to lead influential lives in Victorian religious, social and political life. The extract reprinted below is taken from the editor's preface and offers an account of Hallam's funeral by his father. Tennyson did not attend Hallam's funeral, nor did he visit his grave until after *In Memoriam* was published, so this account provided a source for the imagined gravestones that appear throughout the poem. However, it is perhaps more interesting in its description of Hallam himself, which sets up a set of conventions to which *In Memoriam* later conforms. Hallam is described as 'almost faultless' and the author comes to terms with his son's untimely death by suggesting that he was a young man too good for this world who has progressed into a better one. This idea is taken up by Tennyson, who considers the implications of this progress in detail, worrying that he will never 'catch up' with his friend, who was so far in advance of him in all things, including death. Henry Hallam also expresses difficulty in providing an adequate account of his son and of his own grief, another convention employed by *In Memoriam*.

> The remains of Arthur were brought to England and interred on the 3rd of January 1834, in the Chancel of Clevedon Church, in Somersetshire, belonging to his maternal grandfather, sire Abraham Elton; a place selected by the Editor, not only from the connexion of kindred, but on account of its still and sequestered situation, on a lone hill that overhangs the Bristol Channel.
>
> More ought, perhaps, to be said; but it is very difficult to proceed. From the earliest years of this extraordinary young man, his premature abilities were not

more conspicuous than an almost faultless disposition, sustained by a more calm self-command than has often been witnessed in that season of life. The sweetness of temper that distinguished his childhood, became, with the advance of manhood, an habitual benevolence, and ultimately ripened into that exalted principle of love towards God and man, which animated and almost absorbed his soul during the latter period of his life, and to which most of the following compositions bear such emphatic testimony. He seemed to tread the earth as a spirit from some better world; and in bowing to the mysterious will which has in mercy removed him, perfected by so short a trial, and passing over the bridge which separates the seen from the unseen life in a moment, and, as we believe, without a moment's pang, we must feel not only the bereavement of those to whom he was dear, but the loss which mankind have sustained by the withdrawing of such a light. (Hallam 1834: 35–6)

Hallam Tennyson's *Memoir*

Hallam's memoir of his father, published five years after Tennyson's death, is the first authoritative biography of the poet. Much of it is a collaborative work, put together by Hallam in close consultation with his father.[1] It contains an account of *In Memoriam*'s composition, Tennyson's notes on the poem and a number of draft sections that were not included in the final poem. Like the reviews of the poem (see below), the *Memoir* constructs and frames *In Memoriam* in a way that has been influential for the poem's critical afterlife. Tennyson stresses the 'dramatic' nature of the poem's speaker, describing the voice as one that is both individual and universal. He also insists on the spontaneity of the composition process. By claiming that he never intended the poems to be made into a whole and also that he never intended them for publication, he emphasises *In Memoriam*'s lyric identity; but he also identifies it with Dante's *Divine Comedy*, a comparison that hints at his epic ambition for the poem.

The *Memoir* offers one account of those sections of *In Memoriam* that were written first: sections IX, XXX, XXXI, LXXXV and a version of section XXVII. It also points to a number of possible intertexts, mentioning poems that were composed in the same book of manuscript paper as these opening sections. 'Morte d'Arthur', a retelling of the death of King Arthur, which was eventually worked into Tennyson's Arthurian epic, *Idylls of the King*, is drawn into a close relationship with these early elegiac fragments, suggesting that in the early months of composition, Tennyson was testing out different forms of poetic response to his friend's death.

The other manuscript fragments included in the extracts reprinted below offer a sense of the development of the *In Memoriam* stanza and the inception of some of the poem's central images and themes. In the 'germ' Tennyson is already interested in images of hands; he desires the press of his dead friend's hand and imagines he sees Hallam's ghost, standing with his hands clasped. The lines are written in iambic tetrameter stanzas of four and then five lines, with an ABAB rhyme scheme. It closely resembles the *In Memoriam* stanza, only omitting its innovative rhyme scheme. More like English ballad metre, it provides a bridge between the two forms, demonstrating how Tennyson developed the one from the other. The more complete section, 'The Grave' (the first of a number reprinted in the *Memoir*), also contains traces of other sections. Its opening lines recall the beginning of section CVIII, in which the speaker resolves, 'I will not shut me from my kind' (CVIII, 1), and the voices from the crowd are very similar to the voices of the three travellers that criticise the mourner's solitary mourning in XXI. The *Memoir* notes that this section was originally included as section LVII, which places it between those sections that most directly address the spiritual crisis caused by the science of evolution and the section that begins 'Peace; come away: the song of woe / Is after all an earthly song' (LVII, 1–2). The inclusion of this deleted section therefore has a significant effect on the meaning of this call for 'peace' (or silence). Whereas, in the published version, the mourner breaks off from a series of despairing exclamations about nature's indifference to life and death, in the earlier draft, the mourner is instead called to 'come away' from the side of his friend's grave. This is just one example of the close relationship between structure and meaning in *In Memoriam*, demonstrating the poem's openness to composition, decomposition and recomposition.

Extract 1

On the evening of one of these sad winter days my father had already noted down in his scrap-book some fragmentary lines, which proved to be the germ of 'In Memoriam':

Where is the voice I loved? ah where
Is that dear hand that I would press?
Lo! the broad heavens cold and bare,
The stars that know not my distress!
        *   *   *   *   *
The vapour labours up the sky,
Uncertain forms are darkly moved!
Larger than human passes by
The shadow of the man I loved,
And clasps his hands, as one that prays!

[. . .]

'The Two Voices' or 'Thoughts of Suicide' was begun under the cloud of this overwhelming sorrow, which, as my father told me, for a while blotted out all joy from his life, and made him long for death, in spite of his feeling that he was in some measure a help and comfort to his sister. But such a first friendship and such a loss helped to reveal himself to himself, while he enshrined his sorrow in his song. Tennant writes: 'Alfred although much broken in spirits is yet able to divert his thoughts from gloomy brooding, and keep his mind in activity.'

In the earliest manuscript of 'The Two Voices' a fine verse is found which was omitted in the published edition as too dismal (after 'under earth').

From when his baby pulses beat
To when his hands in their last heat
Pick at the death-mote in the sheet.

Then in the same manuscript-book come the first written sections of 'In Memoriam', in the following order:

Fair ship that from the Italian shore.
            (*written on a stray sheet*)
With trembling fingers did we weave.
When Lazarus left his charnel-cave.
This truth came borne with bier and pall.
It draweth near the birth of Christ.

And between 'With trembling fingers' and 'When Lazarus left his charnel-cave' he has written the first draft of his 'Morte d'Arthur'. (*Memoir* I, 107–9)

Extract 2

'It must be remembered,' writes my father, 'that this is a poem, *not* an actual biography. It is founded on our friendship, on the engagement of Arthur Hallam to my sister, on his sudden death at Vienna, just before the time fixed for their marriage, and on his burial at Clevedon church. The poem concludes with the marriage of my youngest sister Cecilia. It was meant to be a kind of *Divina Commedia*, ending with happiness. The sections were written at many different places, and as the phases of our intercourse came to my memory and suggested them. I did not write them with any view of weaving them into a whole, or for publication, until I found that I had written so many. The different moods of sorrow as in a drama are dramatically given, and my conviction that fear, doubts, and suffering will find answer and relief only through faith in a God of Love. 'I' is not always the author speaking of himself, but the voice of the human race speaking thro' him. After the Death of A.H.H., the divisions of the poem are made by First Xmas Eve (Section XXVIII), Second Xmas (LXXVIII), Third Xmas Eve (CVI. and CV. Etc.). I myself did not see Clevedon till years after the burial of A.H.H. Jan. 3rd 1834, and then in later editions of 'In Memoriam' I altered the word 'chancel', which was the word used by Mr Hallam in his Memoir, to 'dark church.' As to the localities in which the poems were written, some were written in Lincolnshire, some in London, Essex, Gloucestershire, Wales, anywhere where I happened to be'

'And as for the metre of 'In Memoriam' I had no notion till 1880 that Lord Herbert of Cherbury had written his occasional verse in the same metre. I believed myself the originator of the metre, until after 'In Memoriam' came out, when some one told me that Ben Jonson and Sir Philip Sidney had used it. The following poems were omitted from 'In Memoriam' when I published, because I thought them redundant.'

The Grave (originally No. LVII).   (*Unpublished.*)

I keep no more a lone distress,
  The crowd have come to see thy grave,
  Small thanks or credit shall I have,
But these shall see it none the less.

The happy maiden's tears are free
  And she shall weep and give them way;
  Yet one unschool'd in want will say
'The dead are dead and let them be.'

Another whispers sick with loss:
  'O let the simple slab remain!
  The "Mercy Jesu" in the rain!
The "Miserere" in the moss!'

'I love the daisy weeping dew,
  I hate the trim-set plots of art!'
  My friend, thou speakest from the heart,
But look, for these are nature too.
                    (*Memoir* I, 304–7)

Scientific Contexts

One of the most significant contexts for the crisis of faith occasioned by Hallam's death and described in *In Memoriam* is that of pre-Darwinian evolutionary science. There are two publications that appear to have had a direct influence on the elegy's language and thought. The first is Charles Lyell's *Principles of Geology* (1830–3) and the second is Robert Chambers's *Vestiges of the Natural History of Creation* (1844). Although the publication of Darwin's *On the Origin of Species* (1859) has eclipsed both of these earlier texts, they had a huge impact on the Victorian consciousness and were extensively discussed, reviewed and parodied in contemporary newspapers and periodicals. Although both publications try to accommodate their scientific theories within a framework of Christian belief, each presented profound challenges to Judeo-Christian accounts of a divinely authored universe. *Principles of Geology*, which bases its theory about the gradual formation of the earth's surface on evidence gathered from the observation of rocks and fossils, suggested that the earth's creation was a long and gradual process, rather than a single, divinely authored act. *Vestiges of the*

Natural History of Creation is principally concerned with the development of particular species; its most controversial claim being that the human species originated with lower forms of life. Tennyson owned copies of both Lyell and Chambers, but would not admit the influence of Chambers on *In Memoriam*, stating that those sections of the elegy that address theories of evolution were written 'some years before the publication of *Vestiges of Creation* in 1844' (*Memoir*, I, 223). Nevertheless, there are some striking similarities between the language and ideas of both Lyell and Chambers and *In Memoriam*, and the extracts provided below again suggest *In Memoriam* as a kind of textual collage that takes fragments of contemporary cultural material and forms them into poetry so that the poem speaks both with its own voice and with the voice of its age.

Principles of Geology

The vocabulary that Lyell uses to set out his ideas about the changing formation of the earth's surface can be traced throughout *In Memoriam*. *Principles* begins with an examination of earlier geological theories, which Lyell calls 'systems'. Likewise, Tennyson begins his poem by talking about our 'little systems' that 'have their day and cease to be' (Prologue, 17–18); Lyell talks about nature as something that can be read, a figure of speech that is repeated in the Epilogue, which describes nature as 'an open book'; and Lyell employs the metaphorical language of illumination to describe his attempt to discover and reveal scientific knowledge, talking about a partial illumination that might be compared to the 'broken lights' of Tennyson's Prologue. The first of the two short extracts printed below provides context for sections LV to LVII, in which the mourner contemplates the mortality of species. The second, taken from the conclusion of volume I, demonstrates how Lyell struggles to come to terms with the apparent indifference of the geological system he has described.

> The reader has only to reflect on what we have said of the habitations and the stations of organic beings in general, and to consider them in relations to those effects which we have contemplated in our first volume as resulting from the igneous and aqueous causes now in action, and he will immediately perceive that, amidst the vicissitudes of the earth's surface, species cannot be immortal, but must perish one after the other, like the individuals which compose them. There is no possibility of escaping from this conclusion [. . .]. (Lyell 1835: III, 135)
>
> I shall endeavour to point out in the sequel, that the general tendency of subterranean movements, when their effects are considered for a sufficient lapse of ages, is eminently beneficial, and that they constitute an essential part of that mechanism by which the integrity of the habitable surface is preserved, and the very existence

and perpetuation of dry land secured. Why the working of this same machinery should attend with so much evil, is a mystery far beyond the reach of our philosophy, and probably must remain so until we are permitted to investigate, not our planet alone and its inhabitants, but other parts of the moral and material universe with which they may be connected. Could our survey embrace other worlds, and the events, not of a few centuries only, but of periods as indefinite as those with which geology renders us familiar, some apparent contradictions might be reconciled, and some difficulties would doubtless be cleared up. But even then, as our capacities are finite, while the scheme of the universe may be infinite, both in time and space, it is presumptuous to suppose that all sources of doubt and complexity would ever be removed. On the contrary, they might, perhaps, go on augmenting in number, although our confidence in the wisdom of the plan of Nature should increase at the same time; for it has been justly said, that the greater the circle of light, the greater the boundary of darkness by which it is surrounded. (Lyell 1835: II, 291)

Vestiges of the Natural History of Creation[2]

At the heart of Chambers's thesis is his theory of 'Progressive Development'. This model of evolution involves a gradual progress from simple to more complex forms of life that is closely related to the development of the embryo in the womb. Chambers argues that the most compelling evidence for species evolution is the way that an embryo takes on various forms during the course of its development, before assuming a recognisably human shape. These forms, Chambers argues, are the traces of its species heritage. The first of the three extracts printed below outlines this theory, which provides an interesting context for the various infants, metaphorical and real, born and unborn that populate *In Memoriam*, so that, when Tennyson's speaker describes himself as 'an infant crying in the night', his infantilisation might be read in terms of evolutionary progress. The second extract is frequently suggested as a source for section LV, in which the mourner complains that nature seems 'so careful of the type' and yet 'so careless of the single life' (LV, 7–8). Finally, the third extract, in which Chambers emphasises the compatibility of his theory with belief in God bears close resemblance to Tennyson's own reassertion of faith in the Prologue and Epilogue of his poem. Like Lyell, Chambers refers to imperfect 'systems' and expresses faith in humankind's further perfectibility, looking forward to a 'redress' of present suffering that is understood in economic terms.

We have yet to advert to the most interesting class of facts connected with the laws of organic development. It is only in recent times that physiologists have observed that each animal passes, in the course of its germinal history, through a series of changes resembling the *permanent forms* of the various orders of animals inferior to it in the scale. Thus, for instance, an insect, standing at the head of the articulated animals, is, in the lava state, a true annelid, or worm, the annelid being the lowest in the same class. The embryo of a crab resembles the perfect animal of the inferior order myriapoda, and passes through all the forms of transition which characterise the intermediate tribes of crustacean. The frog, for some time after its birth, is a fish with external gills, and other organs fitting it for an aquatic life, all of which are changed as it advances to maturity, and becomes a land animal. The mammifer only passes through still more stages, according to its higher place on the scale. Nor is man himself exempt from this law. His first form is that which is permanent in the animalcule. His organisation gradually passes through conditions generally resembling a fish, a reptile, a bird, and the lower mammalia, before it attains its specific maturity. At one of the last stages of his foetal career, he exhibits an intermaxillary bone, which is characteristic of the perfect ape; this is suppressed, and he may then be said to take leave of the simial type, and become a true human creature. (Chambers [1844] 1994: 194)

It is clear, moreover, from the whole scope of the natural laws, that the individual, as far as the present sphere of being is concerned, is to the Author of Nature a consideration of inferior moment. Everywhere we see the arrangements for the species perfect; the individual is left, as it were, to take his chance amidst the *mêlée* of the various laws affecting him. If he be found inferiorly endowed, or ill befalls him, there was at least no partiality against him. The system has the fairness of a lottery, in which every one has the like chance of drawing a prize. (Chambers [1844] 1994: 377)

To reconcile this to the recognised character of the Deity, it is necessary to suppose that the present system is but a part of a whole, a stage in a Great Progress, and that the Redress is in the reserve. Another argument here occurs – the economy of nature, beautifully arranged and vast in its extent as it is, does not satisfy even man's idea of what might be; he feels that, if this multiplicity of theatres for the exemplification of such phenomena as we see on earth were to go on forever unchanged, it would not be worthy of the Being capable of creating it. An endless monotony of human generations, with their humble thinkings and doings, seems an object beneath that august Being. But the mundane economy might be very well as a portion of some great phenomenon, the rest of which was yet to be evolved. It therefore appears that our system, though it may at first appear at issue with other doctrines in esteem amongst mankind, tends to come into harmony with them, and even to give them support. I would say, in conclusion, that, even where the two above arguments may fail of effect, there may yet be a faith derived from this view of nature sufficient to sustain under all senses of the imperfect happiness, the calamities, the woes, and pains of this sphere of being. (Chambers [1844] 1994: 385–6)

Reviews and Anthologies

On publication, *In Memoriam* received a good deal of attention from contemporary newspapers and journals.[3] Because the poem's anonymity did little to prevent the identity of its author from becoming known, the poem's celebrity had much to do with the reputation that Tennyson had already established for himself and reviews frequently identified *In Memoriam* as the high point of Tennyson's career to date. Reviews therefore provide illuminating context for studies of Tennyson's biography, offering contemporary accounts of his career and growing celebrity. They also help to construct a sense of *how* the poem was read by Tennyson's contemporaries. As well as offering opinions about a published work, reviews also have the power to mediate between the work and the reading public, defining its identity and significance for its audience. In the Victorian period, it was common for reviews to reproduce large sections of a work, so that a reviewer was able to identify what he thought were its most important sections, providing an edited version that supported their reading. Similar work was carried out by poetry anthologies. Macmillan's *Golden Treasury* (1885), edited by F. T. Palgrave, includes a selection of forty-two sections from *In Memoriam*, published in a different order from the one decided on by Tennyson for the 1850 text. This decision effectively rewrote *In Memoriam* for a significant readership who may only have come to the poem via the anthology.[4] In the selected extracts reproduced below, reviewers describe what sort of poem they think *In Memoriam* is and identify the terms by which it should be read and appreciated. Even in the year of its publication, *In Memoriam*'s formal identity was a matter of debate. Reviews tend to talk about *In Memoriam* as a collection of poems rather than as a single text, but also describe it as a diary, a monument, a series of meditations and a soliloquy. There is greater agreement when it comes to the content of the poem. Reviewers repeatedly emphasise the poem's depth, sincerity, earnestness and truth, describing it as different from, and better than, other, more artful or intellectual kinds of poetry. However, they are also keen to recognise *In Memoriam*'s manliness and Englishness. They strike a fine balance between identification of the individuality and privacy of the poem's voice and of its universal application, so that the singularity voiced by the poem becomes one that is 'common to the race' and the author of *In Memoriam* begins to be transformed into the nation's poet. It was partly as the result of this reception that Tennyson was made Poet Laureate a few months after *In Memoriam*'s publication. The first poem that he wrote as laureate, *Ode on the Death of the Duke of Wellington*, an elegy for Arthur Wellesley, military hero and former prime minister, received very mixed reviews. Having crowned their national poet, the Victorian public were dissatisfied with the national, public poetry that he subsequently produced.[5]

J. Westland Marston, The Athenaeum

This volume of verse, though published anonymously, bears such intrinsic proof of Mr Tennyson's authorship that we hazard nothing in at once assuming the fact. Nor probably has the writer any motive to conceal it except the delicate bias which, in raising so solemn and tender a memorial, would not obtrude on the tablet even the name of its founder. The book is a detailed record of that mental experience in a degree familiar to all who have cherished and lost some eminent type of human worth. The tendency of all feeling minds, and of imaginative minds in particular, to incarnate their idea of excellence – so to identify the noblest properties of spiritual life with that special form that displays them as to crowd all the light of existence into one focus of personality – and thence to feel total eclipse when Death's shadow veils that single orb – these are the 'painful passages' of inner life vividly disclosed in the book before us [...] The various poems which are included under the general title of 'In Memoriam' are formally distinguished from each other only by being divided into sections, and are all written in the same stanza. Taking the bereavement recorded at the commencement for their key-note, they embody all the phases of feeling and speculation, which such a loss induces. So elemental are most of these outpourings, that the mere intellect scarcely furnishes any clue to their beauty and their reality. We recognise their power less by any mental estimate than by their vibration on the deepest and most mysterious chords of the heart, – and their effect is analogous to that produced by the unexpected sound of some long absent voice reviving in the breast of manhood the dormant and forgotten sensibilities of childhood. They come on us with all the truthfulness of a diary: – but it is the diary of a love so profound, that though using the largest symbols of the imagination, they appear to us as direct and true as the homeliest language. The beauty and melody of illustration are so absorbed in the pervading feeling, that we become fully conscious of the former attributes only by a recurrence of the poems. (Marston 1850: 629–30)

Anonymous, The Leader

Sacred to the memory of one long loved and early died, this tablet bears neither the name of the deceased nor of the affectionate hand that raised it. Our readers have already been informed that it is erected by our greatest living poet – Alfred Tennyson – to the memory of Arthur Hallam. On first announcing the volume we stated our belief that it was unique in the annals of literature. The only poems that occurred to us as resembling it were the *Lament of Bion*, by Moschus; *Lycidas*, by Milton; and *Adonais*, by Shelley; but these are all distinguished from it both by structural peculiarities, and by the spirit which animates them. They may fitly be compared with each other, because they are all rather the products of sorrowing fancy than of genuine sorrow. Herein note a fundamental difference from *In Memoriam*, which is the iterated chant of a bereaved soul always uttering one plaint, through all the varying moods of sorrow. There is iteration in Moschus, and it is effective; but this ever-recurring burden [. . .] is not the 'trick of grief' but the trick of art. The unity and recurrence in Tennyson lie deeper – they are internal, not external. Tennyson does not, like Moschus, Milton and Shelley, call upon the woods and streams, the nymphs and men, to weep for his lost Arthur; he weeps himself. He does not call on his fancy for images of woe; he lets his own desolate heart break forth in sobs of music. The three great poets are superior to him in what the world vulgarly calls poetry, in the graceful arabesque of fancy, when the mind at ease plays with a grief that is just strong enough to stimulate it, not strong enough to sombre it; but they are all three immeasurably below him in strength, depth, and passion, consequently in the effect produced upon the minds of others. To read Moschus is a critical delight; beautiful conceits are so beautifully expressed that our admiration at the poet's *skill* is intense; but who believes the poet's grief? Who is saddened by his mournfulness, or solaced by his hope? [. . .] The comparison is not here of genius, but of feeling. Tennyson sings a deeper sorrow, utters a more truthful passion, and singing truly, gains the predominance of passion over mere sentiment. (Anonymous, *The Leader* 1850: 303–4)

Anonymous, Fraser's Magazine

We now come to the first of the volumes whose names stand at the head of our article – *In Memoriam*; a collection of poems on a vast variety of subjects, but all united, as their name implies, to the memory of a departed friend. We know not whether to envy more – the poet the object of his admiration, or that object the monument of which has been consecrated to his nobleness. For this latest and highest volume, written at various intervals during a long series of years, all the poet's peculiar excellencies, with all that has been acquired from others, seem to have been fused down into a perfect unity, and brought to bear on his subject with that care and finish which only a labour of love can inspire [. . .] In every place where in old days they had met and conversed; in every dark wrestling of the spirit with the doubts and fears of manhood, throughout the whole outward universe of nature, and the whole inward universe of spirit, the soul of his dear friend broods – at first a memory shrouded in blank despair, then a living presence, a ministering spirit, answering doubts, calming fears, stirring up noble aspirations, utter humility, leading the poet upward step by step to faith, and peace, and hope. Not that there runs throughout the book a conscious or organic method. The poems seem often merely to be united by the identity of their metre, so exquisitely chosen, that while the major rhyme in the second and third lines of each stanza gives the solidity and self-restraint required by such deep themes, the mournful minor rhyme of each first and fourth line leads the ear to expect something beyond, and enables the poet's thoughts to wander sadly on, from stanza to stanza and poem to poem, in an endless chain of

Linked sweetness long drawn out.

There are records of risings and fallings again, of alternate cloud and sunshine, throughout the book; earnest and passionate, yet never bitter; humble, yet never abject; with a depth and vehemence of affection 'passing love of woman' yet without a taint of sentimentality; self-restrained and dignified, without ever narrowing into artificial coldness; altogether rivalling the sonnets of Shakespeare. – Why should we not say boldly surpassing – for the sake of the superior faith into which it rises, for the sake of the proem at the opening of the volume – in our eyes the noblest English Christian poem which several centuries have seen? (Anonymous, *Fraser's Magazine* 1850: 252)

Anonymous, Quarterly Review

It would be very difficult to convey a just idea of this volume either by narrative or by quotation. In the series of monodies or meditations which compose it, and which follow in long series without weariness or sameness, the poet never moves away a step from the grave of his friend, but, while circling around it, has always a new point of view. Strength of love, depth of grief, aching sense of loss, have driven him forth as it were on a quest of consolation, and he asks it of nature, thought, religion, in a hundred forms which a rich and varied imagination continually suggest, but all of them connected by one central point, the recollection of the dead. This work he prosecutes, not in vain effeminate complaint, but in manly recognition of the fruit and profit even of baffled love, in noble suggestions of the future, in heart-soothing and heart-chastening thoughts of what the dead was and what he is, and of what one who has been, and therefore still is, in near contact with him is bound to be. The whole movement of the poem is between the mourner and the mourned: it may be called one long soliloquy; but it has this mark of greatness, that, though the singer is himself a large part of the subject, it never degenerates into egotism – for he speaks typically on behalf of humanity at large, and in his own name, like Dante on his mystic journey, teaches deep lessons of life and conscience to us all [. . .] By the time '*In Memoriam*' had sunk into the public mind, Mr. Tennyson had taken the rank as our first then living poet. (Anonymous, *Quarterly Review* 1859: 458–9)

Modernist Reactions

Having been formed into the image of national poet by the reviewers and having conformed to that image by accepting the laureateship, Tennyson's identity was irrevocably bound up with Victorian Britain. As the nineteenth century drew to a close and confidence in the Victorian ideals of earnest endeavour and faithful progress began to wane, Tennyson became associated with what came to be recognised as the bourgeois conservatism of Victorian culture. *Fin-de-siècle* caricatures of the poet, like the one by Beerbohm that begins this guide, paved the way for a modernist rejection of the poet and his work. Ezra Pound wrote parodies under the pen-name 'Alf Venison' and, in his modernist epic, *Ulysses*, James Joyce renames him 'Lawn Tennyson, gentleman poet'. Virginia Woolf wrote a satirical play called *Freshwater* (1923), which lampooned the poet's family life at their home on the Isle of Wight, and in her influential essay, 'A Room of One's Own', she asks 'Why has Alfred ceased to sing *She is coming, my dove, my dear?* [. . .] Shall we lay the blame on the war? [. . .] But why say "blame"? Why, if it was an illusion, not praise the catastrophe, whatever it was, that destroyed illusion and put truth in its place?' (Woolf [1928] 1945: 16), describing Tennyson's lyric voice (she quotes from *Maud*, Tennyson's poem about the Crimean War) as an illusion that has been shattered or drowned out by the First World War. The war, which Woolf identifies as the beginning of the modern era, caused the deaths of so many young men that poetry was compelled to find new ways to grieve. Through the lens of modernism, *In Memoriam* is often seen as the last traditional elegy, a work that modern writers wrote against or away from.

However, an essay by T. S. Eliot, three extracts from which are reprinted below, attempts to rescue *In Memoriam* for an early twentieth-century readership. His sensitive, influential reading of the poem is set within the context of a sharp critique of Victorian culture and even of Tennyson himself. He suggests that Tennyson's contemporaries misread the elegy and recasts the poem as an expression of doubt rather than of faith, drawing attention to its fine surfaces and arguing that it must be read as single encompassing whole. This reading contrasts sharply and deliberately with early reviews of *In Memoriam* and draws the poem into the twentieth century, tacitly inviting comparisons with Eliot's own work, *The Waste Land* (1922). Eliot's modernist epic, like *In Memoriam*, is a poem that captures the voice of its cultural moment. Like *In Memoriam*, it is a poem about loss and the doubtful possibility of consolation and, like *In Memoriam*, it treads a fine line between fragmentation and wholeness, lyricism and length. In the concluding section of *The Wasteland*, the speaker refers to 'these fragments I have shored against my ruin' (V, 431), describing his own poem in terms that could equally be applied to Tennyson's 'fragments of an elegy'. The modernist *In Memoriam* described in Eliot's essay is not necessarily any more accurate than the Victorian *In Memoriam* described in the reviews; but by remaking the poem in this way, Eliot suggests that *In Memoriam* is a poem that can be formed and transformed with each new reading.

Apparently Tennyson's contemporaries, once they had accepted *In Memoriam*, regarded it as a message of hope and reassurance to their rather fading Christian faith. It happens now and then that a poet by some strange accident expresses the mood of his generation, at the same time that he is expressing a mood of his own which is quite remote from that of his generation. This is not a question of insincerity: there is an amalgam of yielding and opposition below the level of consciousness. Tennyson himself, on the conscious level of the man who talks to reporters and poses for photographers, to judge from remarks made in conversation and recorded in his son's Memoir, consistently asserted a convinced, if somewhat sketchy, Christian belief. And he was a friend of Frederick Denison Maurice – nothing seems odder about that age than the respect which its eminent people felt for each other. Nevertheless, I get a very different impression from *In Memoriam* from that which Tennyson's contemporaries seem to have got. It is of a much more interesting and tragic Tennyson. His biographers have not failed to remark that he had a good deal of the temperament of the mystic – certainly not at all the mind of the theologian. He was desperately anxious to hold the faith of the believer, without being very clear about what he wanted to believe: he was capable of illumination which he was incapable of understanding. The 'Strong Son of God, immortal Love', with an invocation of whom the poem opens, has only a hazy connexion with the Logos, or the Incarnate God. Tennyson is distressed by the idea of a mechanical universe; he is naturally, in lamenting his friend, teased by the hope of immortality and reunion beyond death. Yet the renewal craved for seems at best but a continuance, or a substitute for the joys of friendship upon Earth. His desire for immortality never is quite the desire for Eternal Life; his concern is for the loss of man rather than for the gain of God.

[. . .]

Tennyson's feelings, I have said, were honest; but they were usually a good way below the surface. *In Memoriam* can, I think, justly be called a religious poem, but for another reason than that which made it seem religious to his contemporaries. It is not religious because of the quality of its faith, but because of the quality of its doubt. Its faith is a poor thing, but its doubt is a very intense experience.

[. . .]

In ending we must go back to the beginning and remember that *In Memoriam* would not be a great poem, or Tennyson a great poet, without the technical accomplishment. Tennyson is the great master of the metric as well as of melancholia; I do not think any poet in English has ever had a finer ear for a vowel sound, as well as a subtler feeling for some moods of anguish:

> Dear as remember'd kisses after death,
> And sweet as those by hopeless fancy feign'd
> On lips that are for others; deep as love
> Deep as first love, and wild with all regret.

And this technical gift of Tennyson's is no small thing. Tennyson lived in a time which was already acutely time-conscious: a great many things seemed to be happening, railways were being built, discoveries were being made, the face of the world was changing. That was a time busy in keeping up to date. It had, for the most part, no hold on permanent things, on permanent truths about man and God and life and death. The surface of Tennyson stirred about with his time; and he had nothing to which to hold fast except his unique and unerring feeling for the sounds of words. But in this he had something that no one else had. Tennyson's surface, his technical accomplishment, is intimate with his depths: what we most quickly see about Tennyson is that which moves between the surface and the depths, that which is of slight importance. By looking innocently at the surface, we are most likely to come to the depths, to the abyss of sorrow. Tennyson is not only a minor Virgil, he is also with Virgil as Dante saw him, a Virgil among the Shades, the saddest of all English poets, among the Great in Limbo, the most instinctive rebel against the society in which he was the most perfect conformist. (Eliot [1936] 1999: 328–38)

Notes

1. For a full account of the collaborative authorship of the *Memoir*, see Philip K. Elliott (1995), *The Making of the Memoir*, Lincoln: Tennyson Society.
2. *Victorian Sensation: The Extraordinary Publication, Reception and Secret Authorship of* Vestiges of the Natural History of Creation (2003), by James Secord, provides a full and fascinating history of *Vestiges*.
3. A comprehensive survey of reviews received by *In Memoriam* is provided in Edgar F. Shannon's *Tennyson and the Reviewers* (1952).
4. Marion Shaw writes that Palgrave's selection resulted in 'a poem as uncomplicated, beautiful, and homogeneous as a double string of pearls' (Shaw 1980: 198), a far cry from the complex, multiple character of the complete text.
5. This is an argument that I make more fully in Chapter 3 of *Tennyson's Name* (2008).

Chapter 5

Teaching the Text

This section of the Reading Guide provides a selection of suggestions and starting points for teaching *In Memoriam*. It includes strategies for reading the poem, sample seminar and module outlines and ideas for assessment activities that aim to enable students to engage with those formal elements and thematic concerns addressed in earlier chapters.

Reading the Text

One of the most significant challenges of teaching *In Memoriam* is getting students to read it. Its length and repetitiveness – two characteristics that are key to understanding the poem – also pose problems for students, who will often have one week to 'get through it' in preparation for class. A couple of straightforward solutions to this initial problem are: to spend more than one week teaching the poem (see the outline for an *In Memoriam* module, below) or to ask students to read selected sections (you could take one of the chapters of the reading guide as the basis for this kind of selective approach). However, regardless of whether students are being asked to read the whole poem or just parts of it, in one week or over several, it is important to get students to think about the reading experience: to reflect on how they are reading as well as what they are reading. Students might be provided with a list of questions that encourage this kind of reflection, for example:

- What did you find most difficult about reading the poem?
- Do you think the poem traces a narrative?
- Would you describe the development of the poem as linear or cyclical, or would you say that it failed to develop at all?
- Can you identify any important turning points in the poem?
- Do you think that the poem is best understood as a single long poem or a connected series of short poems?

Questions of this kind encourage students to see the challenges involved in reading *In Memoriam* as a key rather than a barrier to understanding the text; and, because there is no right answer to any of them, they can be used to introduce the formal and generic tensions on which *In Memoriam* is structured.

Initial Responses

Two common – and opposite – responses to *In Memoriam* are that it is impenetrable, repetitive and dull, and that it is deeply moving (sometimes because the reader can relate to the experience of grief that the poem describes). Both of these responses are tricky to develop into a fruitful critical discussion. The first closes down interpretive possibilities; the second leads to responses that are overly evaluative or personal. However, these responses can also be employed to explore *In Memoriam*'s paradoxical double identity, the relationship between fragment and monument, private and public that is discussed at the beginning of this book. In a class where both of these initial responses to the poem are expressed, students can be asked to identify how the poem elicited the response it did from them and then to consider how the same poem can have resulted in such different readings. Emotionally sympathetic responses to the poem can be challenged by drawing attention to the poem's composition and structure: why, if the poem is simply a sincere outpouring of grief, does Tennyson not publish the sections in the order that they were written? Readers who focus on the poem's scale and artificiality should be asked to think about moments when the poem threatens to fracture or break down (see, for example, section XVI). Another common response to *In Memoriam* is that it is self-indulgent. It can be pointed out that this is something that *In Memoriam* thinks about itself (see, for example, section XXI), so that, by levelling this kind of accusation at the poem, apparently resistant readers in fact identify one of *In Memoriam*'s central questions: (how) should we use poetry to respond to loss?

Teaching *In Memoriam* as a Victorian text

In Memoriam is often included as part of core undergraduate modules that survey the literature of the Victorian period. Encouraging students to think about *In Memoriam*'s self-consciously paradoxical textual identity and their own role as readers of the poem introduces the theme of post-Romantic literary doubt that identifies the poem with its historical moment. This can be employed as a starting point for consideration of other ways that *In Memoriam* defines and can be defined as a Victorian text. Again, the main barrier to this kind of discussion is the lyric, apparently personal nature of *In Memoriam* and the fact that it is a poem about the 'universal' experience of grief. For this reason it can be difficult to see how this poem is about, or informed by, the cultural and philosophical concerns of the nineteenth century. To encourage their awareness of the ways that the speaker's grief is informed by its historical and cultural context, students can be asked to pay attention to the identity of the speaker and to the historically inflected themes and motifs that the speaker employs to articulate his grief, so that they begin to see the poem as a construct that assembles and forms (to a greater or lesser extent) a range of cultural and textual materials.

Discussion about the identity of the speaker might begin with Tennyson's comment, recorded in Hallam's memoir of his father, that '"I" is not always the author speaking of himself, but the voice of the human race speaking thro' him' (see 'Contexts and Reception'). What does Tennyson mean by this? What do students make of the implication that the voice is not the same throughout the poem (if '"I" is not *always* the author', this suggests that 'I' is sometimes the author and sometimes something else)? Can students identify parts that they think are spoken by the author and parts spoken by, or on behalf of, 'the human race'? Is it possible to speak on behalf of humanity or is the universal 'I' really a white, masculine, Western, educated, Victorian 'I'? By drawing attention to the problems involved in claiming to speak for everyone, it is possible to think about the relationship between universality and historical specificity, so that by looking at those sections where Tennyson seems to speak with the voice of the race, we can gain insight into the fundamental concerns of a particular nation, gender and class in the first half of the nineteenth century.

Many of the central motifs of *In Memoriam* tread a similarly fine line between the universal and the historical. In the Reading Guide section of this book I trace four motifs through the poem, discussing how they explore and describe Tennyson's grief and also engage with Victorian science, religion, literature and philosophy. A learning activity based on this kind of reading can help students to trace different routes through the poem and to gain a sense of the different cultural materials that the poem weaves together. It will also encourage students to think about the relationship between repetition and progress that structures the poem.

Activity: Mapping the poem

The week before the tutorial, the tutor should assign a word, image or motif to two or three students. Motifs might include: speech and language, hands and touch, economics, circles and cycles, religious ritual, nature, love, family, blood, the country and the city, houses and rooms, daybreak and sunset, light, the sea. Students should be told to read the poem with their motif in mind, marking points where it features and answering the following questions in preparation for the tutorial:

- What is the significance of this motif?
- What does it represent for the speaker?
- How does the speaker represent the motif?
- What language does he use?
- Does the motif engage with ideas or themes that you have come across in other Victorian texts you have read?
- If so, how?
- Do the answers to any of these questions change as the poem progresses?
- What changes occur and why?

In the tutorial, students reading for the same motif should pair up to discuss their readings. They should then be asked to present their readings to the rest of the group.

Thinking About Form

Although students often regard form as the most difficult aspect of reading and writing about poetry, initial responses to *In Memoriam* are frequently dominated by one of its most important formal aspects: length. Discussions of the more detailed aspects of *In Memoriam*'s form can begin with this observation. Students can be encouraged to think about length as a formal feature that represents and performs the experience of three years of mourning, shaping the time of grief as well as describing the experience of grief. Students can then be asked to consider what kind of shape Tennyson gives to his grief in *In Memoriam*. Students might be asked to identify and evaluate different ways in which the poem describes its own form. Is it a series of 'wild and wandering cries', as the speaker claims in the Prologue? Is it a 'sad mechanic exercise', as described in section V; or a collection of 'brief lays', as in XLVIII? Does it 'mingle all without a plan' (XVI, 20)? Or is it 'toil corporate to an end' (CXXVIII)? Is *Fragments of an Elegy* a more apt title than the more monumental *In Memoriam*; or would *The Way of the Soul*, with its implications of progress and development be better still? By justifying why they agree or disagree with these diverse descriptions, students will begin to describe and analyse the different and contradictory aspects of the poem's form.

Bearing these large-scale formal definitions in mind, students might then be encouraged to think about how the details of *In Memoriam*'s form contribute to their understanding of the poem. Below are two activities designed to help students get to grips with the *In Memoriam* stanza.

Activity: Comparative forms

This activity aims to enable students to engage with the *In Memoriam* stanza by comparing it with two poetic forms with which they may already be familiar. The activity deals with short sections of *In Memoriam* and so can be carried out in a seminar or workshop without any preparation. Students can work on their comparative readings individually or in small groups and then present their ideas to the larger group.

Comparison 1: Section LII and Sonnet 43 from Sonnets from the Portuguese *by Elizabeth Barrett Browning*

How do I love thee? Let me count the ways.
I love thee to the depth and breadth and height
My soul can reach, when feeling out of sight
For the ends of Being and ideal Grace.
I love thee to the level of everyday's
Most quiet need, by sun and candle-light.
I love thee freely, as men strive for Right;
I love thee purely, as they turn from Praise.
I love thee with the passion put to use
In my old griefs, and with my childhood's faith.
I love thee with a love I seemed to lose
With my lost saints! – I love thee with the breath,
Smiles, tears, of all my life! – and, if God choose,
I shall but love thee better after death.
        (Barrett Browning [1850] 2010: II, 478)

This comparison takes as its starting point the frequent comparisons drawn between *In Memoriam* and the sonnet sequence (I have suggested a sonnet by another Victorian writer, but a Shakespearean sonnet would be equally appropriate). Students should be asked to read both texts and to think about the following points:

- Use the Browning sonnet (reproduced here) to remind yourself of the sonnet form. Pay attention to the number of lines, rhyme scheme and metre. Think about whether the form encourages you to pause at any point, whether it draws attention to any shifts in the poem's argument, whether you would describe the form as closed or open, complete or incomplete.

- Do the same with section LII of *In Memoriam*.
- Can you identify any significant similarities or differences? Do you think section LII is a sort of sonnet, and why?

Comparison 2: Section XV and 'The Ballad of Sir Patrick Spens', lines 1–20

> The king sits in Dumferling toune,
> Drinking the blude-reid wine:
> 'O whar will I get guid sailor,
> To sail this ship of mine?'
>   2
> Up and spak an eldern knicht,
> Sat at the kings richt kne:
> 'Sir Patrick Spens is the best sailor
> That sails upon the se.'
>   3
> The king has written a braid letter,
> And signd it wi his hand,
> And sent it to Sir Patrick Spens,
> Was walking on the sand.
>   4
> The first line that Sir Patrick red,
> A loud lauch lauched he;
> The next line that Sir Patrick red,
> The teir blinded his ee.
>   5
> 'O wha is this has don this deid,
> This ill deid don to me,
> To send me out this time o' the yeir,
> To sail upon the se!
> (Percy [1765] 1996: I, 72–3)

This comparison is based on the similarities between the *In Memoriam* stanza and ballad metre, which are outlined in the 'Mapping and Making' section of this book. I suggest an extract of the ballad so that the activity can be carried out within a single class, but students could also be asked to read the whole ballad in preparation for the seminar. Again, the following questions should be given to guide discussion:

- What are the key formal elements of this ballad? Pay attention to the stanza form, metre and rhyme scheme.
- A ballad is a type of poem that tells a story. How does the form of this ballad contribute to / affect the story that it tells?

- How does the ballad form compare to the form of this section of *In Memoriam*? What are the main similarities? What are the main differences and how do they affect the way the poem sounds and / or feels?

Activity: Decomposing and recomposing

This activity aims to encourage an understanding of form through practice. Students can reflect on how the *In Memoriam* stanza works by playing around with it, disassembling and reassembling it. Begin by showing the students the 'germ' of *In Memoriam* (reproduced in the 'Contexts and Reception' chapter, above) in order to introduce the idea that the *In Memoriam* stanza was a form that Tennyson developed while he was composing the poem. Having understood that form is the result of a set of conscious decisions on the part of the poet, it is then possible to discuss how those decisions affect the tone and meaning of the poem. One way to do this is to consider how the poem would have looked if Tennyson had made a different set of decisions. What if he had written the poem in rhyming couplets? What if he had placed the line breaks in different places? Choose a section of the poem and ask the students to rewrite it, changing only the form and keeping the sense intact (depending on time and class size, this activity could be carried out in small groups or done as a class). For example, section XXII might be rewritten to look like this:

XXII.
The path by which we twain did go,
Which led by tracts that pleased us well,
From flower to flower, from snow to snow,
Through four sweet years arose and fell;
And we with singing cheered the way,
And, crowned with all the season lent,
And glad at heart from May to May,
From April on to April went:
But where the path we walked began
To slant the fifth autumnal slope,
There sat the Shadow feared of man,
As we descended following Hope;
Who broke our fair companionship,
And spread his mantle dark and cold,
And dulled the murmur on thy lip,
And wrapt thee formless in the fold,
And bore thee where I could not see
Nor follow, though I walk in haste.

I think that Shadow waits for me:
It sits somewhere within the waste.

Ask the students to discuss the new version they have produced. How does the section look now? How does it sound? (How) has the relationship between form and meaning changed? In the example given, students might recognise an increase of pace and might be encouraged to think about how the unbroken ABAB rhyme scheme achieves a different relationship with the interrupted journey that the section describes, building up a momentum that mirrors the mourner's hasty footsteps and carrying the events forward. Having discussed their new versions, students should then be asked to look back at the section in its original form and think about how it looks and sounds in comparison. What happens to its pace and momentum? Is there a change in tone? What is the relationship between form and meaning here? Discussing section XXII, students can again consider the path, the journey and the passing of the seasons: does the form of the section complicate, or create tension with, the events that are described? For example, might the backwards-looking rhyme scheme lead us to question the mourner's sincerity when he says 'I walk in haste,' and draw our attention to his desire to dwell in the past rather than look forward to the future? This section also talks about Arthur being 'wrapt . . . formless in the fold', a reference to form that might help to focus discussion on questions of form and formlessness and the relationship between Tennyson's formal composition and the decomposing body it remembers.

Module Outline: Grieving Forms: *In Memoriam* and the Poetry of Loss

As I have tried to show throughout this Guide, *In Memoriam* is a hugely rich text that yields to multiple readings and stands in vital relation to a great number of other texts. These readings and relationships might form the basis for a stand-alone module for either undergraduate or postgraduate students. The outline below suggests texts, discussion topics and assessment ideas for a ten-week module. It begins by establishing *In Memoriam*'s place within the elegiac tradition and moves on to explore the questions of voice and performance, raised by Tennyson's mourner, through other, more overtly dramatic responses to the death of Hallam. Week five encourages students to think about the poem's faltering religious belief alongside other Victorian poetic expressions of faith and doubt, and week six explores the poem's engagement with pre-Darwinian evolutionary science by reading Tennyson's descriptions of 'nature red in tooth and claw' alongside its scientific intertexts. In week seven discussion focuses on the ways poetry articulates sexuality, reading the elegy as love lyric alongside the Sapphic poetry of Swinburne and the Michael Field poets; and in week eight students are invited to think about the ways in which this anonymous poem contributed to and also complicates the public spectacle of Victorian grief. The module ends by moving into the twentieth century, concluding with T. S. Eliot's modernist, elegiac epic, *The Waste Land*.

Outline

Selections from *In Memoriam* will be set each week alongside the following texts:

Week 1: Mapping Grief: Fragments, Cycles and Wholes
  Introductory Tutorial
Week 2: Remembering the Elegy 1
  Spenser, *Astrophel* (1595)
  Milton, 'Lycidas' (1637)
Week 3: Remembering the Elegy 2
  Gray, 'Elegy Written in a Country Churchyard' (1751)
  Shelley, *Adonais* (1821)
Week 4: Performing Grief
  Tennyson, 'Ulysses' (1842), 'Tithon' (1833)
Week 5: Loss of Faith
  Christina Rossetti, 'When I am dead my dearest' (1862)
  Emily Brontë, 'No coward soul is mine' (1850)
  G. M. Hopkins, 'The Wreck of the *Deutschland*' (1918)
Week 6: The Science of Mourning
  Charles Lyell, *Principles of Geology* (1830–3) (extracts)
  Robert Chambers, *Vestiges of the Natural History of Creation* (1844) (extracts)
Week 7: The Grief that Dare not Speak its Name
  A. C. Swinburne, '*Ave Atque Vale*: In Memory of Charles Baudelaire' (1878)
  'Anactoria' (1866)
  Michael Field, 'Sometimes I do despatch my heart' (1893)
Week 8: Private Grief, Public Spectacle
  Tennyson, *Ode on the Death of the Duke of Wellington* (1854)
  Wordsworth, 'Essays on Epitaphs' (1810)
  Robert Browning, 'The Bishop Orders His Tomb at Saint Praxed's Church' (1845)

Week 9: Afterlives 1
  Matthew Arnold, 'Thrysis' (1866)
  Thomas Hardy, 'The Going' (1912), 'Your Last Drive' (1912), 'Rain on a Grave' (1913), 'The Voice' (1914)
Week 10: Afterlives 2
  T. S. Eliot, *The Waste Land* (1922)

Assessment – Option 1: Edited Edition

This assessment activity is designed to offer students a hands-on engagement with *In Memoriam*'s forms and meanings by asking them to construct their own *In Memoriam* out of the poem's elegiac fragments. Students are required to edit and introduce a select edition of *In Memoriam*, choosing a collection of lyrics that relate to a particular theme, influence or context. Their introductory essay to the edition will combine close readings of their chosen sections with relevant critical, theoretical and historical material. One way to introduce this assessment activity is to show students a range of select editions (from Palgrave's selection for the Macmillan *Golden Treasury* to the Norton edition) and invite them to consider the editorial decisions that have been made and the effect that they have on the poem's textual identity. Certain editions emphasise particular themes; others alter the order of the lyrics so that the poem follows a different line of development. If students are made aware of the creative potential of editorial work, they will be encouraged to think carefully about the implications of their editorial decisions and produce editions that communicate their own reading of the poem.

Assessment – Option 2: Essay

This assessment method is designed to lead on from the 'Mapping the Poem' activity, outlined above. Rather than responding to a set essay question, students can be asked to perform a close-reading of the poem that traces the development of a particular motif or idea. As above, students might choose from a list of options, or might be invited to identify their own image / idea. This assessment requires a combination of detailed close-reading and a sense of the way the poem works as a whole.

Annotated Bibliography

The tradition of modern scholarly writing about *In Memoriam* is so rich and wide-ranging that it is impossible to do justice to it in the space available. The briefly annotated, highly select bibliography provided here lists some of the best introductions to Tennyson's poetry, as well as a handful of the most influential work on *In Memoriam* itself.

Editions

Gray, Erik, ed. (2004), *In Memoriam: Norton Critical Edition*, New York: W. W. Norton.
An accessible edition that provides helpful explanations of many of *In Memoriam*'s literary allusions and contexts. Also includes a selection of extracts from critical essays that samples a range of approaches and perspectives.

Ricks, Christopher, ed. (1987), *The Poems of Tennyson in Three Volumes*, 2nd edn, Harlow: Longman.
The definitive modern edition of Tennyson's poetry. Generously annotated, providing information about the poem's composition and revision, and suggesting connections with other works by the poet. *In Memoriam* is also included, in full, in Longman's select edition of Tennyson (2006).

Shatto, Susan and Marion Shaw, eds (1982), *In Memoriam*, Oxford: Clarendon.
A single-volume scholarly edition, annotated in meticulous detail, with information about composition and manuscript variation, as well as extensive commentary.

Companions and Introductions

Culler, A. Dwight (1977), *The Poetry of Tennyson*, New Haven: Yale University Press.
This sensitive study charts the development of Tennyson's poetic identity in relation to his work, focusing on literary rather than biographical contexts. It includes chapters on many of his major works, including *In Memoriam*.

Perry, Seamus (2004), *Tennyson*, Tavistock: Northcote House.
A brilliant introduction to Tennyson's style, including a series of deft close-readings. Essential reading for anyone coming to Tennyson for the first time.
Ricks, Christopher (1989), *Tennyson*, 2nd edn, Basingstoke: Macmillan.
Another indispensable introduction that provides an illuminating account of Tennyson's life and work.
Shaw, Marion (1988), *Alfred Lord Tennyson*, Hemel Hempstead: Harvester Wheatsheaf.
One of the best feminist accounts of Tennyson's poetry. Engages with psychoanalytical theory, taking in a range of work, including *In Memoriam*.
Sinfield, Alan (1986), *Alfred Tennyson*, Oxford: Blackwell.
A concise introduction written from a Marxist, deconstructionist perspective that reads the poems with an eye to their political context.

Biographies

Martin, Robert Bernard (1980), *Tennyson: The Unquiet Heart*, Oxford: Clarendon.
The best recent biography. Offers a lively, detailed account of Tennyson's life and some interesting psychological insights.
Ormond, Leonee (1993), *Alfred Tennyson: A Literary Life*, Basingstoke: Macmillan.
A useful critical biography that reads Tennyson's work in its biographical and literary contexts.
Tennyson, Hallam (1897), *Alfred Lord Tennyson: A Memoir by his Son*, 2 vols, London: Macmillan.
Hallam Tennyson's personal, partial memoir of his father remains an essential biographical resource. The narrative incorporates journal extracts, letters, unpublished poems and the reminiscences of many of Tennyson's friends.
Tennyson, Sir Charles (1949), *Alfred Tennyson*, London: Macmillan.
A biography by Tennyson's grandson. The first to provide details of Tennyson's troubled family history.

Studies of *In Memoriam*

Armstrong, Isobel (1992), 'Tennyson in the 1850s: From Geology to Pathology – *In Memoriam* (1850) to *Maud* (1855)', in *Tennyson: Seven Essays*, ed. Philip Collins, New York: St Martin's, pp. 102–40.
One of the best treatments of *In Memoriam*'s engagement with evolutionary science.
Bradley, A. C. (1901), *A Commentary on Tennyson's* In Memoriam, 3rd edn, London: Macmillan.
An important early work of criticism and analysis that draws on biographical detail and identifies significant themes.

Peltason, Timothy (1986), *Reading In Memoriam*, Princeton: Princeton University Press.
A lively account of the poem, influenced by deconstructionist criticism.
Sacks, Peter (1985), *The English Elegy: Studies in the Genre from Spenser to Yeats*, Baltimore: Johns Hopkins University Press.
Sacks's reading of the elegiac tradition in England is influenced by Freudian theories of mourning and melancholia, and includes an excellent chapter on the psychology of *In Memoriam*'s mourner.
Sinfield, Alan (1971), *The Language of Tennyson's* In Memoriam, Oxford: Blackwell.
Very different from Sinfield's later, post-Marxist account of Tennyson's life and work, this fine, nuanced reading focuses on the different traditions that inform *In Memoriam*'s rich, allusive language.

Works Cited

Anonymous (1850), '*In Memoriam*', *Fraser's Magazine*, September, pp. 245–55.
Anonymous (1850), '*In Memoriam*', *The Leader*, June, pp. 303–4.
Anonymous (1859), 'Tennyson's Poems', *Quarterly Review*, October, pp. 454–85.
Armstrong, Isobel (1982), *Language as Living Form in Nineteenth-Century Poetry*, Sussex: Harvester.
Armstrong, Isobel (1993), *Victorian Poetry: Poetry, Poetics and Politics*, London: Routledge.
Attridge, Derek (1995), *Poetic Rhythm: An Introduction*, Cambridge: Cambridge University Press.
Auden, W. H. (1973), *Forwards and Afterwords*, London: Faber & Faber.
Austin, J. L. [1955] (1976), *How To Do Things With Words*, ed. J. O. Urmson and Marina Sbisà, 2nd edn, Oxford: Oxford University Press.
Barrett Browning, Elizabeth (2010), *The Works of Elizabeth Barrett Browning*, ed. Sandra Donaldson, 5 vols, London: Pickering & Chatto.
Barton, Anna (2008), *Tennyson's Name: Identity and Responsibility in the Poetry of Alfred Lord Tennyson*, Aldershot: Ashgate.
Beerbohm, Max (1904), *The Poets' Corner*, London: W. Heinemann.
Bell, Catherine (1993), *Ritual Theory, Ritual Practice*, Oxford: Oxford University Press.
Bevis, Matthew (2003), *Lives of Victorian Literary Figures*, part 1, vol. 3, London: Pickering & Chatto.
Blair, Kirstie (2001), 'Touching Hearts: Queen Victoria and the Curative Properties of *In Memoriam*', *Tennyson Research Bulletin* 5, pp. 246–54.
Blocksidge, Martin (2010), *A Life Lived Quickly: Tennyson's Friend Arthur Henry Hallam and His Legend*, Eastbourne: Sussex Academic Press.
Bradley, A. C. (1901), *A Commentary on Tennyson's* In Memoriam, 3rd edn, London: Macmillan.
Buckley, Jerome Hamilton (1960), *Tennyson: The Growth of a Poet*, Cambridge, MA: Harvard University Press.
Chambers, Robert [1844] (1994), *Vestiges of the Natural History of Creation*, ed. James Secord, Chicago: University of Chicago Press.

Coleridge, Samuel Taylor (1969–90), *The Collected Works of Samuel Taylor Coleridge*, ed. Kathleen Coburn, 16 vols, London: Routledge & Kegan Paul.

Derrida, Jacques (2001), *The Work of Mourning*, ed. Pascale-Anne Brault and Michael Naas, Chicago: University of Chicago Press.

Eliot, T. S. [1936] (1999), '*In Memoriam*', *Selected Essays*, 3rd edn, London: Faber & Faber, pp. 286–95.

Eliot, T. S. (2004), *The Complete Poems and Plays*, London: Faber & Faber.

Elliott, Philip K. (1995), *The Making of the Memoir*, Lincoln: Tennyson Society Monographs.

Fish, Stanley (1998), *Surprised by Sin*, 2nd edn, Cambridge, MA: Harvard University Press.

Forster, John (1850), '*In Memoriam*', *The Examiner*, June, pp. 356–7.

Freud, Sigmund [1917] (2005), 'On Mourning and Melancholia', trans. Shaun Whiteside, *On Murder, Mourning and Melancholia*, ed. Maud Ellman, Harmondsworth: Penguin.

Gray, Thomas, William Collins and Oliver Goldsmith (1969), *Poems*, ed. Roger Lonsdale, London: Longman.

Hair, Donald S. (1991), *Tennyson's Language*, Toronto: University of Toronto Press.

Hallam, Arthur Henry (1831), 'On Some of the Characteristics of Modern Poetry and on the Lyrical Poems of Alfred Tennyson', *Englishman's Magazine*, August, pp. 616–28.

Hallam, Arthur Henry (1834), *Remains in Verse and Prose*, ed. Henry Hallam, London.

Homer (1987), *The Iliad*, trans. Martin Hammond, Harmondsworth: Penguin.

Homer (2006), *The Odyssey*, trans. Robert Fagles, Harmondsworth: Penguin.

Janowitz, Anne (1998), *Lyric and Labour in the Romantic Tradition*, Cambridge: Cambridge University Press.

Joseph, Gerhard (1992), *Tennyson and the Text*, Cambridge: Cambridge University Press.

Keats, John (1972), *The Complete Poems*, ed. Miriam Allott, Harlow: Longman.

Kennedy, David (2007), *Elegy*, Abingdon: Routledge.

Knowles, James (1893), 'Aspects of Tennyson', *The Nineteenth Century*, January, pp. 164–88.

Leighton, Angela (2007), *On Form: Poetry, Aestheticism and the Legacy of a Word*, Oxford: Oxford University Press.

Lukács, Georg [1916] (1971), *The Theory of the Novel*, trans. Anna Bostock, Cambridge, MA: MIT Press.

Lushington, Franklin (1850), '*In Memoriam*', *Tait's Edinburgh Magazine*, August, pp. 499–506.

Lyell, Charles (1835), *Principles of Geology*, 4th edn, London: John Murray.

Marston, J. Westland (1850), '*In Memoriam*', *The Athenaeum*, June, pp. 629–30.

Martin, Robert Bernard (1983), *Tennyson: The Unquiet Heart*, Oxford: Clarendon.

McGann, Jerome (1996), *The Poetics of Sensibility: A Revolution in Literary Style*, Oxford: Clarendon.

Milton, John [1667] (1968), *Paradise Lost*, ed. Christopher Ricks, Harmondsworth: Penguin.

Milton John (1971), *The Complete Shorter Poems*, ed. John Carey, London: Longman.

Newlyn, Lucy (2001), *Paradise Lost and the Romantic Reader*, Oxford: Oxford University Press.

Nunokowa, Jeff (1996), '*In Memoriam* and the Extinction of the Homosexual', in *Tennyson*, ed. Rebecca Stott, London: Longman, pp. 197–209.

Percy, Thomas [1765] (1996), *Reliques of Ancient English and Poetry*, 3 vols, London: Routledge.

Perry, Seamus (2004), *Alfred Tennyson*, Tavistock: Northcote House.

Plato (1993), *The Last Days of Socrates*, trans. Hugh Tredennick and Harold Tarrant, Harmondsworth: Penguin.

Proust, Marcel [1913–1927] (1981), *Remembrance of Things Past*, 7 vols, trans. C. K. Scott-Moncrieff and Terence Kilmartin, London: Chatto & Windus.

Ramazani, Jahan (1994), *The Poetry of Mourning: The Modern Elegy from Hardy to Heaney*, Chicago: University of Chicago Press.

Ricks, Christopher (1989), *Tennyson*, 2nd edn, Basingstoke: Macmillan.

Ross, David (1953), *Plato's Theory of Ideas*, 2nd edn, Oxford: Clarendon.

Sacks, Peter (1985), *The English Elegy: Studies in the Genre from Spenser to Yeats*, Baltimore: Johns Hopkins University Press.

Secord, James (2003) *Victorian Sensation: The Extraordinary Publication, Reception and Secret Authorship of* Vestiges of the Natural History of Creation, Chicago: University of Chicago Press.

Sedgwick, Eve Kosovsky (1985), *Between Men: English Literature and Male Homosocial Desire*, New York: Columbia University Press.

Shannon, Edgar Finley, Jr. (1952), *Tennyson and the Reviewers: A Study of his Literary Reputation and of the Influence of the Critics upon his Poetry 1827–1851*, Cambridge, MA: Harvard University Press.

Shaw, Marion (1980), 'Palgrave's *In Memoriam*', *Victorian Poetry* 18.2, Summer, pp. 199–201.

Shelley, Percy Bysshe (1970), *Complete Poems*, ed. Thomas Hutchinson, 2nd edn, London: Oxford University Press.

Sinfield, Alan (1971), *The Language of Tennyson's* In Memoriam, Oxford: Blackwell.

Sinfield, Alan (1986), *Alfred Tennyson*, Oxford: Blackwell.

Sinfield, Alan (1994), *The Wilde Century: Effeminacy, Oscar Wilde and the Queer Movement*, New York: Cassell.

Tennyson, Alfred [1850] (1981), *In Memoriam*, ed. Susan Shatto and Marion Shaw, Oxford: Clarendon.

Tennyson, Alfred (1987), *The Poems of Tennyson*, ed. Christopher Ricks, 3 vols, 2nd edn, Harlow: Longman.

Tennyson, Hallam (1897), *Alfred Lord Tennyson: A Memoir by his Son*. 2 vols, London: Macmillan.

Tucker, Herbert (1988), *Tennyson and the Doom of Romanticism*, Cambridge, MA: Harvard University Press.

Tucker, Herbert (2008), *Epic: Britain's Heroic Muse 1790–1910*, Oxford: Oxford University Press.

Woolf, Virginia [1928] (1945), *A Room of One's Own*, Harmondsworth: Penguin.

Wordsworth, William (1982), *The Poems*, 2 vols, ed. John O. Hayden, London: Yale University Press.

Wordsworth, William and S. T. Coleridge [1798–1800] (1991), *Lyrical Ballads / The Text of the 1798 Edition with the Additional 1800 Poems and the Prefaces*, ed. R. L. Brett and A. R. Jones, 2nd edn, London: Methuen.

Index